WITH LOVE
AND PRAYERS

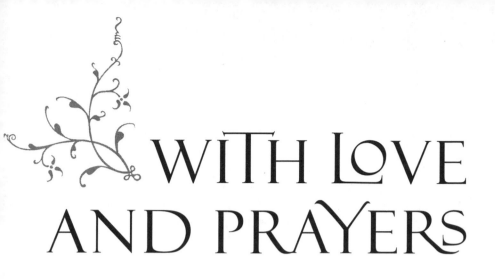

WITH LOVE AND PRAYERS

A Headmaster Speaks to the Next Generation

F. WASHINGTON JARVIS

FOREWORD BY *PETER J. GOMES*

DAVID R. GODINE · PUBLISHER · BOSTON

David R. Godine, Publisher, Inc.
P.O. BOX 450 JAFFREY, NEW HAMPSHIRE 03452

ISBN 1-56792-143-4 (HARDCOVER)
ISBN 1-56792-233-3 (SOFTCOVER)

Design and Typography by
Scott-Martin Kosofsky at The Philidor Company,
Cambridge, Massachusetts.
Set in Philidor Bell and Philidor Fairfield types.

SECOND PRINTING
Printed in the United States of America

Cotton Mather in his *Life of the Renowned John Eliot* (1690)
quotes Melchior Adam on the calling of a schoolmaster:

Pulverulentam ac molestissimam quidem,
sed Deo longe gratissimam functionem.

Schoolmastering is a dusty and disagreeable vocation,
but by far the most favored by God.

WITH GRATITUDE TO
THE MASTERS AND STAFF OF
THE ROXBURY LATIN SCHOOL

You have been an inspiration every step of the way,
and you have made God's favored vocation
the most agreeable profession.

Ye, like angels, appear,
Radiant with ardour divine.
Beacons of hope, ye appear!
Langour is not in your heart,
Weakness is not in your word,
Weariness not on your brow.

Eyes rekindling, and prayers,
Follow your steps as ye go.
Ye fill up the gaps in our files,
Strengthen the wavering line,
Stablish, continue our march.
On, to the bound of the waste,
On, to the City of God.

Contents

Part Two: Values to Live By

Foreword

An Anachronism for Our Time:
Tony Jarvis and the Roxbury Latin School

All the world's a school:
To save it from disaster
I bear viceregent rule
For God, the great Headmaster.
    —GEORGE ROSTREVOR HAMILTON
    (*Epigrams*, 1928)

HE REVEREND F. WASHINGTON JARVIS and the Roxbury Latin School over which he has presided for a quarter of a century are each anachronisms and proud of so being; and in the crowded field of private secondary education in North America they both stand out because neither fits in. Dr. Jarvis is an unrepentant Episcopal clergyman with Catholic tendencies, who sees as a priestly vocation his office of headmaster in a decidedly secular age. Boys routinely call him "Father." He is never seen without a collar and, on the frequent state occasions of the place, is clad in a scarlet cassock with academic bands, gown, and hood; indeed, like a character from *Ruddigore*, Jarvis could easily have stepped out of any of the framed portraits of his seventeenth- and eighteenth-century predecessors. He prays for his boys and tells them that he loves them, and he does this in public, and regularly.

The School? It too remains steadfast in its chosen way, vigorously masculine and proudly singlesex in an era of remorseless co-education. Its curriculum is fiercely classical: Greek and Latin are not fancy *hors d'œuvres* but a central part of the required diet, and formal "Halls," as assemblies are known at Roxbury Latin, open each day with the Head in the chair. At the start of each term Dr. Jarvis addresses the boys as would a father, a pastor, or a mentor, and while he loves them, he is not their pal: he is the Head, and the boys seem to like it that way.

Since 1645, this "nursery of piety," as no less an observer than Cotton Mather called it, has seen as its God-given mission to "fit [students] for public service both in Church and Commonwealth." That ambition is not unique, for there are many independent schools in North America that can find similar language in their founding documents. What is unique about the Roxbury Latin School is that it has never wavered from that founding principle and continues to this day in its prosecu- tion. Avoiding the temptation to bigness, Roxbury Latin has chosen to remain small, while at the same time its resources have been so wisely husbanded for so long that it is able to provide the very best education to all who meet its requirements, without regard to ability to pay.

To the uninitiated, such an institution as this would appear to be an elite bastion of unentitled privilege for the ruling classes, but, like many cherished myths, that one would be quite wrong. It is a point of pride for this, the oldest school in continuing existence in North America, that from its foundation it was designed to be an instrument of civic virtue, preparing diverse boys for citizenship in a diverse culture. The founder, the pious John Eliot, was universally known as "Apostle to the Indians" for his work among the native Americans. He also labored for the welfare of the progeny of the African slaves who had been brought to Boston. His fervent hope was that the children of blacks, whites, and Indians could be educated together at his School—an aspiration that earned him much criticism from his contemporaries and the admiration of later generations—such as our own—that claim the notion of 'diver- sity' for themselves.

Not every school with a distinguished pedigree, however, can live as well in the present as it can in the past, and for many such schools the past is a burden to be overcome in the present as quickly and faddishly as possible. The story of independent secondary education over the past twenty-five years is in far too many instances a sad narrative of a colossal loss of nerve and a crisis of identity and purpose, with the mission of many such institutions simply to survive the enormous societal revolutions of the last generation. In order to do this they have had to adapt their mission to market forces, and often have found themselves at the mercy of a consumer society with its insatiable desire for the most user-friendly bargain.

That this is hardly an accurate description of the Roxbury Latin School at the end of the twentieth century is due in large measure to the twenty-five-year tenure of the present headmaster. In 1838, when Roxbury Latin was one hundred ninety-three years old, Dr. Thomas Arnold began his radical reforms of England's Rugby School upon his appointment as its headmaster. Of his new school, Arnold famously said, "What we must look for here is first, religious and moral principles; secondly, gentlemanly conduct; and thirdly, intellectual ability." Few people quote Thomas Arnold today, but in even a casual glance at this collection of timely addresses of Tony Jarvis, it can easily be seen that Arnold's ideals, as radical in their own day as in ours, are alive and well and flourishing in Roxbury. The founders of Roxbury Latin directed the schoolmaster to "use his best skill and endeavors, both by precept and example, to instruct [students] in all scholastical, moral, and theological discipline." The current catalogue, in the prose of which can be detected the fine Italian hand of Headmaster Jarvis, translates that mandate as a continuing commitment to a "comprehensive philosophy of education [that] seeks to help a student grow and develop not just academically but morally, aesthetically, physically, and socially." The catalogue continues: "it is . . . the end towards which a boy uses his intellectual training that is our principal concern. *We care, most of all, what kind of person a boy is.*" [Emphasis added.]

That caring quality comes through clearly over and over again in these school talks: the very title, *With Love and Prayers*, says it all. As a life trustee of the school—full disclosure is called for here, at last—I receive vast quantities of printed materials from it, all of which must in good conscience be read and digested in advance of the quarterly meetings of the board: the one publication to which I look forward and read first is the one that contains the Opening of Term addresses by the headmaster. Some of them I have heard upon their delivery in the school, and after all, like a good sermon the addresses are meant to be heard. An early morning audience of boys under compulsion is no easy challenge to meet, and for this, as for many other reasons, many schools have forsaken the assembling of themselves especially for the purpose of hearing from the headmaster. At Roxbury Latin, however, the headmaster takes naturally and regularly to his bully pulpit. Wonder of wonders, the talks read as well as they sound, with the ring of authenticity about them and hence a natural, moral authority, because one can sense in and through them the authentic and natural moral authority of the speaker.

As the author explains in his introduction to this collection, he thinks and writes in narrative form, meaning that he is given to telling stories and that he draws upon his own life and experience to do so. Moral principles abstracted from real life are as easily forgotten as they are uttered, while moral principles that derive from a lived life communicate to the lived lives of others: one's own life is the illustration of one's own story. Nearly all of Dr. Jarvis's talks begin with an existential situation, such as, "I was returning on the last train from downtown Boston. . . ." "I was in London on the first day of spring vacation, standing in line at the Aldwych Theatre. . . ." "Ten days ago in Virginia I visited Appomattox. . . ." "If you're a schoolmaster, you inevitably come into contact with parents. . . ." In the hands of a lesser master of this form so easily parodied—"The queen and I dislike namedroppers. . . ."— we might grow weary of travels with Tony, but as he is always going to interesting places and learning interesting things along the way, which he is more than willing to share, we are drawn into his words and not put off by them.

One of his most intriguing talks is entitled "Lies Teenagers Are Told," which he begins: "One night this past vacation I came to realize afresh that no segment of the population is more lied to than adolescents. . . ." Now, adolescents have an instinctual sense that that is true, but they are stunned to hear their own headmaster in Hall confirm their worst fears, and so they are bound to listen, as are we. He then goes on to discuss "The TV Family" lie, with its gross oversimplifications and Brady Bunch morality. There is "The Best Years of Your Life" lie told often at commencement time—a sad commentary if it is true; and the "There Should Be No Pain" lie fails to prepare the young for a pain-filled life and world. "We grow more through our sufferings than through our successes," he concludes.

The strength of these talks consists in their uncommon common sense reading of reality. Dr. Jarvis is able to articulate truths whose power is found not in their obscurity or profundity but in that ordinary accessibility that so often eludes those who confuse the impressive with the important, the simple with the simplistic. His talk on lies might conclude with the cynical notion to trust no one and nothing, but it doesn't, and he concludes with an extended riff on "Living Constructively with the Truth." Sometimes the truth tells us that there is no answer, no way out, no neat and tidy solution as on television, and that is when we face up to our need for help, both human and divine. "Prayer," says Headmaster Jarvis toward the close, "is what we offer up when there is nowhere else to go, nothing else to be done or said." If he had begun by saying that this was to be a talk about prayer, no one would have been with him at the end, but the journey from lies to prayer has been so fascinating, so amply illustrated, so clearly put that we are surprised to discover that there could have been no ending other than this.

In another talk, entitled "David and Goliath," the author begins with an account of a conversation. "Recently I was introduced to someone as the headmaster of Roxbury Latin. He immediately said, 'What can you possibly say to young people as they look to the future?' He didn't really want my answer, and he launched more salvos of pessimistic, gloom-doom rhetorical questions before walking away. I actually thought a good deal about his first question: 'What can you possibly say to young people as they look to the future?' and since *you* can't walk away, I'll share my answer with you. It is, simply, the biblical story of David and Goliath." This could be just another reprise of the famous Bible story, or worse, a Sunday sermon cut down and rehashed, but happily, and characteristically, it is not. Tony Jarvis tells the story with relish and the point, of course, is not what the story says but rather what it means. He amplifies the meaning with historical and contemporary examples of apparent weakness prevailing over giant odds, which he calls the "triumph of weakness," never forgetting that the motivation for this talk was the annoying pessimist who wondered what was worth saying to boys in the face of the world's seemingly overwhelming troubles. Facing the troubles of our age full on and with a visibly stiffened spine, the headmaster concludes, "I do not despair for you. I rather rejoice. Times of maximum danger provide maximum opportunity. . . . Some of you who are sitting here this morning will find the faith and courage to place your lives in the service of the living God, confident that He can use what little you have in His great purpose, and, like David, in His service you shall prevail."

This is strong stuff: God, courage, service, faith. In any context it would be worthy of notice and comment, but in an age in which the young are fed little more than self-confirming drivel from elders who fear to lead and at best can only sell, this kind of thinking out loud can seem positively incendiary. It is also seditious, which is to say that it goes against the conventional wisdom, the received opinion, the prevailing consensus. The culture that celebrates low self-esteem as its only original sin cannot easily cope with one who argues that the problem is not low self-esteem, but rather low expectation.

If what Dr. Jarvis says is novel to his boys, it ought to be familiar to an older generation that may well remember a time when inspiration, aspiration, and consecration were foundational concepts for the education of the young. I did not have the benefit of a Roxbury Latin education, but fifty years ago, in the public junior high school of Plymouth, Massachusetts, we began our day with the following school song, the verses of which I still recall:

Be strong!
We are not here to play, to dream, to drift,
We have hard work to do, and loads to lift.
Shun not the struggle, face it, 'tis God's gift. Be strong!

Be strong!
Say not the days are evil—who's to blame?
And fold the hands and acquiesce—O shame.
Stand up, speak out, and bravely, in God's name. Be strong!

Be strong!
It matters not how deep-entrenched the wrong,
How hard the battle goes, the day how long;
Faint not, fight on! Tomorrow comes the song. Be strong!

—MALTBIE DAVENPORT BABCOCK

One might easily write off all of this as the bombast of the British public schools of a century ago, or the sweaty virtue known in America as the "muscular Christianity" much admired by Phillips Brooks and Theodore Roosevelt. But there is so much more here than cold showers, corporal punishment, and the worship of brute strength—none of which, in fact, obtain at Roxbury Latin. Among the Jarvis addresses are to be found pastoral sympathies sometimes so acute in their simplicity and clarity as to bring tears to the eyes of those who know far more of the vicissitudes of life than these boys could possibly yet imagine. In a talk entitled "Coping with Pressure," he concludes that "Happiness in life is not the absence of pressure and stress. Happiness in life is finding a way to deal with the inevitable pressure and stress of life." In another talk, "Standing on Our Own Two Feet," he speaks to that boy—that person—who, from time to time and despite the best of wills and efforts, simply is overwhelmed by the dangers and demands of life and thus feels helpless, hopeless, inadequate. Instead of saying in headmasterly fashion, "Buck up," Dr. Jarvis concludes:

If you are honest with yourself as you feel your way along the human journey, you will experience times when you lose the vision, times of discouragement, times of loneliness, times when you feel powerless or lost, times of suffering, despair, emptiness. In all these darkest moments you are never, ever separated from the love of God, no matter how insignificant or worthless you feel. You need not wait until the darkest hour to place your hand in the hand of God. The truly strong man—the man who can stand on his own two feet—is the one who realizes his own weakness, his own limits. The truly strong man knows that he needs to ask for help from his companions on life's journey, and from God.

One adult friend of the Roxbury Latin School, and a regular reader of the headmaster's addresses, said somewhat ruefully that he feared that all of this was wasted on boys who, at eight o'clock in the morning, are more eager to get on with classes rather than with life. It is an understandable conceit to think that only adults can appreciate the pearls cast before them, but I have always had some sense that the headmaster knows the audience before him, and that what he says to the boys he means for them. True, in later life they might cherish all the more and in a deeper way the morning wisdom that they may have so readily taken for granted, but, for example, just as in order to have a second hearing of a Beethoven quartet there must first be a first and that first hearing must be thought to count, so it is with these addresses. Boys will not necessarily read this book, not even the unusual boys of the Roxbury Latin School, but men and women will, and they and their children will have the benefit of this anachronistic headmaster who wears his soul on his sleeve so that others may recognize that they have one of their own. When the full worth of Tony Jarvis's words and stewardship is taken and he joins that great company of his predecessors on the portrait wall, John Dryden's 1684 elegy on the grammarian Lewis Maidwell, of Westminster School, will sum it up:

Let then our Reverend Master be ador'd
And all our grateful Penns his praise Record;
I dare not name my selfe, yet what I am
From his examples and his precepts came.
Our Noblest witts from his instructive care
Have grac'd the Senate and have judg'd the Bar;
But, above all, the Muses sacred Bank
Have been transplanted from his Eden Land.

—Peter J. Gomes

Sparks House
Cambridge, Massachusetts
September 1999

Introduction

N MAY 10, 1940, as the Nazis poured into France, King George VI summoned Winston Churchill to Buckingham Palace and asked him to form a national government as prime minister. Churchill later wrote: "As I went to bed at about 3 A.M. . . . I felt as if I were walking with Destiny, and that all my past life had been but a preparation for this hour and this trial."

I felt much the same way when I was elected headmaster of Roxbury Latin twenty-five years ago, and my life ever since has been little less than a dream come true. People say you can call yourself fortunate if you are happy with two-thirds or more of your life; I love ninety-nine percent of mine. My brother-in-law Craig Smith has been organist and choirmaster at Groton School for twenty-two years. Recently, he pointed up to the great Aeolian Skinner organ in the Groton Chapel and said to me, "I'll never get over the fact that they actually pay me to play this!" In so saying, he perfectly expressed my sentiments about being headmaster of Roxbury Latin. For me, it has been a marriage made in heaven. There have been difficult times, as there are in every marriage, but I can truthfully say I have never had an adulterous moment. I have never "lusted in my heart" (as Jimmy Carter famously put it) for any other life than the one I have been blessed to have here.

I was thirty-four when I became headmaster of Roxbury Latin, and I bragged to my father that I was the youngest of the forty-four new independent school heads that year. My father, as was his wont, suggested that I had better acquire some other virtues, since that one wouldn't last long. When my mother died, my father moved to Boston and lived nearby. People from the school very kindly visited him.

Several—politely struggling to find some conversational common ground—told him how much they enjoyed my addresses to students printed in the school's newsletter. His reply was invariable: "I keep my son's speeches right by my bed. If for some reason I can't sleep, I turn on the light and read what he said. I'm sound asleep in five minutes!"

EVERY SO OFTEN people ask me, "Don't you get tired of working with teenage boys year after year?" I never do, because no boy is like any other. You have to win kids one by one. You have to find the key to each individual boy—and that is utterly engrossing and endlessly intriguing. In the last analysis, we have only two weapons we can bring to the battle of winning kids over: love and prayer. In my experience, strong and persistent love has the power to transform even the toughest and seemingly most unreachable boy. Ultimately, in my experience, nearly every boy surrenders to love. But since we understand so little about adolescent behavior, since we often don't know how best to go about loving a boy, even more important than love is prayer. The Irish Catholics in Boston have a wonderful saying: "Offer it up." By far the most important thing I do as headmaster is to offer up each boy in prayer every morning and evening.

Love and prayer are all we have and all we need to have. That is why I usually sign my letters to members of the Roxbury Latin community, "With love and prayers," and that is why so many people have suggested these words as the title of this book.

All the talks in this book are variations on these two great themes.

The summer I became headmaster, I attended a two-week conference for new heads. One of the experts running the conference announced grandly, "The time when headmasters can get up in front of their schools and give speeches or sermons is over. Young people today just won't listen." I knew he was wrong, terribly wrong. Young people are searching for meaning in their lives, and one source of that is the adults they encounter. Like it or not, those of us who work with teenagers are always speaking to them—both in what we say and in what we do. Adolescents are almost always willing to listen to adults who actually value something, who actually stand for something. And if young people believe you genuinely care about them, they will almost always give you a hearing.

This is no time for principals and teachers to stand timidly aside, sounding either an uncertain trumpet or no trumpet at all. The makers of music videos and porn films, the editors of teenage magazines, and the rock and rap idols are sounding no uncertain trumpets in advancing their agendas of hedonism—in drugs and sex—and aggressive and even violent self-expression. Those of us who believe that life has meaning and purpose—who believe that honesty, simplicity, respect, and concern for others are eternal and life-enhancing values—cannot in good conscience remain silent.

JOHN ELIOT, who founded Roxbury Latin in 1645, said that his school's purpose (indeed, the purpose of all education) should be "to fit students for public service." When, a century and a half later—in 1789—Samuel and John Phillips founded their academy at Andover, they wrote:

> *But above all, it is expected that the Master's attention to the disposition of the Minds and Morals of the Youth, under his charge, will exceed every other care; well-considering that, though goodness without knowledge . . . is weak and feeble; yet knowledge without goodness is dangerous; and that both united form the noblest character. . . . [T]he first and principal object of this institution is the promotion of PIETY and VIRTUE.*

Unlike some of their modern counterparts in education, the Phillipses saw that education outside the moral context was dangerous. Will Rogers corroborated their view when he wrote, "A poor man will steal from a railroad car. Give a man a college education and he'll steal the railroad." Surely, there has never been a more important time than now for headmasters and teachers to speak up about the meaning of life and about values to live by. That is what I have tried to do.

FOR TWENTY-FIVE YEARS, I have spoken on the opening day of each of the three terms. I have selected forty of these addresses to include in this book. They are arranged not by chronological order, but by topic.

Let me remind you that the spoken word is meant for the ear and not the eye. I am keenly aware that the talks in this book lose something when they are "reduced" to print. But it would be futile, I think, to try to turn these talks into written essays. I *spoke* these words. It has seemed equally futile to remove the topical—sometimes dated—references. These talks were given in a specific context, and much of their vitality depended on contemporary references. Repetition is one of the qualities of good teaching, and I have made no effort to cover up the fact that I repeat themes and retell stories. Likewise, I have not tried to disguise the fact that I was speaking to boys, and furthermore to boys of a particular school. However, as these talks have appeared one by one in the school newsletter, it has been very gratifying to receive letters from adults and from teenagers—girls as well as boys—whose parents or grandparents have shared my remarks with them.

Finally, let me add that people often remark that my addresses are essentially anecdotal. I have, of course, been influenced by the fact that the greatest of all teachers spoke in parables. If it is true in general that a picture is worth a thousand words, it is ten times as true when you are speaking to teenagers. Teenagers love biography; they are fascinated by the concrete reality of life experiences and they quickly drift away when you go abstract on them. Perhaps I have never grown up, but I have to confess that it is, most of all, people's stories—their own testimonials about what it is that has changed and influenced them—that move me. And, though I have not held high office, led armies in battle, or invented a cure for anything, I enjoy sharing with my beloved students the ups and downs of my own little life, the experiences—often seemingly trivial—that have caused me to stop and consider the meaning and purpose of existence. This book, then, is really my story.

I am grateful beyond expression to the trustees of Roxbury Latin for appointing me to the best job on earth and for their generous and unfailing support through good times and bad. They have made this book possible. My thanks go also to the original victims of these talks, the boys of the School. Their willingness to suspend disbelief and to listen with hope has touched me deeply and pushed me to try to be worthy of their attention.

In preparing these addresses for publication, I have once again had the good fortune to work with David Godine, alumnus of Roxbury Latin and renowned publisher. I have, therefore, happily renewed my friendships with Scott-Martin Kosofsky, the book's designer, and Marlowe Bergendoff, its copyeditor. I have benefited greatly from the wisdom of these three geniuses. I want especially to thank the person who has patiently typed and retyped these talks over the years, my incomparably wonderful and long-suffering assistant, Joanna Buxton Gormley. Finally, let me express my gratitude to my old and dear friend Peter Gomes who has written a most generous (and amusing) Foreword.

—F. WASHINGTON JARVIS

PART I
The Search for Meaning

1

What Am I Doing Here?

WAS RETURNING on the last train from downtown Boston, the 10:30 P.M. from South Station. Seconds after I sat down, a recent graduate of the School noticed me and came to join me. He's now in his early thirties. In his triumphal progress through school and college and graduate school, he won all the glittering prizes. To his contemporaries, his meteoric rise in business defines the word "success."

Our conversation began with superficial chitchat—he lamenting that the train—the 10:30 P.M.!—"left so early," since he still had more work to finish at the office. Then his tone changed and he added, in a different voice, "You know, ever since I was in school, almost all my days have been like today—never enough time to do everything I need to do. I worked incredibly hard in school. I worked incredibly hard in college. I worked incredibly hard in business school. And now I work incredibly hard at my job. Through school, college, and graduate school I never really asked myself, 'Why am I doing this?' I was always just focused on getting the crucial next credential. Every now and then, however, over the last few years—for a few frightening moments—I have actually stopped and asked myself, 'Why am I doing this? Why have I chosen this life? Why am I working so hard?' As hard as I try to repress these questions, they keep popping back up."

By the time he finished this confession, the train was nearing my stop and I was ever so slightly daunted by the task of disclosing the entire meaning and purpose of human existence in the remaining seventy seconds of my journey. For some reason James Thurber flashed through my mind, and I asked if he had ever read Thurber's short story,

"The Sea and the Shore." He hadn't, so I faxed it to him the next morning and it became the focus of our next conversation.

Thurber writes about the lemmings, the small rodents that live in Scandinavia and are best known for their inexplicable periodic tendency to rush from the land into the sea—to certain death. In Thurber's story, one "single excited lemming" looks at the setting sun on the ocean and cries out, "Fire! The world is coming to an end!" as he rushes precipitously into the sea. Mass hysteria grips the other lemmings, and in tumultuous flight—amid rumors and panic—the other lemmings follow him headlong into the sea. As they drown, some shout, "We are saved!" while others cry out, "We are lost!"

In case we miss it, Thurber tells us the moral of his story: "All men should strive to learn before they die what they are running from, and to, and why."

I read recently about a seventeen-year-old high school senior in Fremont, California, who received double 800s on her SATs and a perfect 8000 on the University of California acceptance index, something, I understand, no one had ever achieved before. She was apparently known to her high school friends as "Wonder Woman." A reporter interviewed her for the inevitable story and in the course of the interview he asked her, "What is the meaning of life?" She replied, "I have no idea."

Knowledge—which she had perfectly acquired—and wisdom are not the same. The possession of knowledge does not guarantee the possession of wisdom. You can accumulate vast stores of knowledge and still not be able to answer the question, "What am I running from and to and why?"

A couple of weeks ago I shared the story of the double-800 girl from California with a Roxbury Latin alumnus who graduated *summa cum laude* last June. He said, "I don't want to reach the age of sixty or even forty and have someone ask me what the meaning of life is and have to reply, 'I have no idea.'" Then he added, "I see so many people just going through the motions: get into a good school so you can get into a good college so you can get a good job so you can get a better job so you can get rich and die. I want more than knowledge; I want wisdom. I don't want to exist; I want to live."

Each of us is engaged in a lifelong search for wisdom and for a life worth living. I cannot stand before you and claim to have achieved either complete wisdom or the perfectly fulfilling life, but I can say to you—from my personal experience—that what little wisdom I have attained comes from two insights—both given to me by others.

Remember to Be Modest

The first is this: remember to be modest. That is the principal insight of both the Judeo-Christian tradition and of classical literature. You are mortal, you have but a comparatively short time on the planet, and then you are gone. Much in the universe is vastly beyond either your understanding or your control. To the Hebrews, the principal error of human beings is their pride: we forget that we're human—we think we're the brightest and best and that we can act as if we're God. And when humans think they're God, tragedy ensues—for all concerned. After Adam and Eve eat the forbidden fruit of the tree of knowledge of good and evil, their lives cease to be a paradise garden and unhappiness ensues.

The Greeks reached essentially the same conclusion as the Hebrews. Sophocles, for example, saw that hubris (pride, human presumption) was the path to ruin. Listen to what his Chorus says at the end of *Oedipus Rex*:

> *Men of Thebes: look upon Oedipus.*
> *This is the king who solved the famous riddle*
> *And towered up, most powerful of men.*
> *No mortal eyes but looked upon him with envy,*
> *Yet in the end ruin swept over him.*
> *Let all of us in our human frailty*
> *Consider life's last days; and let none*
> *Presume on our good fortune until we find*
> *Life, at our death, a memory without pain.*

"Presume" is exactly what Oedipus does: his life defines hubris because he forgets he is a mere man, forgets that he is not in control of the universe, forgets that he is mortal, subject to forces beyond his control.

To both the Hebrews and the Greeks, modesty was the gateway to wisdom. "The fear of the Lord," said the Hebrews, "is the beginning of wisdom." The acknowledgment of our temporary humanity in the presence of the Eternal God was, to them, the starting point. To the Greeks also, modesty (humility) was the greatest virtue. Not so much modesty as an ethical virtue (though they admired that) but modesty as an existential virtue. Sophocles portrays Theseus, the great king of Athens, as the incarnation of this existential modesty in *Oedipus at Colonus*. King Theseus says to Oedipus:

> *I know I am only a man, I have no more*
> *To hope for in the end than you have.*

Albert Einstein possessed this existential modesty; arguably it is what made him the greatest scientist of his time. Listen to what he said:

> *The most beautiful and most profound emotion we can experi-*
> *ence [is the awareness] of the mystical. It is the source of all*
> *true art and science. . . . this insight into the mystery of life . . .,*
> *[this knowledge] that what is impenetrable to us really exists*
> *. . . is at the center of true religiousness. . . . My religion consists*
> *of a humble admiration of the illimitable superior spirit, who*
> *reveals himself in the slight details we are able to perceive with*
> *our frail and feeble minds.*

Sir Isaac Newton possessed this same humility, this same existential awareness of the brevity of our human lives and the limits of our human minds:

> *I do not know [how] I may appear to the world, but to myself I*
> *seem only like a boy playing on the seashore and diverting*
> *myself now and then finding a smoother pebble or a prettier*
> *shell than ordinary, whilst the great ocean of truth lay all*

undiscovered before me. . . .

The first truth, then, that I would leave with you is this: mod-esty—the realization that you know very little and that life is very short—is the beginning of wisdom.

Greed Does Not Bring Happiness

The second insight (about wisdom and life) I can put more concisely: Greed (or even enlightened self-interest) does not bring happiness. Real happiness comes only to those who are able to grow beyond self-interest.

As children, we all love receiving things: What will I get for my birthday? What will my father and mother bring me home from their trip? What game or toy will I get if I'm good? Children believe that it is more blessed to receive than to give.

As we mature, we come to enjoy giving as much as or more than get-ting. We see a child's face light up when she receives a gift, we enjoy the gratitude that comes from doing a favor for a friend. We discover that "it is more blessed to give than to receive." We are happier giving than receiving. And, in the great mystery of things, we discover that the more we give of ourselves the happier we are.

Someone recently conducted a survey of retirement home residents. "Do you have any regrets?" they were asked. Here's what they said:

First, they wished they'd spent more time loving people.

Second, they wished they'd taken more risks.

Third, they wished they'd done some good that would remain after they are gone.

These three regrets encapsulate the second insight I want to suggest to you about the meaning of life: if you want to be happy, you have to go beyond self-interest. You have to take the risk of reaching out to others. You have to pay the price in time, talent, and treasure now in order to do something that will endure after you're dead. This is part of what Willa Cather meant when she said, "Happiness is to be dissolved into something complete and great." Happiness comes when you get beyond self-interest: when you dare to risk loving people and when you involve yourself in some costly cause that benefits others more than it benefits you.

Choose to Live

I am aware that it is fashionable to be cynical, and I could reel off most of the aphorisms attributed to Vince Lombardi. Cynicism is nothing new. It has always been fashionable to be cynical. Frances Cornford cynically described the young poet Rupert Brooke this way when he was about your age:

> *A young Apollo, golden-haired,*
> *Stands dreaming on the verge of strife,*
> *Magnificently unprepared*
> *For the long littleness of life.*

The too-little-recognized eighteenth-century poet and playwright Edward Young plaintively lamented: "Born originals, how comes it to pass that we die copies?" We might ask, with the same sadness, "Given the opportunity to live, how comes it to pass that so many choose only to exist?"

The tired and the worldly-wise view "the long littleness of life" with cynicism and despair. And the way most people—in every generation—choose merely to exist seems to corroborate this cynical and despairing outlook. If your generation is like those that have gone before it—and it is—the majority of your contemporaries will choose unreflective, shallow, comfortable, self-indulgent existences. They will die "copies."

T. S. Eliot memorialized this majority in these words:

> *A Cry from the North, from the West and from the South*
> *Whence thousands travel daily to the timekept City;*
> *Where My Word is unspoken,*
> *In the land of lobelias and tennis flannels*
> *The rabbit shall burrow and the thorn revisit,*
> *The nettle shall flourish on the gravel court,*

And the wind shall say: "Here were decent godless people:
Their only monument the asphalt road
And a thousand lost golf balls."

That will be the epitaph of most people in your generation as it is the epitaph of most people in my generation. It is the epitaph of the dull, of the copies, in every generation.

There is another way. It is the way chosen by the few in every generation who are courageous enough to face the existential reality of their own mortality, of their own modest place in the universe. It is the way of the few who—fully aware of the smallness of their own lives— are somehow, nevertheless, empowered to use what little they have for causes and concerns beyond—and greater than—themselves. The way of the few is the harder, more lonely, more costly way. Someone asked Mother Teresa of Calcutta shortly before she died, "Why did you choose to give up family and money and security to go and live among the destitute and hopeless?" In a flash, she replied, "I wanted a very hard life."

I am not cynical or despairing about you because I believe that most of you will dare to choose the hard life, because I believe that most of you will dare to be among the few in your generation who will make a difference. Most of you already know that the only life worth living is the hard life. The hard life is the better way. Whatever else the harder way is, it is not dull. It is, I would submit, much more exciting, much more rewarding, and, dare we say it, much more fun.

2

Lies Teenagers Are Told

NE NIGHT this past vacation I came to realize afresh that no segment of the population is more lied to than adolescents. Last Tuesday night, after a particularly grueling sequence of days and nights, I crawled home for a late supper and—foolish optimist that I am—I grabbed the weekly TV guide and looked eagerly for something that would entertain me on my first night of TV in months. I recognized nothing on the schedule, but after perusing the blurbs under 8 P.M. I settled on *Who's the Boss?* It was a charming little story about a dumb but lovable father who found it hard to trust his teenage daughter to go out on a date. Upshot: father falsely accuses daughter, daughter is innocent, father apologizes, much hugging.

Done in by this gripping drama I was too weak to change channels and soon found myself engrossed in the epic that followed at 8:30: *Growing Pains.* The subject of this story was a dumb but lovable teenage son who decides to take a part-time job with a former buddy who is a bad guy. Upshot: son takes job, son realizes former buddy is a bad guy, son comes home to worried but trusting parents to tell them that they (the parents) were right all along, much hugging.

The TV Family Lie

As I watched I suddenly realized that these two shows have been playing on TV for at least thirty-five years—only under different names—*Ozzie and Harriet, Flipper, My Three Sons, The Brady Bunch, The Partridge Family, Eight Is Enough,* to name a few from decades past.

American audiences never tire of these two relentlessly and endlessly recurring plots: parents who come to realize their kids are basically good and who then apologize for not trusting them; kids who come to realize their parents' values are right and who then apologize for doubting their loving parents.

Both these plots are reassuring and I predict your children and grandchildren will watch them reenacted on TV (or whatever replaces TV) for years to come. Why, then, make a big deal about them?

The reason I make a big deal about them is that they oversimplify life's complexity to such a degree that they are lies—quite damaging lies about the way life really is.

The first conversation I had with an adolescent in my first parish began by his saying to me, "Unfortunately, I don't come from the typical All-American family." After he had talked a bit about his family's various difficulties, I said to him, "By the way, how would you describe the typical American family?" And he rattled off a list of characteristics of his idea of the typical family and then concluded by saying, "You know, like the Brady Bunch."

I've had a thousand conversations like that one with adolescents over the last twenty-three years: all based on the misconception that these TV families are "typical." But, of course, they are not typical. Real parents usually are not cute and lovable, they have serious problems of their own, they have to earn a living, they have to deal with disappointments, they are not always there, they can't always understand. Conflicts are rarely resolved in twenty-two minutes (thirty minutes minus eight minutes for commercials) and sometimes never resolved at all. Real adolescents are usually not very cute and lovable, they have zits and body odor, they aren't always surrounded by pals or by adoring members of the opposite sex, they make bad mistakes with long-range consequences, they don't get out of every scrape unscathed, they don't resolve disagreements neatly, they don't get their hurts all nicely and immediately nursed. Family fights do not always end in hugging.

It is not you or your family that is atypical or abnormal. It is this TV fantasy of problems-easily-resolved in twenty-two-minutes-and-all's-well that is false to reality. Real parents and real adolescents are not like that. Real life is not like that.

The Best-Years-of-Your-Life Lie

Another lie adults tell adolescents is the one that goes, "These are the best years of your life. These are the happy, carefree years."

Last summer I was briefly back in my hometown—Painesville, Ohio. And I was having dinner at the home of one of my old school buddies and his wife and kids who were about your age. The minute we all sat down at the supper table, he began regaling everybody about the great times he and I had had as kids. Now I had, I think, about as happy a childhood and adolescence as anyone could have. I'd duplicate it for all teenagers if I could. But this guy's description of life in the fifties in a Midwestern small town was a wildly idealized picture of a golden age of innocence and fun that simply never existed. I finally said (and he was not at all happy to hear his fantasies disturbed): "Come on, George, we were bored stiff a lot of the time."

Every afternoon after school I delivered the evening paper to eighty-nine customers in my neighborhood, and then went home for supper, which, typically in the Midwest, was at 5:30. In the school year I then went up and did my homework. Boring. In the summer I went down to the Sohio gas station with my friends and hung around listening to Elvis Presley and other avant garde cultural luminaries on the radio. Months—maybe years—after movies had played everywhere else in the nation, they came to Painesville's one and only theatre—the Lake Theatre —and we skipped the gas station to see each new movie on the opening night of its weeklong run. Otherwise, we hung around. Oddly, I don't recall ever asking myself whether or not I was happy, but had I been asked if I was happy, I'm certain I'd have said, "Sure." But, objectively, no one could legitimately recall these years as some sort of golden age of adolescence.

Adults remember selectively. They recall selectively a few golden moments: the time someone told them how wonderful they were, or the walk on the beach with the girl as the sun was setting. Adults forget the wrenching trauma of breaking up with a girlfriend, the dreary hours devoted to homework in history or Algebra II, the hurts inflicted by friends we trusted, being left out, the ennui and emptiness of nothing-to-do on a summer's night.

I rebuked a parent the other day for laughing about what she called "the puppy love" of her son who had broken up with his girlfriend. I rebuked her because I think such events hurt adolescents more deeply than they hurt adults who have been through them before and who know they'll survive. There is much about adolescence that is painful. Fortunately, human beings—over time—tend to sift out unhappy memories and remember the good things about the past. That's what an adult is doing who tells you, "These are the happiest years of your life." But whatever tricks memory may play, the reality is adolescence is not the happiest time of life—but rather a time of often painful self-discovery, of confusion about who you are and what you want, of self-doubt, fear of failure, and dread of rejection.

I thought I was pretty happy as a teenager, but I have found the years after adolescence far happier and more fulfilling. And I believe you will.

The There-Should-Be-No-Pain Lie

The third lie adults tell adolescents is that the teenage years should be years without pain, without suffering. I am touched but appalled at how far some parents go to protect their children against any kind of defeat or disappointment or rejection or unhappiness. As a result, their children are deprived of learning how to deal with these inevitable realities of adult life.

Parents say to me such things as, "You don't realize how hurt my son was not to be invited to his friend's party." But life does not consist of always being included in everything or even in most of what we want to be included in. How will adults cope when they're not invited to things they'd like to be invited to if they have had no experience of being left out when they're younger?

Parents sometimes say to me, "You don't realize how terribly hurt my son was to be cut from the team," or a variation, "I'm worried about his self-image; you don't realize how hurt he was by getting so little playing time." But I *do* realize—because I was bitterly disappointed on both counts myself as a teenager. I was cut and I sat on the bench. And in retrospect, I think I probably learned more from those "defeats" than I learned from the many and celebrated successes I had in school. I had to dig deep and find self-respect. I had to pick myself up out of the dust and find reasons to go on cheerfully. And I did. And the experience of doing so has prepared me well for all the defeats and reverses that real adult life dishes out to everyone.

A parent said to me last spring, "You don't realize how deeply hurt my son is by not getting into his first-choice college. It's cruelly unfair. He should have gotten what he wanted after all the work he's put in for it. He's just been destroyed by being rejected." I said at the time what I have often said in similar circumstances. It may sound glib but I mean it with all my heart: "I'm never sure each spring who's luckier: the ones who get into their first-choice college or the ones who don't."

I have a friend who was—as a youth—the proverbial "fair-haired boy." Handsome, charismatic, smart. Everything broke his way. He always made the team and was always elected captain. Mr. Popularity. He starred at everything. He got into his first-choice college, and again at college everything broke his way and he went from success to success. But when he got his first job, his boss didn't instantly love him or instantly promote him. And so my friend quit, loudly proclaiming what a jerk his boss was. This first job experience quickly repeated itself in his next job and gradually a pattern developed—he quit one job after another, and in every case his boss "was a jerk." His youthful success had terribly misled him into thinking that everything would always break his way. He had been deprived of the experience of defeat and disappointment and therefore was unable to cope when real life brought him defeat and disappointment.

How often at Roxbury Latin I have seen boys rejected by their first- or second-choice college—disappointed, crushed. How often have I seen these very boys dig deep to discover much more profoundly who they are, what they're worth, and what they want to accomplish in life. How often these boys have said to me later: "I was bitterly disappointed at the time. But in retrospect I'm really glad things worked out the way they did."

It may well be that the most valuable experiences we have in adolescence are not our triumphs or our successes or our popularity, but rather our disappointments and defeats and rejections. We grow more through our sufferings than through our successes.

Living Constructively with the Truth

I've been talking about the lies adults tell. What, then, is the truth about life? The truth, I submit, was stated succinctly by Jesus of Nazareth: "In the world ye shall have tribulation." Life is not easy. Life has its troubles.

The cynic will state that truth bitterly. "Expect the worst in life," the cynic says, "and you'll rarely be disappointed." And people build whole lives around bitter disappointment. We all know adults who complain incessantly about life—how burdened they are by this or that family obligation, how underrecognized they are, how put upon in every way. Complaining becomes a way of life to such people. A variation on this theme is practiced by those who go around angrily trying to affix blame—if I can find someone to blame I'll feel better. The lives of such people become self-fulfilling prophecies: almost every event becomes a verification of the complainer's outlook. Every action is cynically analyzed so that it becomes further cause of complaint. How many people waste their lives complaining!

But we do not have to be among the pathetic who react this way to life's realities. There are constructive responses to the reality that "in the world ye shall have tribulation." And I want to share with you— briefly—some constructive responses I have found useful—and which you may, as well. This is not an exhaustive, objective list, but a short, quite personal, list.

1. I sometimes wake up at night—or become aware in the midst of the day—that dozens of obligations and commitments are jangling through my brain: I've got to do this; don't forget that. All of them seem priority obligations, and amid the swirl, I feel incapable of facing any of them. When I feel overwhelmed by priority obligations, I find it helpful to sit down and make a list of all the things I have to do, all the obligations, all the worries. Writing them down gives me at least the illusion of control and sometimes is the key to organizing the reality of control. There is also something psychologically soothing about transferring the various conflicting jangling worries from one's mind onto a piece of paper.

2. A second tactic I have found useful is just to do something—anything—to get my mind off my own problems. In the middle of the night, reading for a while can help do that. In the day, some small act of kindness toward another can sometimes pull me out of myself.

3. Another useful tactic is to cut problems up in smaller pieces. In order to bribe myself to grade papers, I lay them all out in sets of four on Sunday afternoon, and then I give myself a present (a section of the *New York Times* or something I want to do) after I have graded each set of four.

4. Another useful attitude is one that my grandmother used to try to convey to me whenever I complained about something as a child. She would say, "Count your blessings." It's my experience that adolescents (and adults) spend a great deal of time and energy counting the curses in their lives, and little time counting their blessings. We look at the two percent of the world's population that are better off than we are and not the ninety-eight percent who are less well off than we are. We always compare up to the two percent and never down to the ninety-eight percent. We conveniently forget that a third of the world's population goes to sleep every night hungry. I say "goes to sleep" rather than "goes to bed" because much of the world's population—and a good many right in our own prosperous city—don't have a bed to sleep in or a roof over their heads. There is something obscene—even blasphemous—about much of our self-pity. Less than two percent of the

world's population is as well off as every one of us in this room is. We need now and then to take stock and count our blessings, to realize that we are in so many ways better off than almost all the people around us in the global village.

5. Having grown up in an era dominated by the "I'll-tough-this-out-alone" philosophy of life, it took me quite a while to realize that, from time to time, we all need to ask help from our fellow human beings as we try to cope with our lives and sort out our troubles. It takes courage to ask for help. We like to be in control; we like others to think we're tough, that we don't need anyone's help, that we can do it on our own. It takes guts to say, "I'm having trouble dealing with this." It takes guts to say, "I'm really hurting from what happened to me." It takes guts to say, "I don't know what to do about things." Everybody needs help getting through life. The gutless man is afraid to admit he needs help or to seek help. The man of courage is willing to express that need and to seek that help.

6. Finally, and closely related to that asking for human help, is the seeking of Divine help in prayer. When I was a small boy my father went off to war and my mother and sister and I went to live in my grandparents' house in a small town in western New York. It was a large house because until the depression they had been quite wealthy. Living in the house was their sometime maid, an older woman who had come as a girl from Ireland to work for my great grandparents. Her name was Mrs. Jackson; we called her "Mrs. Jacky." One wartime day (when I was four or five) my mother and I were in the laundry room with Mrs. Jacky and I suddenly realized that my mother was crying. (A parent crying makes a strong impression on a small child.) She was talking to Mrs. Jacky about her brother, my uncle George, a Marine pilot who was missing in the Far East. When my mother finished, Mrs. Jacky said, "Offer it up, Prudy. Offer it up."

That is, of course, what prayer is. And, of course, many people don't discover prayer until they are faced with problems they cannot solve. A year or two ago a boy said to me, "I never really prayed until I watched my mother try and fail and try and fail and try and fail again to control her drinking." Recently a father said to me, "I never prayed until the doctor told me that my sixteen-year-old son is going to die of cancer."

There are many things in life we are not in control. Jewish parents of a sixteen-year-old girl said to me a few months ago: "We don't belong to any temple, but when we see our daughter walk down the front steps and go off in a car with a boy who just got his license, we pray." And a Roxbury Latin wrestler who won the Graves-Kelsey Tournament said to me a while back, "I don't get down on my knees, I don't cross myself or anything, I don't look like I'm praying before a match, but I'm totally praying."

There is much in life we are not in complete control of—much that we simply have to offer up. That's what prayer is: the crying out, the offering up of the mess we're in. "I don't know if I can hack this. I don't see a way out of this mess. Help!"

3

Attitude

WHEN I THINK of myself at your age, the words that, like a wave, keep rolling in and washing over me are the words: "I don't like your attitude." These words could be uttered in a variety of tones. My grandmother spoke them reproachfully: "Do you think that's the right attitude to have?" Uttered by my father—"I don't like your attitude"—they were a warning that the line had been drawn. On my street lived Mr. Reniger—whose evening paper I had the misfortune to deliver six nights a week on my paper route. On the rainiest or snowiest of days, he would stand—practically stopwatch in hand—waiting just inside the front door of his house to pounce on his paper when I delivered it. If I was late by five minutes, he'd pounce on me. I quickly learned to keep silent, for if I made the slightest excuse he was off to the races on a four hundred-hour tirade that began with "Son"—every man in Ohio in those days addressed every boy as "son"—"Son, I don't like your attitude. If I'd made an excuse like that when I was your age . . . blah, blah, blah." I'll skip ninety-nine percent of his harangue—because only the final line is memorable. He always concluded with this rousing finale: "Son, I don't like your attitude. It's a perfect example of everything that's wrong with this country."

Since, at so early an age I attained the distinction of having an attitude that was "a perfect (note the word!) example of everything that's wrong with our country," I am obviously a certified expert on the subject I'd like to address this morning: the all-important question of attitude.

Get a Real Life

Last year at this time I described in detail an obnoxious preppie adolescent who sat in front of me on a transatlantic flight. She was the picture of entitlement: miserable because she (poor baby) had to endure a seven-hour flight from London when she was tired. "This seat's uncomfortable," "I don't like this food," she groaned. Her life was constructed on the premise that she should have everything she wanted. She should never have discomfort of any sort; every need should be met at once, every desire gratified.

This attitude of entitlement is not, of course, confined to preppie adolescents. It is present—though cleverly disguised in many adults. I know adults who expect that everything in their marriage or their job should be perfect, all their feelings understood, all their needs met; and then, when they are not, they expend enormous energy blaming someone else.

Last year after the first marking period, a set of parents came in to see me: "For the first time in three years here," they said, "our son doesn't like one of his teachers. The two of them just don't communicate well and he's not happy in the class. We don't think he should have to spend a whole year this way, and we want you to move him to another teacher."

My response was deliberately overstated. I said, "I'm glad he's unhappy. He now has the opportunity to grow by discovering how to cope with someone he doesn't like. It will be very interesting to see how he handles it." The premise on which these parents were operating was that life—childhood, adolescence, adulthood—shouldn't contain anything that makes us unhappy. That premise is exactly the same premise as that of the entitled preppie on the airplane.

If a school is preparing young people for life—and it is—it would be cruelly wrong to give young people the impression that life is devoid of pain, to give adolescents the impression that in life you don't have to get along with people you don't like or perform tasks that are difficult or unpleasant.

If you approach life with the attitude of expecting that life is a rose garden that will offer you nothing but beautiful sights and pleasant fragrances, you are in for a huge disappointment. Happiness comes to those who have realistic expectations about life. I picked up a couple (who are friends of mine) at the airport this summer and, trying to get out of the short-term parking lot, I got caught in a line of traffic that barely moved, because, instead of several toll booths being open, only one was, and that one was manned by an imbecile without any change. As a result, it took us forty minutes to go seventy-five feet. Now it's not as if we were going to be late for a meeting with the governor. We were just heading to my house for a bologna sandwich. Nonetheless the husband launched into a tirade about Boston, modern math (because the toll booth attendant was an adolescent who couldn't count), the heat, the decline and fall of the United States, and ultimately, the unbearable stress of modern life.

The premise of all these histrionic lamentations, of course, was that, for him, the lights should all be green, the path before him always clear, the weather sunny but cool. Life, in short, should never present any difficulties.

I have often said that anyone who drives to Logan Airport should expect trouble. Anyone who travels should expect delays and inconvenience. A mature attitude toward life begins with the premise that life does not accommodate itself to us; we must accommodate ourselves to life. And life often presents us with difficulties. How stupid not to expect life to be difficult, when it usually is.

I spent a week downtown this summer doing research at the Boston Athenæum. As I crossed Tremont Street the first day, I witnessed something I would see each successive morning: a traffic jam (exactly what any reasonable person driving on Boston's narrow downtown streets would expect). What struck me, therefore, were the many drivers who were red in the face, profusely sweating, pressing on their horns in apoplexy because they were stalled in traffic. Most of these people were familiar with Boston's morning rush hour, and yet they were still upset, still stressed, still fighting it. They had still not made their peace with reality. But I could also see, looking in the windows of other cars, that there were at least as many mature adults who drove to work each morning expecting difficulty, expecting a traffic jam, expecting delay. They sat quietly—even serenely—until things sorted themselves out, knowing that outrage and impatience would not affect the tide of traffic in the least. Their attitude was that trouble should be expected in life, and this attitude of realistic expectation enabled them to be at peace.

Life does not adjust itself to us; we have to adjust ourselves to life's inconveniences, to life's disappointments. We don't get everything we want. We can waste a lot of energy blaming people (it sometimes feels good to kick someone around), we can waste a lot of energy complaining or lamenting. But people who have a mature attitude expect that they'll have to come to grips with the disappointments life doles out.

And life is filled with disappointments. When I was a freshman in high school in Ohio, a friend of mine—also a freshman—was about 6'1" or 2" and weighed 180 pounds. He not only won a place on the varsity football team, but he played a lot as well. Naturally, he was drawn more and more away from me and our circle of freshman friends and into a circle of older boys. And this upset us. One night in mid-fall, I said to my father, "Jack is really conceited" (actually I said, "Jack is really stuck up," which was Midwestern for conceited). "Jack is really stuck up. Just 'cause he's playing varsity football, he thinks he's better than me."

My father's response was withering: "Well, actually he's bigger than you, he's stronger than you, and he's a much better player than you."

A few years ago I recounted my father's comment to a child psychiatrist and he replied, "That's child abuse. What a terrible thing for a father to say!" "No," I said, "that's the kind of reality that someone who really loves you confronts you with." My father was not saying, "You are a loathsome worm because you're not the biggest, strongest, and best football player in the ninth grade." My father was saying, "You must adjust to life because life is not going to adjust to you. You may want to have Jack's body, but you don't. You may want to be a better player, but you're not." To put it in the language of today, the essence of what my father was saying was this: "Get a real life. Others have things you'll never have; accept that and get on with real life."

My first point, then, is this. If you want to be happy in life, get real: approach life with the attitude that life has many problems and that life has many disappointments. Lower your expectations.

We Are Not Victims

My second point is this: just because life does not fulfill your every hope does not mean that you have to adopt the attitude of a victim. The other day, as I sat in a hundred-plus-degree Red Line subway car stuck somewhere near (but not in) Park Street Station, a baby started to cry—I mean all-out throbbing wailing. Babies do that if they don't have what they want. They signal their unhappiness to the world, until someone gives them succor. Adolescents and adults don't cry like babies, but I know adolescents and adults who are figurative crybabies. They're always complaining about not having just what they want. You all probably know an adult hypochondriac, someone who is not really sick but who forms his whole personality around being sick, so he can be waited on, sympathized with as a victim. There are psychological hypochondriacs: people who form their whole personality on some real or imagined hurt. If you believed the anecdotal evidence of Oprah or Geraldo (speaking of great moments in American culture), you would conclude that most of the population of the United States had cruel or abusive parents who said and did terrible things to their children that scarred them for life.

Some of these people were, in reality, abused victims of their parents' sickness. Others were not—they just approach life with the attitude that every need at every moment in their childhood should have been perfectly met and satisfied (which, of course, never happens in real life).

Whether they are real victims or—as I believe, in many cases—imagined victims, these people form their whole attitude toward life as victims, forever looking back at some scarring experience or relationship.

Such an attitude is a guaranteed recipe for unhappiness. The great Viennese psychiatrist Viktor Frankl articulated the opposite view when he wrote about his ghastly imprisonment in a Nazi concentration camp where everything was stripped away—his clothes, his possessions, his professional standing, all personal dignity—and he was reduced to slave labor and near starvation and death. But Frankl did not adopt the mantle of victimization. He did not wallow and sulk in self-pity. He adopted instead the attitude that he was in control of his own mind. The one thing they couldn't take away from him was his ability to respond positively. And he built a rich interior life of the mind, an unassailable mental kingdom. This mental strength, this attitude, enabled him to survive.

Some years ago, Billy McDonald sat in the seats you now occupy. Captain-elect of football, he was diagnosed with leukemia at the end of his Class II year; he was seventeen years old. Chemotherapy that summer reduced his two-hundred-pound body by almost a hundred pounds; all his hair fell out. At first he felt sorry for himself. Until he was seventeen, everything had gone well for him. A golden future had seemed to beckon. Now he was dying. Of course, he felt self-pity.

Then one day his whole attitude changed. He went down to the cancer ward for little children and saw tots two, four, and six years old who, like him, were facing almost certain death from cancer. When I visited him that night, the first words he said were, "I guess I'm really lucky." "Why's that?" I asked. And he told me about visiting the little kids, and then said, "At least I've had seventeen years." And tears filled his eyes as he told me about an eight-year-old boy who had asked him, "Billy, do you think I'll ever play football like you?"

From then on, Billy was no longer a victim. He could not change the cruel reality life had dished out to him; he knew he was going to die (and, in fact, he was dead by the following March, two months before he would have graduated). But, even though he could not change the cruel realities life dished out to him, he did not become a "victim." He took control of his response to life's realities. His attitude was not one of victimization and complaining and lamenting, but rather: I will face all this horror cheerfully and positively and with dignity. And he did.

Life does not adjust itself to us, we must adjust ourselves to life. We must expect disappointments, and when they come we must try to find the strength to respond to them courageously. When we are handed a lemon we must (as the old cliché puts it) try to make lemonade.

Seeing Life's Possibilities

The final point I want to make about attitude is this: while we must expect that life is hard, that life does not give us all we want, and lower our expectations about what life will bring us, we must not, on the other hand, become lugubrious pessimists who see life only in terms of its bad possibilities. Just as we must lower our expectations about life, we must also raise our sights and see life in terms of its highest possibilities.

This summer marked the seventy-fifth anniversary of the events that led to the building of the great shrine at Fatima in Portugal. And in July (as I said) I made a pilgrimage there—as millions do every year. I've been amazed at how people respond when I tell them I was at Fatima. I guess I expected they'd say something like, "Oh, was it 'wonderful' or 'meaningful' or some such?" The first response from three out of four, however, is, "Oh, wasn't it terribly commercial?"

Now, in one way, such a response is just the sort of mature lowering of expectations that I've been advocating. And, of course, if you visit a place that's visited each day by hundreds of thousands of people, all of whom want some souvenir of their visit, then, of course, you will expect Fatima to be commercialized. But what struck me was that, coupled with such realism in these people, there was absolutely no idealism. Almost no one said, "Oh, I bet it was wonderful" or "Was the shrine beautiful or moving?" Lowering of expectation alone as an attitude can be nothing more than craven pessimism, disillusioned cynicism. It must always be accompanied by idealism. Before I went to Fatima I knew that it would be commercialized. And it was. But before I went I also hoped it would be a place where I could worship and pray and offer my life up again to God and find refreshment and renewal. Since I had expected to find commercialism, I was not dismayed when I found it there. But I also found what I had hoped to find: inspiration and renewal. My experience in life is that we often find what we ardently hope to find, what we idealistically dare to search for.

In George Bernard Shaw's play *Saint Joan*, Joan of Arc urges the French king and the archbishop to continue the fight against the English. Her "voices," she says, ordered them to so do.

"Oh, your voices, your voices," says the king, despairingly, cynically. "Why don't your voices come to me? I am the king, not you!"

To which Joan of Arc replies: "They do come to you, but you do not hear them. You have not sat in the fields in the evening listening for them. When the angelus rings you cross yourself and have done with it: but if you prayed from your heart and listened to the throbbing of the bells in the air after they stop ringing, you would hear the voices as well as I do."

Joan knew all about the trials one could expect in life. But she did not stop seeing life in terms of its possibilities.

That is the attitude I dare to hope you will adopt towards life: to be realistic and yet to remain idealistic; to expect life to be difficult and disappointing, but to remain positive and cheerful, listening for the beautiful sounds, looking for the ennobling sights, seeking to discover: to see and perceive, to hear and understand, to know and affirm.

Stop—Look—and—Listen

GREW UP in a small town in Ohio crisscrossed by four
different railroads. You couldn't go very far without coming to a railroad crossing. A few major crossings had
blinking lights and bells automatically set off by an
approaching train, but most simply had large white wooden signs with
the words Stop—Look—and—Listen in black letters. Mrs. Curry, my
first grade teacher, wrote those words on the blackboard. Stop—
Look—and—Listen were the first words we learned to read because
most of us crossed tracks on our daily walk to school. Mrs. Curry even
taught us a little song—which I shall restrain myself from singing to
you—the refrain of which was: "Stop—Look—and—Listen."

On the theory that everything we need to know in life we learn by
the age of six, I want to take that refrain as the topic of my remarks this
morning.

Stop

"Stop!" was often the advice I needed most when I was your age,
and—from all I see—you need it, too. When I was your age I needed to
be told now and then to stop. And even today—in my infinite wisdom—
I still need that advice. Stop acting that way. Stop being a jerk. Stop
complaining. Stop procrastinating. Stop indulging yourself. Stop
goofing off. Stop wasting time. Stop rationalizing.

"Stop!" is often good advice. And I want to focus on two kinds of
stopping that are particularly important. From time to time I feel
unhappy—angry, depressed, fed up. Sometimes I feel that way because
I'm brooding day and night about some specific problem. More often,

it's not something specific but rather a general sense of unhappiness—of malaise and lethargy—that hangs like a dark cloud over my life.

Matthew Arnold speaks, in one of his poems, about

> *. . . this strange disease of modern life,*
> *with its sick hurry, its divided arms,*
> *Its heads o'ertaxed, its palsied heart. . . .*

When Arnold speaks of "this strange disease," he is using the word disease in its original meaning: dis-ease, being on edge, often for reasons we cannot quite understand, feeling uneasy, at odds with things, disturbed, downhearted, devoid of energy and enthusiasm. Dis-eased.

I find, at such times, that the most valuable action I can take is simply to stop, take out a pad of paper, and ask myself, "OK. What's wrong? What's bothering me?" It's often at the busiest and most pressured times—when you're stressed to the hilt and least able to stop—that you have to stop, take inventory, and analyze your dis-ease.

I talked to a Roxbury Latin boy two days before midyears and could tell he was stressed by his impending exams. I asked him what his first exam was, and he told me. Then I said, "What do you have on Friday?" He had no idea. He was completely dis-eased. His exams loomed as a huge unmanageable problem. I said, "Look, I want you to sit down before you go today and draw up a chart, showing when each exam is and when you're going to be studying for it." He snapped at me, "I don't have time to do that! I have to use all my time to study." And he was furious when I made him sit down and do it. Fortunately, he almost immediately saw that stopping and planning ahead were actually relieving his anxiety. When exams were over, he said to me: "Just writing all the exams down on one sheet of paper made me feel better. I got control. I could see that there was time for me to deal with each one."

When you feel upset—dis-eased—in general or specific, it is extremely healthy just to stop, to write down everything you can think of that bothers you. Rather than jangling around in your brain and psyche, what is dis-easing you is then transferred to a piece of paper—and you can then diagnose and treat it. You can get control, you can break down the problem into manageable smaller pieces. The time to stop and take such an inventory is often precisely when you tell yourself you don't have time to stop.

There's another kind of stopping that I've also found useful: stopping not just when I'm in a crisis, but at certain regular intervals in my life. I choose certain points in my life when I stop and reclarify what my goals and objectives are. Some people do this at New Year's, making resolutions for the coming year. Some people do it at Rosh Hashanah or during Lent. Some students do it at the start of each school year. I stop for this purpose several times a year. When I stop I find that it is critically important to do a written inventory: what I'm happy and unhappy about in my life and what my new goals (or resolutions) will be for the days ahead. I find my own mental health is deeply dependent on these regular times of stopping. And sometimes I add a very special stop. Last summer I went to the great shrine at Lourdes in France for two days of prayer and reflection. It was an amazingly helpful experience to reclarify all the goals and priorities of my life.

Some years ago I was asked to speak at a summer conference for school heads and their spouses. We met in June and we were all exhausted. Feeling very tired and spent, I got up very early that morning to write my talk, and the words that came to me were from the prophet Isaiah: "They that wait upon the Lord shall renew their strength; they shall mount up with wings like eagles, they shall run and not be weary, and they shall walk and not faint." Isaiah says—in essence—if you want to be healed, restored, reinvigorated, you must stop and wait upon the Lord, stop and take stock.

To my amazement, as the day progressed, four couples who had heard my talk spoke with me about it. The response of one of these couples was brutally honest. They said, "We're afraid to stop. We're afraid to take inventory of our lives. We both work and play obsessively so we won't have to reflect on life. We're afraid of what we'd find out if we stopped." Three of the couples felt their marriages were disintegrating.

Something a Class IV boy said to me (before the holiday) brought back a long-forgotten fragment of memory of myself at his age. I was fourteen—sitting alone in my bedroom with the radio blaring. My door was closed so it really didn't bother anyone. I'd have isolated myself with a Walkman, as some of you do, but Walkmans hadn't been invented. My father came in and said, "Turn your damned radio off. You can't think listening to music like that." To which I replied vehemently, "I don't *want* to think."

There is something in our natures that makes us resist thinking, resist helping ourselves. There is a fear of stopping, a fear of taking stock, of thinking about ourselves. We need to overcome that inner rebelliousness to take control, to take charge of our own lives. We need to stop. The Quakers call this "centering down"—quieting ourselves, waiting upon the Lord.

Franz Kafka (of all people) put it this way: "You do not have to leave your room. Remain sitting at your table and listen. Do not even listen, simply wait. Do not even wait, be still and solitary." I have to tell you that the most important thing I do in my own life is to stop when I am depressed or when I am stressed, in order to catalogue my dis-ease. And the second most important thing I do in my own life is to stop at regular intervals, to be still and solitary and revisit the goals and objectives of my life.

Look

We stop in life in order to look and listen for clues about the meaning and purpose of our lives. We find meaning only if we're looking and listening for it.

If we look for things, we have to believe they exist. If we look, we must suspend disbelief, in the hope and expectation of seeing something.

If you're not looking, you won't see. I was at Chartres Cathedral last summer, listening to one of Malcolm Miller's brilliant afternoon lectures. In front of me was a girl about sixteen or seventeen with a Walkman. She closed her eyes and crawled into the music. When the group got up to move together to another part of the cathedral, she took off the Walkman briefly and said to her parents, "How long is this going to go on? When can we go shopping?" She was in the greatest cathedral on earth, but she never saw anything.

When I was nineteen I first visited the Brancacci Chapel in Florence to see the Masaccio frescoes. Five other college guys and I went all over Europe for a hundred days. We spent nearly two weeks in Florence and went to most of the places we were "supposed" to see. I'd never had an art history course and the book said these Masaccio frescoes were a must. At least I was willing to go and look. But I only spent about ten to fifteen minutes with them, and they had very little impact on me. I did look—sort of—but saw very little. Since that time I have studied art history. And in the intervening years I've looked at the Masaccio frescoes probably a dozen times (sometimes, as in 1995, for a whole day). Each time I've seen something new. What I now see was there all the time, but I didn't see it when I was nineteen, or even when I was forty. And the next time I go I'll see things I've never seen before.

Two days ago in New York I went to the Metropolitan Museum of Art exhibition of the work of the twentieth-century Scottish architect Charles Rennie Mackintosh. I saw it first in the morning, then left the museum for lunch, and returned about three. I decided to go through the exhibit again—even though I'd spent two hours going through it in the morning. For the next two hours I kept seeing things I'd looked at in the morning but not seen. These things were there all the time; I just didn't see them.

Mr. Kerner and Mr. Randall and I frequently comment that, though we've been teaching *King Lear* for eighteen years, we keep seeing things we didn't see before. These things were there all the time; we just didn't see them.

I have often retold my experience as an elementary school boy being made to go and hear the Cleveland Orchestra play classical music. How I hated those boring concerts. How authoritatively I said, "There's nothing there." Then I had a course in music listening and I heard it and realized that it had been there all the time. I just hadn't heard it.

You never see unless you stop and look diligently. At this time of year, Christians celebrate the visit of the Magi (variously, three kings or three wise men) to the baby Jesus. They were led by a star. The story has always—to me—had the ring of truth about it as history. But whether it's true or not as history, it's true in a far greater way as myth: three well-to-do and powerful men—whose lives were somehow incomplete and unfulfilled, who were rich but poor—were looking, searching for the meaning of life. And, looking hard, they saw a star that led them to the truth. If you stop and assiduously look for the meaning of your life—your goals and objectives—a star will always appear and guide you, perhaps not where you think you want to go, but to a truth greater than you can imagine.

Listen

I overheard a conversation at my church in Dorchester a few weeks ago. We have a men and boy choir and at an evening service they sang—among other things—the "Hallelujah Chorus" from Handel's *Messiah*. One ten-year-old choirboy had invited a school friend to hear him sing. After the service, the friend said to our choirboy, "What was so great about that?" To which our choirboy responded, "Man, you were there, didn't you hear it?" The friend didn't hear it, but the choirboy knew it was there because he heard it. That's why he said—so plaintively—"Man, you were there, didn't you hear it?"

In early December, one Monday morning, I overslept because somehow, before I went to bed, I inadvertently jarred the tuner on my clock radio so that when the radio went on it wasn't tuned to WBUR. Instead there was just that faint hissing sound between stations that didn't wake me up.

Naturally, I was annoyed, but I could only be annoyed at myself. I correctly assumed it was not the station's fault (the station hadn't closed down) or my radio's fault. I correctly said, "This is my problem—the station was there to be heard; I just wasn't tuned into it."

We stop in life in order to look and listen for its meaning. If we're listening and not hearing, it's a safe bet that the problem is ours. And we have to try to adjust our listening. It is up to us to figure out how to tune in.

We have to realize that we also make ourselves deaf to some things. All the accounts of the life of Winston Churchill describe him as deaf, but almost all note that he was selectively deaf. If he was interested in a subject, he heard everything. If he was not interested, he tuned out. We are all, to a degree, selectively deaf. In my old school, we experimented for a time in the 1960s with giving students written comments rather than grades. The results were disastrous because—surprise, surprise—the kids heard only the good part of the comments and discounted the criticisms. They were selectively deaf. When we went back to giving grades, the kids were shocked at how poor their grades were. They had listened selectively. You must be careful, when you are listening, not to hear only the things you want to hear.

Important things happen all the time and we are unaware of them. We don't see or hear them. One of the biographies of Abraham Lincoln records the conversation of two farmers at the general store on the morning of Abraham Lincoln's birth: "Any news?" says one. "No," says the other. "Nothin' happened, 'cept a birth down at the Lincolns' house." One of the greatest men in the history of the world had just been born, but they didn't realize it.

On the night of Jesus' birth, the powerful figures of Rome heard nothing about it. They were wrapped up in their busy and important lives. They heard nothing. The nice middle-class folk of Bethlehem—who had no room in their inn to accommodate Mary and Joseph—were sound asleep in their nice middle-class homes. They heard nothing. St. Luke tells us in his Gospel that when the angels sang their song that night, only the shepherds heard it. The shepherds were the lowest class of society (looked down upon because their occupation kept them from practicing all the intricate rituals of their religion). They were out in their fields—in the silence of the night—watching their sheep, listening. "And there were in the same country shepherds abiding in the field, keeping watch over their flocks by night. And the angel of the Lord came unto them and the glory of the Lord shone round about them."

If you think you have it all, have seen it all, have heard it all, you will be among those who are not listening. It's very unlikely that you'll listen if you think there's nothing more for you to hear. And if you do not listen you cannot hear.

Let me conclude with the advice my first grade teacher, Mrs. Curry, gave us: "Children," she said, "you must first stop. Then you must look and listen. If you don't first stop you can't really look carefully or listen carefully." She was uttering an eternal truth. What she taught us in the first grade—which I have had to relearn many times since—is true. You cannot deal with the dis-ease of your life unless you first stop and take inventory of yourself. You cannot find meaning in life unless you first stop and consider your goals and objectives.

After you stop, then you need to look and listen diligently. The foolish among you will say, "Because I don't see it, it isn't there," "Because I don't hear it, it isn't there." The wise among you will realize that to see and hear you have to stop and be quiet. You have to center down. You have to shut up. You have to wait. Then you will see and then you will hear.

5

More Than Meets the Eye

WANT TO BEGIN with a quotation. The speaker is Albert Einstein, perhaps the greatest scientist of the century. Einstein argues that we need to go beyond the surface of life (what we can see, hear, touch, and smell) to experience a greater and deeper Reality:

> *The most beautiful thing we can experience is the mysterious. It [the mysterious] is the source of all true art and science. He to whom this emotion is a stranger, who can no longer pause to wonder and to stand rapt in awe, is as good as dead; his eyes are closed. This insight into the mystery of life . . . [this knowledge] that what is impenetrable to us really exists, manifesting itself as the highest wisdom and the most radiant beauty which our dull faculties can comprehend only in their most primitive forms— this knowledge, this feeling, is at the center of true religiousness.*

As Good As Dead

Standing up here I can see your faces. Judging from your faces, some of you didn't even hear the first word of the quotation. "Be reasonable, Jarvis," some of you are thinking. "Einstein at 8:25 A.M. on the first day of term? My mind is still on vacation. Wake me up at 8:55." I'd estimate that at least twenty percent of you missed every word of the quotation. Maybe another twenty percent gave the quotation a fainthearted shot, and managed to follow it though the first sentence. Some of you got farther than that. And maybe twenty percent of you, at the other end of the spectrum, followed the quotation and understood what Einstein said.

And in a way, that illustrates what Einstein is saying and what I'm trying to say at one remove. Einstein is talking about awareness—awareness of our sensual surroundings and awareness of a deeper Reality beyond the things around us that can be seen or heard.

But let's go back and look at the twenty percent who heard nothing. I was in London this vacation at the same time the Glee Club was there. Two weeks ago today I tagged along on their visit to Cambridge, Ely, and Little Baddow. These are places I've been many times, and I have to admit that what made the day fascinating to me was not so much observing the historic sites, as observing the Glee Club members observing the historic sites. In my group I would say that at least twenty percent wandered about all day seeing almost nothing. You could observe them looking at the ground, talking to one another, waiting for lunch, or wondering how long they had to walk before they got back on the bus. These were not evil kids, they were not uncooperative or mean-spirited or badly behaved. They were simply, as Einstein said, "as good as dead; their eyes were closed."

The next day the Glee Club journeyed to Windsor and Eton. After three hours in Windsor—including a tour of Windsor Castle—the group walked across the bridge to Eton College. After seeing the school, the Club was invited for cokes in the headmaster's living room. Mrs. Anderson, the wife of the headmaster, asked one boy where he'd been earlier in the day. "Well," he said, "that's a good question. Let's see. It was some town nearby. Ah, I forget the name." "Windsor?" she said. "Oh, yeah, Windsor," he said, "that's right." Brain dead. Absolutely brain dead.

For those in this same twenty percent as-good-as-dead category, London will not be a memory of the National Gallery or Westminster Abbey or the Tower of London but, rather, a memorable sampling of the Burger King, McDonald, and Kentucky Fried Chicken outlets around Piccadilly Circus. This twenty percent did not have the faintest inkling that they might be missing something important.

Another twenty percent felt some obligation to see the major sites of London—even if they didn't have any natural desire to do so. I met three seniors in the Underground on Wednesday, and one of them said to me plaintively, "Is St. Paul's Cathedral a must?" Here, at least, was some sense of obligation (even if not desire) to open one's eyes to see something others regarded as valuable.

Having myself lived in a glass house, however, I cannot throw stones. My first year at St. Mark's School, I wandered up to the music listening rooms to play one of my 45 rpm popular favorites. I looked through the small window of the door to the next room and saw a senior—a boy I really liked and admired (a prominent jock and popular leader)—listening to a piece of classical music. He was my dorm prefect and I said to him that night, "Why were you listening to that stuff? What was it, anyway?" "That's the Bach B-Minor Mass," he said. "Who made you listen to it?" I asked. "No one made me, you idiot! I like it." I couldn't believe this kid—this normal, popular, respected kid listening to this boring music. But, of course, it was I who—in Einstein's words—was "as good as dead." My eyes—or, in this case, my ears—were the ones that were closed.

I think I've told the story before of an American friend who visited me at Cambridge when I was a student there. Those Glee Club members who were not brain dead two weeks ago will attest, I think, that Cambridge is one of the most beautiful places on earth, even in the dregs of March. But it was during the lushness of May that I walked this friend of mine through the ancient courtyards and buildings, the lavish gardens. He talked the whole time so he never heard anything. He was looking at me as he talked so he never saw anything. And he smoked the whole time so he never smelled anything. Even at the sensual level, then, even at the level of things we can see and smell and hear, he was "as good as dead." His eyes and ears were closed.

There are people—some in this room—who are, at this point, incapable (for whatever reason) of seeing anything on a tour, incapable of having their consciousness raised, incapable of being pulled out of their self-enveloped, narrow, and constricted little world. They have not taken the most rudimentary baby steps towards sensual awareness. They may see, but they do not perceive. They may hear, but they do not understand. They are, therefore, light years away from any perception or understanding of Reality beyond the things one can see and hear and smell. They do not even perceive and understand the things around them that can be seen and heard.

Degrees of Awareness

All of life should be an awakening of awareness. Some of you in this room are profoundly awakened to—aware of—the things around you. I was enormously impressed by the perceptions some of you had visiting Cambridge and Ely. I think in particular of three boys who seemed to see things (perceive and understand things) that I myself didn't perceive until I'd seen them two or three times.

A few years ago four Roxbury Latin boys—recently graduated from college—toured Europe together. When they got to Florence, each sent me a postcard—obviously in happy remembrance of the undoubted highlight of their Roxbury Latin experience: my Western Civ Renaissance art lectures.

The first wrote: "We've had some great times here in the main square. Italian beer is great and so are Italian women. Don't worry, we're seeing all that stuff you taught us about."

The second wrote, "Florence has been the high point of our trip. I keep thinking I've seen the best thing here—first the Michelangelo captives at the Academy, then the Fra Angelico frescoes at San Marco, then the Bargello. Today the Boticelli's [*sic*] at the Uffizi. We didn't allow enough time here."

The third wrote: "You didn't tell us how hot Florence is in summer. We're being bitten alive by mosquitoes. The museums are so full and so hot you can only last about fifteen minutes. Really long lines for everything. Heading north tomorrow at last."

The fourth wrote, "Just as you said, the Bargello is the highlight of Florence. I've spent over four hours in this room with the Ghiberti panel and the three Donatello statues. I feel I've been here before, and can't wait to come back."

These four Roxbury Latin graduates illustrate the different levels at which you can perceive the sensual world around you. Their perceptions are all accurate, but two of the four perceived and understood Florence at a far deeper and more profound level than the other two. They saw and perceived. They heard and understood.

The Reality Beyond the Sensual

There are, of course, sensual realities that we as humans are incapable of experiencing. You will sometimes see a dog prick his ears; he hears sounds you and I can't hear. Last week I read about a police dog who smelled out two thieves hiding in an attic who had covered themselves in insulation. Though you and I couldn't smell them, the dog could.

But I want to move beyond our awareness of the sensual world—the world we can see and feel and smell—to the deeper level of awareness that Einstein talks about, to our awareness of that Reality that cannot be seen or touched or heard or smelled, to our awareness of that Reality that, "though impenetrable to us, really exists."

Here Einstein is talking about realities that are not sensual. One analogy might be gravity. No one can see gravity itself, for instance. We experience its existence; it explains what happens to things we can see. No one can see electricity itself, but we know it is really there. No one can touch or see or smell team "spirit" but we know team spirit is real; we know when it's there and when it's not. We cannot see love. We can see certain physical expressions of it, but we cannot see love itself— real though we know it to be.

Robert Kennedy expressed this same insight in a somewhat different way when he said:

> *The gross national product [the measure of our nation's wealth] does not include the beauty of our poetry or the strength of our marriages, the intelligence of our public debate or the integrity of our public officials. It allows neither for justice in our courts, nor for the justice of our dealings with others. The gross national product measures neither our wit nor our*

courage, neither our wisdom nor our learning, neither our compassion nor our devotion to our country. It measures everything, in short, except that which makes our life truly worthwhile.

There is, then, a whole realm of Reality that is "impenetrable" to our eyes and ears: this Reality cannot be quantified, cannot be seen or heard, but it is more profoundly real even than the very real sensual world around us. It cannot be seen, but it can be perceived. It cannot be heard, but it can be understood.

That is what Einstein is saying when he remarks: "The most beautiful thing we can experience is the mysterious. It is the source of all true art and science. He to whom this emotion is a stranger, who [cannot] pause to wonder and to stand rapt in awe, is as good as dead; his eyes are closed."

Another great scientist—Sir Isaac Newton—put this same thought this way toward the end of his life:

I do not know what I may appear to the world, but to myself I seem only like a boy playing on the seashore and diverting myself in now-and-then finding a smoother pebble or a prettier shell than ordinary, whilst the great ocean of truth lay all undiscovered before me. . . .

Sharing Einstein's "rapt awe" in the face of the Mystery of things, Newton likened himself to a child playing by the ocean—"whilst the great ocean of truth lay all undiscovered before me. . . ."

This is the same realization Job experienced: the recognition in the whirlwind of his puny humanness in the presence of the God who is the Creator of all things.

It is an experience both Newton and Einstein describe as essentially religious, the discovery of the Eternal Mystery that comes when we reach the limits of our human powers and our human strengths. Hear Einstein:

This insight into the mystery of life . . . [this knowledge] that what is impenetrable to us really exists, manifesting itself in the highest wisdom and the most radiant beauty (which our dull faculties can comprehend only in their more primitive forms)— this knowledge, this feeling, is at the center of true religiousness.

Conclusion

Every year in the spring term I experience a certain despair. I look out on those who are about to graduate and I wonder if we have failed to teach here the most important things. I think of the Roman philosopher who wrote: *"Propter vitam vivendi perdere causas."* ("In the process of life we lose the reason for life."). We have made you—members of the graduating class—learn a lot of stuff, a lot of information. But have we stressed enough that you need to open yourselves to the sensual realities around you, and even more that you need to open yourselves to that whole realm of Reality beyond the sensual—"the Mysterious," as Einstein puts it, "the Ocean of Truth," as Newton puts it?

When I taught junior English at my old school, we read *Huckleberry Finn*. Every year one or two boys would tell me, "I've already read it— I read it years ago; it's a kid's book." Of course they *had* read it, but when they read it as juniors they read it at a much deeper level, and when they read it again in college they read it at an even deeper level still.

Some of you have a close-minded attitude toward the realm of Mystery, toward the Ocean of Truth that Einstein and others describe as religious experience. You say: "I did religion when I was a kid. I know all that stuff." I ask you to do what I asked the juniors I taught *Huckleberry Finn* to do: "Approach it with an open mind. I think you'll find something there that you didn't see earlier."

Open your heart and mind not just to the possibility of ever increasing sensual awareness of the things around you that you can see and hear—but open your heart and mind to that realm of Reality that is beyond the sensual, to the great Mystery, to the Ocean of Truth, to the profoundest Reality of all.

6

How Can I Be Happy?

 WAS in Penn Station in New York a few days ago waiting for the Boston train. Up came this lady to a man sitting near me, stared at him intensely and asked, "How can I be happy?" Then she accosted the rest of us, one after another, repeating, "How can I be happy?" She obviously had a screw loose. I'm rarely at a loss for words and I thought of about a dozen responses: some angry, some funny. But by the time she got to me I could think of nothing—sweet nothing—to say. It's been my experience, that it's often the nuts who ask the ultimate questions, and her question keeps echoing in my ears: "How can I be happy?" It's the question we're all asking.

Escapes from Unhappiness

When I was in college, I worked summers on the Fairport, Painesville, and Eastern Railroad. I was a member of the section gang; we laid rail and raised and straightened track. One summer we worked for quite a while laying a new spur to the Industrial Rayon Company. Each day at mid-morning and mid-afternoon the workers at the plant piled outside, where we were working, for their ten-minute smoking break. Their jobs required them to do the same mindless task several thousand times a day, so they lived for these cigarette breaks. Out they poured, speechless, vacant-eyed, amid the bleakness of their lives, to grasp a brief moment of pleasure—a cigarette. Happiness to them was escape, relief from the pain of life.

Outside school from time to time I counsel kids your age who are alcoholics or drug addicts. The theme that runs through their stories is this: their lives are empty and purposeless, so they get drunk or get stoned to escape the pain. They can't face the realities of their lives, so they run away. One boy said to me recently: "I just want to get away from the pain." Happiness for him is getting drunk, escaping the pain, even though when he wakes up from the alcoholic haze, the problems and the pain are still there.

I can feel some of you thinking, "He's not talking about me. I'll never have a mindless job like the workers at that plant," or "My life isn't so painful I'm running away into booze or drugs." But just this vacation I talked at length with a prominent physician who said to me, "If any of your boys want to become doctors, send them to me, I'll tell them why they shouldn't. I no longer enjoy what I do." "Why do you keep doing it, then?" I asked him. "Because I like the things I can buy with the money I make." And he talked about his cars, his stereos, and the other adult toys he buys to give him moments of pleasure amid a life he hates, moments of escape from the pain.

I've just finished reading the *Journals of John Cheever*. In my view, Cheever is one of the preeminent authors of our time; he had one great literary success upon another. But his journals show a man living on the edge—desperately unhappy in his marriage, desperately trying to stave off taking his first drink until 10:30 in the morning, desperately trying to endure the reality of life for a few hours before he anesthetizes himself with drink.

I can think of nothing sadder than a person whose life—like those I've just talked about—is reduced to trying pathetically to grasp, in the midst of the fundamental unhappiness of his life, a few moments of pleasure (a cigarette, an adult toy, an escape into an alcoholic haze).

Inadequate Visions

Let me share with you the stories of three other lives, lives perhaps more relevant to your own than the four I've just talked about.

At the alumni reception over the holidays, a recent Roxbury Latin graduate—now at one of the nation's most prestigious colleges—cornered me and said, "When I was a senior you said, 'I don't know who the lucky ones are—the ones who get into their first choice college or the ones who don't; the ones who don't are often happier than the ones who do.' I thought you were making that up to make those who didn't get their first choice feel better. I didn't think you really meant it. I also thought you were stupid to say it because everyone would know you didn't really mean it. I knew that when I got into Brand X College the rest of my life was set—I'd never be unhappy again. I really believed that—I really knew that. But I was wrong. If anything I'm less happy because I now realize that in the future when I get something I think I want—like a good job—that won't make me happy either."

In New York during exam period I saw a young man in his twenties who poured out the story of his marriage and subsequent divorce. I had married this couple, and I remarked to him how madly in love both of them had been at the time. He responded by saying, "When I was pursuing her I knew—knew with my whole being—that if I could marry her I'd never be unhappy again—and I think she felt the same way. When we came to see you to arrange the wedding you tried to talk to us about how hard marriage was, about the bitter arguments we would have, etc. When we got to the car after seeing you we just laughed about what you'd said. We knew you were wrong. But, as things turned out, we were wrong. After the first year or so it was nothing but unhappiness—every minute was hell."

At Thanksgiving I was talking with my sister about a childhood friend of ours. This guy had everything—good looks, a brilliant mind, winning personality. He was a schoolboy athletic hero, went to the best college, married a gorgeous—and nice—wife, climbed speedily to the top in business, made a bundle of money, bought an estate in the 'burbs, had three kids, a dog, a cat, a lawn service, and three cars. The perfect model of success. My sister had just seen him at a high school reunion. He had just up and left it all—his estate, his wife, his family, and he was talking about quitting his job. "You remember what I was like as a kid," he said. "We didn't have much money. I knew what I wanted—the whole package of success. I looked around at some of my friends' parents and said, 'I'm going to have a house like that and three cars and a big job.' I knew I'd be happy if I realized that dream. But when I got it, it turned to dust. I just got sick of it all," he said. "Sick of the whole rat race. It wasn't worth it. I've had enough of all the pressures. I want the rest of my life to be happy."

These three people are arguably better off than the ones I talked about earlier. These three people at least had a vision—a picture of what would make them happy. The first said, "I really want Brand X College," and that desire, that vision, enabled him to work hard and to achieve well in order to realize that vision. The second—who envisioned a happy life if only he could marry the woman he was in love with—was, in many ways, made a better person by that vision: "I always exercised, I always dressed well, I worked harder in my job to get ahead. She gave me a reason for being," he said to me. The third person, who dreamed of being a success (and having all the accoutrements of success—top job, estate, and all), was motivated every day by that vision to push himself hard and go for the gold.

All three had a vision which made all their efforts day by day worth it. Sadly, however, when each achieved his vision, the gold turned to dust. Achieving the vision didn't bring the happiness they expected.

A Long-Term Vision

They each had a vision, but the vision was not an adequate one. The boy whose vision extended only to getting into Brand X College (which would bring him fulfillment for the rest of his life) had never really considered—in a wider context—*why* he wanted to go to Brand X College. There's nothing wrong with wanting to get into a good college. (I hope you all want to do that.) But, far more, I hope you know why you want to do that in terms of a much larger vision for your life. Getting into college is a good short-term goal, but it is not an ultimate vision for life.

I know some of you are saying, "I don't believe him. Let me get into Brand X College and I will be happy for life. Let me get the good job, the house in the 'burbs, a beautiful wife, 2.3 kids, etc., and I will be happy for life." But I promise you that many have said what you are saying and come away unhappy, unfulfilled. Their goals were not part of a larger vision.

In answering the question, "How can I be happy?" the first requirement is that we see all our short-term goals as part of some long-term vision for our lives.

Any worthy long-term vision must take life's most basic realities into account. Do not think me morbid when I begin by pointing out that nothing is more real—nothing more certain—about our lives than our own deaths. How desperately we try to avoid considering death! I was talking with an AIDS patient recently who said, "I just never thought about dying." I've heard the same words from a hundred others over the years whose lives are threatened by cancer or some death-dealing disease. But we are all going to die. If you want a great vision for your life, you need to begin by dealing with that single most certain reality.

Happiness in life comes from a worthy vision of all of life—in all its reality including the inevitability of our own death. Try to imagine yourself at your own funeral. What is it that you want people to say about you? That's the question you have to answer if you want to find a long-range vision for your life. What do you want people to say about you when you're dead?

After we have some idea of the ultimate vision for our lives, we can then develop short-range goals. There is nothing wrong with wanting to go to Yale, there is nothing wrong with wanting to marry a particular woman, there is nothing wrong with wanting to be successful in business, as long as we don't confuse such short-term goals with the ultimate vision for our lives (who we want to be).

An immensely successful boyhood friend of mine said to me recently, "I never really thought about why I wanted all this. I just went along— college, marriage, job—I just went along. For the rest of my life I want to choose who I want to be."

It has been said that the saddest words in any language are "It's too late." For many people my age, it *is* almost too late. They find themselves trapped. You have the greatest treasure of all on your side: time.

For you it is not too late. You are not trapped. You do not have to go along. You can choose a worthwhile vision for your whole life; you can choose who you want to be.

Will your ultimate vision at age sixteen or seventeen be unchanged for the rest of your life? Probably not. Your vision of who you want to be will become deeper and richer and wiser as you mature. But the very fact that right now you step aside from the day-to-day concerns and pressures and ask the ultimate questions will prevent you from just "going along" in life. The very fact that you try now to find a vision that will encompass all the years you will be here on earth will help prevent you from drifting through life, mistaking short-term goals (such as college) for long-term visions.

Being Open to Life's Possibilities

Such a vision is essential to your quest for happiness, but it is not the only thing you need. In addition to a long-range vision, there is a critical second ingredient to happiness: namely, approaching day-by-day life affirming the possibility of happiness in all its events.

In every senior class I see two or three boys who seem never to have imagined the possibility that anything they're studying could be interesting or valuable. It's all something that someone else is inflicting on you, something "they" think you should do. I admire these guys because I think they must have tremendous inner strength to plod—with utter joylessness—through the daily requirements of School. I think many adults regard their jobs that way—and their marriages.

To find happiness in the midst of daily life—in our school work, or job, or marriage—we must approach them positively, affirmatively. I've said to several of you sitting here this morning, "Try to imagine that your school work could be good for you, that it could even be interesting." And, every once in a while, one of you will say, "I've changed my attitude toward my work and it really helps." You will never find happiness in relationships, in your work, anywhere, unless you start with the belief, the trust, the assumption, that you might possibly find it there.

Happy people are those who are open to the possibility of happiness; they therefore discover it in small things—in relationships with their fellow workers or schoolmates, in the work itself. By the same token, those who approach life negatively, critically, complainingly, fulfill their own prophecies and are unhappy. Much of life's happiness depends on the attitude we bring to the day-to-day events of life.

Happiness Has to Do with Others

If happiness requires a worthy long-term vision and an affirmative attitude that happiness is a possibility in life's day-to-day events, it also, I believe, requires a third and final ingredient. Happiness almost always has something to do with others.

Show me an unhappy person and I'll show you a person wrapped up in himself. Dante in the *Inferno* says the inner circle of hell is reserved for those "lost people" who are enveloped in themselves, trapped in their own lives—unaware either of God or other human beings.

The happiest person I know is a monk. His life—far from being a living hell—is, in a way, a living heaven. "What is your secret?" I asked him. His reply? "Every day, in every encounter with every person," he said, "I tell myself, 'I could die at any moment. This person I'm speaking to now may be the last person I ever speak to. I need to love him—to care about him—more than any other person I've ever met.'"

I visit several older people on a regular basis as part of my duties as a clergyman. They are people for whom the prospect of death has now become real—as it will for us someday. I've noticed that when these people reminisce about their lives, they rarely brag about making a lot of money or achieving some high position. If they speak with pride or with joy about their lives, it is almost always to talk about something they did for someone else. That, ultimately, is what brought them happiness in life—some person they helped at a key moment, some good piece of advice they offered, some gift they gave, some act of kindness they performed.

Today we embark on a new year—replete with possibilities, filled with opportunities. Now—while so much of life lies before you—think about these things so that someday you don't utter those saddest words of all: "It's too late." For you it's not yet too late. I pray that you will not just "go along," that you will not confuse short-range objectives with a lifetime vision. Be tough enough to contemplate the prospect of your own death, your own temporariness, and ask yourself: "Who do I want to be?" Seek the great vision. "What do I want to accomplish before I die?" Each one of our lives is passing away. Grasp each moment as if it were your last: approach each moment thinking of it in terms of its possibilities. So much of life's happiness is what you make of each moment, the hope you bring to it, the willingness to see each moment in terms of its positive possibilities. Finally, remember that you can be happy only if you are able to break out of your shell, to burst the prison of self-envelopment. Happiness comes most of all from caring more about others than you care about yourself.

The Pursuit of Happiness

 WAS in London on the first day of "spring" vacation, standing in line at the Aldwych Theatre in hopes of getting a ticket to see Maggie Smith in *The Importance of Being Earnest*. She had received rave reviews and I was eager to see her. The sign in the theatre said the show was sold out through April, but I stood in line anyway, hoping I'd luck out and get a single ticket for one of the nights I was in London.

A little ahead of me in the queue was an American couple. When they got to the window, the woman soon started shouting at the ticket salesman: "I've come all the way over here to see this show. What do you mean you have no tickets?" Then to her husband: "Do something. Will you just *do* something!" It was his turn: "My wife and I have spent a lot of money to fly over here to London. Are you telling me there are no tickets?" This little duet went through several variations, but each time the couple received the same answer: the theatre was sold out the whole week they were in London.

They finally left the ticket window, but the wife was not finished. In front of all of us standing there, she assailed her husband: "You're such a loser, you let him walk all over you. Have you ever put up a fight about anything? Our whole vacation is ruined and you just stand there and take it!"

Happiness Is Not a Right

I share this vignette because it seems to me to illustrate a widespread attitude that everything in life should go our way, that things should always work out, and if they don't, then the first thing to do is to take it out on someone, to blame someone, to kick someone around.

Perhaps this attitude springs in part from advertising. One commercial after another urges us: "You deserve this! Treat yourself. You owe it to yourself." The premise of these ads is that life should go well. You deserve to have things go the way you want them to go. If you fly to London, you should expect that every theatre will be eager to give you front row seats to every play you want to see. And if things don't go the way you want, then, by God, you have every right to be angry.

A few years ago a Roxbury Latin boy didn't get into his first-choice college and his father was on the phone to me that night. "I sent him to Roxbury Latin so he'd get into Brand X College. He deserves it and I want him in. What are you going to do about it?" (Actually, the boy did deserve it, but the most competitive colleges have many more "deserving" candidates apply than they can accept. You therefore need to be more than good, you need to be lucky and this boy wasn't.) I said to the father, "We have already done everything we can do, but the college had a lot of great kids to choose from and your son was not among the lucky ones. There's nothing more we can do. Let's start looking at his future elsewhere." "I'll never agree to that," said the father. "I will not take no for an answer. You've made a mess of this, now what are you going to do about getting him into Brand X?"

Again, the underlying premise: we should always get what we deserve. Life should go just the way we want it to. And, if it doesn't, then we have every right to kick someone around.

Some time ago the mother of one of our boys came to see me. The family lived in a large house in a posh suburb and were members of an expensive country club. Her husband had recently lost his job, and she wanted Roxbury Latin to give her son a scholarship. I said that I doubted they'd qualify for financial aid, and suggested she first consider modifying their lifestyle a bit—perhaps they could give up the country club. Not on your life! "We've worked hard to make it to this town and into this country club. Do you really expect us to give that up?" Her premise: she deserved the town, the house, the country club, and if they were short of money, she deserved a school that would pay for her son's education. When I said no, she was outraged and called me heartless and unsympathetic, and even threw in a final zinger: "I thought you were supposed to be a clergyman."

The Constitution guarantees to each of us "life, liberty, and the pursuit of happiness." Some people forget the words "pursuit of." They think happiness itself is a right. But the Constitution does not establish happiness itself as a right. It doesn't guarantee the happiness of each citizen, only his or her right to *pursue* happiness.

Happiness Is Not the Absence of Criticism

The "I deserve to be happy in life" attitude often goes hand in hand with a similar attitude: the "I am wonderful and if you say otherwise you're assaulting me" attitude.

This attitude was prevalent among adolescents in the sixties when I was a young teacher. In my first year of teaching, I told a boy his spelling and grammar were atrocious. His response: "Do you really think that spelling and grammar are still important? Is that what you care about?" "Yes," I said, "I do care about spelling and grammar." "Well," he responded, "it's not what *I* care about, and I'm not going to let you destroy my creativity—I'm going to express myself however I like, and I don't care about spelling and grammar."

I failed him for the marking period. Not just because of grammar and spelling, but even more because the content of what he was writing was shallow and self-indulgent rubbish. I didn't use the words "shallow and self-indulgent rubbish" when I talked with him; I was gentler and more constructive. My comments, however, enraged him, and he lashed out at me: "You're a terrible teacher," he said, "because you're so judgmental." Now "judgmental" was the worst thing you could say about someone in the sixties. But I accepted the accusation, telling him that I was being judgmental because I wanted him to be a better writer. I then had his mother on my hands. My criticisms, she said, were "hurting his self-esteem." A lot of teachers in the sixties were held hostage by this self-esteem gambit. Any suggestion of criticism was immediately labeled harsh and judgmental, and destructive of a student's self-esteem. Teachers therefore backed off. They were intimidated, and they harmed a whole generation by not giving students the sort of positive criticism that makes us all do better.

I keep thinking this sixties attitude is dead and then it rears its ugly head again. Recently I was visiting an elementary school classroom and saw a large poster with these words: "I am perfect just the way I am."

Now I believe children (and adolescents) should receive positive reinforcement about who they are, and I think teachers who do nothing but carp and criticize and tell you only what's wrong should not be in the teaching profession. But when you mislead a child into thinking that he is perfect just the way he is, you are not giving him positive reinforcement, you are lying to him—and most children know it!

The teacher who put up this poster said to me, "My role is to find things all day long to praise. Children thrive on praise." Since she declared this viewpoint as an undeniable eternal truth, I didn't argue with her. But I will tell you that she is exalting one truth to the exclusion of all other truths. Children do need praise (and that is a truth), but they also—and this is also a truth—need criticism. If a child is praised for everything, he sees no reason to do something better. If a child is praised for everything, when he does something truly praise-worthy, you have no way to praise it. Visiting her classroom I could observe that by this point in the school year the pupils treated this teacher's praise for what it was worth: they placed no value on it. Praise is like chocolate cake. The occasional piece of chocolate cake is delicious, but chocolate cake morning, noon, and night loses its appeal and becomes sickening.

You may have read about a recent incident in England in which two ten-year-old boys kidnapped a two-year-old at a shopping mall and murdered him. Commenting on the murderers' inability to tell right from wrong and their lack of remorse, Prime Minister John Major commented: "I feel quite strongly that society needs to condemn a little more and understand a little less."

The adult who is always "understanding," who is not willing to pull a student up short and judge his behavior or his performance, is actually harming the child, is actually encouraging him to be less than his best self, to settle for mediocrity. And the adult who tells a child or adolescent that he is "perfect just the way he is" is guilty not just of encouraging mediocrity, but of lying.

I experienced another variation of this "I am wonderful" attitude the other day in a context outside of school. An adult came to see me to persuade me to take a particular action. But I wasn't persuaded. "I don't think you're hearing me," he said. "No," I said, "I hear you but I don't agree with you." We went back and forth at this for a while—he using all the current buzz words to manipulate me into doing what he wanted me to do. At one point, for example, he said: "I'm trying to share myself with you, but you're not accepting me." At another: "I'd like you to try to be sensitive to my point of view."

With this sort of adult, you can't have a simple disagreement. He sees himself as so invincibly right that to disagree with him amounts to moral imperfection on your part: you are insensitive, you don't "accept" him, you aren't listening to him. He wants to live in a world in which he gets his way. By not letting him have his way—by disagreeing with him—you have wronged him.

Happiness Does Not Expect Life to Be Just

Some years ago, I was telling a fellow school head my hurt and disappointment with the parents of one of our students. Many of us on the faculty had reached out in extraordinary ways to try to help this boy. In the end, however, things didn't work out, and the boy had to leave. The parents launched into a bitter diatribe about how little we cared and how little we'd done. It was very painful to hear since we had gone way, way beyond the call of duty with this kid. I concluded my self-pitying account to my fellow headmaster with the words, "It's so disillusioning."

My fellow headmaster snapped at me: "How old are you?" I told him, and he said, "You're far too old to be disillusioned."

It was a well-deserved rebuke. I am old enough to know that you don't get what you deserve in life, that life isn't just. (I never complain, by the way, when I get undeserved praise, which I do frequently.)

Those who approach life thinking you get what you deserve have not yet made their peace with reality.

If you think you are wonderful and that things should break your way, you are in for a huge disappointment.

A few years ago a junior came to see me. He'd started the year with high expectations about a certain course: "I really thought I could get an A. But I got Mr. So-and-So." After some further beating around the bush, the boy finally got to the heart of the matter. It was "unfair" that he'd gotten someone whose teaching he found uncongenial, and this particular teacher was wrecking his plans, destroying his dreams. As the weeks dragged on the boy became angrier and angrier, and devoted more and more energy to brooding about all the alleged injustices that Mr. So-and-So was inflicting on him day by day.

This boy reminded me of an immature basketball player. If you want to be a good basketball player, one of the things you have to do is to forget the shot you just missed, leave it behind, let it go, and focus on the next opportunity. I see endless schoolboy basketball games, and you can watch the immature player look backwards—you can watch the immature player focus on a pass he just threw away or on the shot he just missed—long after play has moved on. Sadly, of course, the player who is focused on the past goes on to make further mistakes in the future.

This junior, who was angry at Mr. So-and-So, was squandering enormous amounts of energy looking back with anger at all the teacher's supposed injustices. He was therefore missing all sorts of opportunities to improve things in the present. Like the woman at the theatre, this boy was clinging to the fallacious theory that he deserved to have things go well in life. When he didn't get his way, like the woman, he wasted his energy looking back in anger. Like the woman, he saw himself as a victim.

Captains of Your Own Destiny

The Declaration of Independence does not assert that happiness is a right in life. It asserts that we have the right to pursue happiness. It declares that we have the right to take control of our own life and to say, "I am not a victim, and I will not squander my life looking back and wishing life were some other way."

If you want to be happy, you begin by accepting reality—and the reality is that you don't deserve anything in life. Life doesn't owe you a damned thing; and you don't always get what you want.

You approach life expecting trouble, expecting that you won't get the theatre tickets you want, you won't get the teacher you want, or the ideal parent, or the dream college. If you approach life realizing you deserve nothing, that life doesn't owe you anything, you will be prepared to deal with the inevitable disappointments.

Then when those disappointments come, you will not look back—like the raging wife at the theatre or the immature basketball player—but you will look forward constructively.

I'm happy to say that this junior came to grips with the unalterable reality that he was stuck with this teacher he didn't like. He then stopped looking back in anger and started looking forward constructively. And, inevitably, his grades shot up.

Let me, then, summarize the bad news: you are not perfect just the way you are and the world was not created to satisfy your every need and desire. Happiness is not guaranteed you as a right. As you make the pursuit of happiness your goal, you can be guaranteed that you will encounter many a barrier, many a trouble. You will not get what you think you deserve; often you will not get even what you do deserve.

Face life's realities expecting trouble. Face life's problems—not like the woman at the theatre squandering all her energy looking backwards in anger like a victim. But face life's inevitable problems looking forward constructively. Above all, ask for help. Ask for the help of God in prayer—nothing is more efficacious than that. It takes guts to do that, to admit you are not in control of the universe, to acknowledge you are a temporary little speck and that the world does not revolve around you. And ask for human help. There are plenty of people around you who have also had to learn to come to grips constructively with life's disappointments.

You have a choice about your life: you can run away from reality and try to convince yourself that life will give you whatever you think you deserve. If you adopt this view, you will, sooner or later, be crushed by disappointment and see yourself as a victim. And you will squander your energies looking back in anger.

Or you can face reality, expect trouble, and work constructively to deal with whatever life dishes out to you. Then, instead of being a victim, you will be the captain of your own destiny in the pursuit of happiness: expecting obstacles and roadblocks along the way, willing to seek the help of God and man, looking always ahead, with hope and cheerfulness, for new opportunities.

8

Having Your Cake and Eating It Too

Life Should Have No Consequences

N THE SMALL Midwestern town where I grew up, only one or two kids in each class came to school by bus. They ate their packed lunch in the classroom with the teacher. Most of us, however, walked home every day for lunch.

One day in the fall of my fourth grade year, my mother had to take my grandmother to Cleveland to have some dental work done. The journey back and forth to what we regarded as the Cultural Center of the Universe was an all-day undertaking. And so, after giving me a large breakfast, my mother packed me a lunch, since she wouldn't be home at lunchtime. "Here," she said. "Here's the lunch I've fixed for you to eat at school. I've packed everything you like—now don't eat any of it till lunch time!"

Postponing gratification was not one of my strong points in fourth grade, and as most of you know, apodictic commands ("Don't do this"; "Thou shalt not") often have counterproductive results. So about three minutes and twenty-seven seconds into my ten-minute walk to school, I opened the bag. My mother had packed my favorite: an egg salad sandwich. "I'll just have half of it," I said to myself. I was midway through the Van Dusens' backyard—which we all cut through to get to school. So I sat down on the ground right there and unfolded the waxed paper in which the sandwich was wrapped. The aroma of egg salad bursting forth enveloped my entire body with rapture. I carefully rewrapped the other half and delightedly consumed half the sandwich.

Purring with pleasure, I resumed my journey, crossing the street and sauntering across the large school yard. As I reached the side entrance to the school, however, I was seized again with hunger pains I can only describe as rapacious. I felt absolutely starved, and there was just nothing to do but sit down on the steps, unwrap the remaining half sandwich, and relieve the agony of famine. I finished the delectable egg salad just in time to take my seat in Mrs. Safick's fourth grade class at 8:10 A.M.

I settled down to a morning of serious intellectual endeavor. At 11:45, the bell rang signaling lunch time. Mrs. Safick said to me, "Tony, where are you going?" I said, "Home." She said, "I thought your mother was away and you were having lunch at school." "No," I quickly said. "I'm going home." Now amazingly, this was the first thought I had devoted to my existential condition of lunchlessness. "I know what I'll do," I said to myself. "I'll go to my grandmother's." She lived a street away from us and she doted on me. Off I trotted to her house—arriving almost there when suddenly it dawned on me that she was in Cleveland with my mother. What to do? I stopped right in the middle of the sidewalk. "I know," I finally said in my ongoing dramatic monologue, "I'll go get some lunch at 'Old Lady' Harriger's." Mrs. Harriger was our next-door neighbor. She was probably younger than I am now, and yet she was known to all of us as "Old Lady" Harriger.

As I gazed through the screen on her backdoor, I could see Mrs. Harriger sitting alone at her kitchen table having a bowl of soup. "Come in, Tony," she said, looking up from her sumptuous repast. "Mrs. Harriger," I said, "my mom's in Cleveland and I don't have anything to eat for lunch." After some discussion she got the "whole truth" from me, and then she said, "Well, I guess you'll just have to go hungry. You can't have your cake and eat it too."

"What?" I said.

"You can't have your cake and eat it too. Do you understand what I mean?"

"No," I said.

"You can't eat your lunch on the way to school and then have it to eat at noon. You can't have your cake now and eat it later."

"But I'm starved," I said.

"That's too bad," she replied.

"But that's not right," I said.

To which she replied, "That's the way it is."

My mother told me years later that it nearly killed Mrs. Harriger to send me away with an empty stomach. But if she'd fed me I would probably never have learned the lesson I did learn that day: that you cannot have your cake and eat it too. The corollary of that lesson is revealed in the final exchange between Old Lady Harriger and me.

When I said, "That's not right," I was asserting my right to a life free of consequence or pain. What Mrs. Harriger was asserting when she said, "That's the way it is," is the reality that there's no free lunch in life, the reality that you cannot have your cake and eat it too, the reality that you have responsibility for your own life and no built-in right to have someone or something take care of you if you mess up.

Life Should Be Cost Free

This story goes very much against the grain of our times, and that's why I told it to you. We are living in a time when most talk is about rights and very little about responsibility, when most talk is about getting what we deserve and very little about our duty to others.

Perhaps you read this summer about Shannon Faulkner, the young woman who applied to The Citadel—the small all-male military college in South Carolina. The admissions committee actually took her, believing (because of her ambiguous name) that she was a man. She asserted that it was her right to attend, even though The Citadel has for 152 years been a men's college. The Citadel experience, she asserted, couldn't be duplicated anywhere else and she wanted it: "It's my right."

Now let me say at the outset that I cannot possibly imagine why anyone—male or female—would voluntarily choose to go to The Citadel. Underclassmen have to walk in the gutters, submit to all sorts of bizarre and puerile punishments for ridiculous infractions, do push-ups till they vomit, and have their heads shaved. I can't imagine anyone deliberately choosing such an experience. However, in this wonderfully diverse country of ours, apparently a sizable number of men and this one woman—are eager to gain admission. Even though I cannot imagine myself going to The Citadel, in principle I like peculiar institutions that dare to be different and that do things in an unconventional way. And truth to tell, I had a kind of secret admiration for Shannon Faulkner. She's right—this odd Citadel experience is not duplicated elsewhere, and part of me was rooting for her when she asserted: "I want the Whole Citadel Experience, and I can get it only at The Citadel."

Part of me was rooting for her until, that is, she announced that she—alone of all those admitted—should be excused from having her head shaved. But the haircut, of course, is one of the defining elements of the Whole Citadel Experience that she claims she wants.

As it turns out, of course, what she really wanted was not the "Whole Citadel Experience," but rather those parts of it that appealed to her. She wanted the Whole Citadel Experience not as The Citadel defined it, but as she defined it. It was her right to pick and choose. She perfectly exemplifies the desire to have your cake and eat it too. She perfectly incarnates the desire to have rights without any of the bad consequences of those rights.

Let me give you another example. Back in the sixties I was at Resurrection City in Washington—one of the big national protests during the Vietnam War. I can't remember now whether it was spring or fall, but we were all living in tents and the rains came down. The whole scene was quickly reduced to a squalid muddy uproar. One of the flaky Cleveland suburbanites who'd been on our bus to Washington came over to me and said, "Hey, man, I'm going home. This is ridiculous. I didn't expect to get soaked like this. I gotta go home." He wanted to protest the war, but not at the cost of being uncomfortable. And, of course, the next day he and others like him were the subject of a searing article in the *Star*, Washington's now-defunct evening paper, entitled (I think) "Fair Weather Friends," about those who had deserted the protest when the rains came down. When you analyze it, the philosophy of these deserters was: I'll hold onto my convictions as long as they aren't too costly.

That is the theme of our age—rights without consequences, the willingness to stand up for something as long as it doesn't cost us anything.

Our age also despises guilt. A fellow headmaster told me this summer about a boy who was caught stealing at his school. The parents' first reaction was to dispute all aspects of the evidence. When the evidence turned out to be incontrovertible, one of them asked, "What sort of counseling do you give students about not stealing? Obviously it wasn't good enough. It's not my son's fault that he stole things, it's the school's fault." The basic problem this boy had, of course, was his parents, who by their unwillingness to have the boy face the consequences of his actions all his life, had bred a son who really believed he could do whatever he wanted without any bad consequences.

It is painful to feel guilt, so we try to banish guilt from our lives, to absolve ourselves of guilt. Last spring, after an Roxbury Latin boy did something outrageous, I called him into my office and pointed out to him—in clear terms—the callousness of what he'd done. With remarkable chutzpah, he said to me, "You're laying a guilt trip on me." I said, "Ooh! Light bulb! That's exactly what I'm doing." "But guilt trips are bad," he said. "I thought adults weren't supposed to lay guilt trips on kids." I replied, "Your basic problem is that you've been deprived of guilt trips all your life. What you've done is awful, and you should feel guilty. Since you don't 'get it', let me explain again what you've done wrong and why you should feel guilty."

In addition to the right to live without consequences and the right to live without guilt, it is also more and more frequently asserted nowadays that it is our right to have a good and happy outcome whenever we work hard to achieve something.

In an admissions interview here a few years ago, both parents of an applicant stated emphatically how much they wanted to send their son to Roxbury Latin because "he needs to be challenged." They criticized the school he was attending for being too easy: "He does no work and gets all A's." And they repeatedly expressed the desire to see him stretched intellectually, something that would only happen if he came to Roxbury Latin. We took him. By early January of his first year, his parents were in my office in a state. For the fall term, their son had received two C's. I thought he was off to a reasonable start, but that was not his parents' view! Their tune had changed considerably since the admissions interview. Now they felt the School's standards were "brutal" and their son's self-esteem was being "shattered" by receiving the two C's. One of the parents said, "This school is a Marine boot camp." When I rather quietly remarked that a few months earlier they had wanted Roxbury Latin because it would challenge their son, they were further enraged by what they called my "insensitivity."

These parents wanted the right to the Roxbury Latin challenge, but only if it came risk-free, cost-free, defeat-free. Fortunately, the boy's attitude was much more positive, and he redoubled his efforts and met the challenge in the succeeding months.

I dealt with another irate parent whose son (to the boy's relief) was placed in a C section of math. The father—one of that brand of conservative who is forever denouncing the declining values of our society—was furious. After explaining to me all the evils of sectioning by ability, he ended his diatribe by asking the rhetorical question, "Are you telling me that my son is inferior in math?" I answered, simply, "Yes." This, as I might have expected, had the predictable effect of pouring gasoline on his fire, and I hunkered down in order to survive his second assault.

Finally, I pointed out that his son was a starter on the basketball team (it wasn't basketball; I'm changing the story's details), and I asked him, "Do you think he deserves to start?" "Yes, of course he does, he's very good." "Well," I said, "Is it really fair to have a team consisting only of the better players? Shouldn't we—to be fair—just choose a team at random out of all the interested players? Why should all the better athletes be on one team?" He responded, as you'd expect, by stating that sports and academics are utterly different. He simply could not bear to accept the reality that his son might be a great kid (which he was) and work quite hard (which he did), and not be particularly good at math—at least in the rarefied little world of Roxbury Latin. But to that father, his son had a right to no bad outcomes. His son should have his cake (a challenge) and eat it too (with the guarantee of coming out on top in the challenge).

Speaking myself as both a mediocre math student and as a mediocre basketball player, I have to say I'm glad I grew up in an era when nobody put the notion into my head that if you're a good kid who works hard you should always get in the A section of math and be guaranteed the right to start in basketball. I had to accept the reality that you can be a good kid and work hard—and the outcome may be far less than you hoped for. I had to work that through. I'm glad I had to work that through. I want you to work that through. Because there is no right in life to a good outcome.

Mrs. Harriger's hard words to me in 1948 are as true now as they were then. "That's the way it is." Life does not confer upon you the right to make decisions that have no consequences, to have your cake and eat it too. Life does not confer upon you the right to do stupid and thoughtless things without any cost or any guilt. Life does not confer upon you the right to a good outcome for every effort you make.

The Secret to Happiness in Life

The Judeo-Christian tradition—upon which our School is founded—says precious little about rights. When, in fact, the Judeo-Christian tradition does address the issue of rights, it talks mostly about giving up rights, about denying yourself rights in order to help others.

The Judeo-Christian tradition focuses not on the right to a good outcome, but rather on the duty of a noble effort.

The first great virtue of the Judeo-Christian tradition is courage. The courage to face reality. The courage to look at the bad consequences of your actions as well as the good. The courage to take responsibility for your mistakes, the courage to feel the full brunt of guilt whenever you ought to feel guilty, the courage to face the reality that your hard work and virtue are not always rewarded the way you want them to be—and that you can't go through life blaming other people for reality.

Or to state things more positively, the courage to attempt great things in the face of heavy odds, to be David against Goliath, and the courage to accept with grace and magnanimity the defeats and disappointments life will inevitably dish out to you. The courage to face bravely the suffering involved in postponing gratification. The courage to turn off the TV and do the work. The courage to tell the truth rather than to waffle and evade like a coward.

Secondly, the Judeo-Christian tradition focuses not on your right to be comfortable, but rather on your duty to be uncomfortable for the sake of others, to sacrifice yourself for others. When Mother Teresa was asked why she gave up everything to go and live among the poor, she said nothing about her right to happiness or her right to be comfortable or her right to success or her right to anything. She said, "I wanted a very hard life." She chose to "do something beautiful for God," something costly, something painful, something exhausting, something that brought her poverty and heartache and unending hard work. She says nothing about rights. She lays down her rights for others and talks of self-sacrifice, costliness, giving. "I wanted a very hard life."

The third great virtue of the Judeo-Christian tradition—along with courage and self-sacrifice—is gratitude. This, of all the Judeo-Christian virtues, seems the most in eclipse. And yet, the older I get, the more it seems to me the mother of all the virtues.

If there is any secret to happy living, I believe it is in living thankfully. I have seen some very ugly entitled boys over the years—not very many here, but a few who are memorable. It is their right to have everything go their way—and the least thing that doesn't go their way embitters them.

But I have seen many, many more of the opposite kind of boy here. Right now sitting amongst you—and few if any of you will ever realize it—are boys with alcoholic parents, boys from dysfunctional families, boys living in situations where they are physically and/or psychologically abused, boys living with parents who are dying painfully or whose parents have died. Most of these fellow students of yours are living with these realities cheerfully and even gratefully. A boy whose mother was dying a hideous and painful death a few years ago said to me: "I'm grateful that she's still there. I'm grateful for every additional day. I'm grateful I may be able to bring her some small comfort by something I do and say each day." No bitterness. No "Why me?" No entitlement to a trouble-free life. This boy had hit upon the key to human happiness—to focus on all that is good and to be thankful for it.

Life entitles you, my dear boys, to nothing. As Mrs. Harriger said, "That's the way it is." You have no right to actions without consequences and without guilt. You cannot have your cake and eat it too. You have no right to a happy outcome for all your efforts.

If you want to be happy, you must begin not with rights but with responsibilities: with the courage to face reality, the courage to attempt great things at the risk of losing, the courage to lose bravely, the courage to suffer with patience, the courage to tell the truth.

If you want to be happy, you will find happiness arises not so much from getting your way and asserting your rights as it does from sacrificing your rights, sacrificing your time and treasure for the sake of others.

If you want to be happy, you will find happiness not from dwelling on all you do not have in life and feeling bitter about it. You will find happiness by dwelling on all that is good and true and beautiful in your life and being thankful for it.

9

Great American Teenage Tragedies

UOTATION from an advisor letter written to the parents of a senior whose grades this fall were somewhat lower than usual: "It may just be a coincidence, but several of your son's teachers have noticed—and quite a number of his classmates have commented on the fact—that Harry [we'll call him] has been absent at least three times this fall on the day of a major test or paper. We are also disappointed that you saw fit to add an extra day to his college trip by taking him sightseeing in San Francisco."

When I was shown this letter—about a senior at another school—my reaction was that it was the mildest of rebukes, far milder than what he'd have received from this school. However, his parents replied with a blistering twelve-page indictment charging the advisor both with maligning the boy's reputation and (in response to the day of sightseeing) with trying to deprive him of a close relationship with his parents: "We find precious quality time with him whenever we can and, quite frankly, we're just not going to let the school stand in the way." Then, turning to the subject of their son's grades, they said, "All fall we've been concerned about his teachers' insensitivity to the pressure he is under. Now you tell us they doubt his honesty. Our lawyer tells us we could sue you for impugning his motives. You have some very dissatisfied customers on your hands. We're paying a lot of money for his education and we're not happy with what we're getting. Next term we want him to have a fresh start with five new teachers who will not destroy his confidence by tearing him down."

No. This is not a typical parent letter. And no, I have never received one like it at Roxbury Latin. I quote from it because its excessive and hysterical tone throws into bold relief feelings that normal, stable, rational parents and boys sometimes have. Underneath the crude, gauche, emotionally volatile response of these particular parents lies a philosophy or (if philosophy is too pretentious a word) an attitude that I think other boys and parents share and that is worth our while to consider. That attitude might be summarized this way. If parents are paying a lot of money and boys are working hard, then everything should work out and there shouldn't be any problems: hard work should be rewarded with good grades and success in extracurriculars; everything should go well. This attitude is most openly expressed by new seventh graders here. Many a new boy—after getting his first C—has wept: "I worked really hard and I only got a C. So-and-so hardly did anything and he got an A." As we get older, we're no longer as open about our feelings as we were at twelve, but the attitude still persists.

It is hard for us to come to grips with the sad reality that life is not fair, that some people are better than others at certain things, that hard work is not always rewarded, that things don't always work out the way we want them to. Perhaps we never quite fully accept that painful reality and that is why, when we are a good deal older than twelve, we still sometimes want to scream, "That's not fair."

Getting Cut from a Team

Many a Roxbury Latin boy has cried (or tried hard not to cry) upon hearing that he's been cut from a team. Coaches understand the enormous emotional investment boys make when they try out for a team, and they try to do the cutting—which sadly they have to do—privately and sensitively. And yet, of course, no amount of privacy and sensitivity can do much to soften the crushing reality that someone else was chosen—and I wasn't.

Occasionally—and I mean only occasionally—a boy or parent will murmur that he wasn't given a fair chance or a long-enough look. I remember one father saying, "Why couldn't the coach just have looked a little longer to see what we see there? Being cut has humiliated our son with his friends and destroyed his self-confidence." Again, the father's underlying philosophy was that life should always reward effort, that no one who tries should ever lose, that losing is destructive and humiliating. At such times, frankly, I wonder if we (and schools in general today) are too sensitive, too gentle. In the schools I attended in the fifties, coaches just posted the names of those who made the team. I was cut a number of times. No coach ever took me aside and shared his regret. I found out when I looked on the board and saw my name wasn't on the list. Read all about it.

Yes, I felt crushed, embarrassed, even humiliated—and yes, I felt on several occasions that I was better than some of the players the coach chose for the team. And yes, I suppose that, at least for a while, my self-confidence was shaken.

I was blessed, however, by having parents with a healthy perspective. They realized how much I wanted to make the team and they understood how badly I was hurting. But they didn't make things worse by overreacting, by treating my being cut as if it were the disaster of the decade. I remember my father—and he was a fanatic sportsman—saying, "That's the breaks. That's the way the cookie crumbles. Life isn't fair. The sun will still rise tomorrow."

Looking back, I'd have to say that getting cut was among the most valuable experiences I had as a boy. It prepared me well for the reality of life. For life brings many disappointments and defeats, many cuts. Each time I was cut—or each time I made a team but didn't get the playing time I was hoping to get—I had to dig deep within myself to find an inner confidence I never would have found without those defeats. I can think of at least one friend of mine—an athlete who was never in danger of being cut—whose success in sports as a teenager left him badly prepared for life's disappointments and who was knocked down in his twenties, because nothing in his life had prepared him for life's inevitable reverses.

Perhaps we gain more self-confidence digging deep to deal with our defeats than we gain by succeeding or winning. Perhaps we learn more about ourselves from failure than we learn from success.

Working Hard and Getting Low Grades

The same may be said of academics. Every one of you is gifted or you wouldn't be here. But the cruel reality is that you are not equally gifted.

Some years ago when we were interviewing a boy for admission, the mother and father talked on and on about how they were looking for a school with standards. "This nation is shooting down the tubes. The whole country lacks standards. There's no discipline any more," incanted the father. When their son was admitted, and the School's vaunted standards were applied to him, the father's tune changed: "Our son has always gotten A's before. His teachers are ruining his self-confidence by making everything so hard. "

In my experience, most boys have a pretty realistic picture of their academic abilities. When they do poorly in a subject, they have a pretty good idea about the degree to which that is due to having somewhat less aptitude for a particular subject and the degree to which that is due to not working as hard as they should have. Parents are not always as reasonable as their sons. Sometimes a parent will look for an external cause: a teacher, or sickness, or stress: It must be the teacher's fault ("He's too hard" or "He doesn't explain things well" or "He has certain favorites"). "My son wasn't feeling well that day" or "He's been depressed by getting so little playing time in football" or "He's worried about whether he'll get into Brand X College." (As if every boy ought always to find every teacher perfectly congenial, or as if every test should be taken or paper written in perfect conditions without any out-side pressures.) The only explanation that's not acceptable to such par-ents is the real one: the boy just didn't do particularly well.

School is a great deal like life: in school you can expend enormous quantities of time on writing a paper and still receive only a C. In life you can work very hard at planning some project or selling some prod-uct and still not succeed.

I know of an elementary school in which every child gets a prize, in which grades are based mostly on effort. Far be it from me to determine whether such a policy is advantageous for little children. But I am certain it is not advantageous for adolescents. It is not advantageous because a high school should prepare its students for life, and life is not like that. To alter reality at this level—to finagle things so that a student's effort is always rewarded—would leave that student defenseless in the future in the face of real life—which does not work that way. "In the world," says Jesus, "you shall have tribulation." In digging deep now to cope with the disappointments of school life, you learn how to deal with the setbacks that follow in later life.

Not Being Admitted to the College You Want

In another city a few days ago I watched a colleague of mine deal with the mother of a boy who was deferred at an Ivy League college. "I just don't understand it," she said. "If they don't want him, who do they want? He's a brilliant student [he's good, but not brilliant]; he's a superb quarterback [he'd never play in Division I]. Did you call the director of admissions? You didn't? You only called the school's contact in the admissions office? I thought so. You've got to go right to the top [the worst tactic in this circumstance]. I want you to call him today and get this decision reversed. My son's self-esteem has been shattered. [Do you notice the recurring theme?] A terrible injustice has been done. You're going to call up and get him in—today! "

Her son is a strong candidate from all I can see, though by no means a sure bet. But even if he walks on water, there is a very good chance he will not get what he thinks he wants and what he—in so many ways— "deserves." You have to be both very good and very lucky, and he may not be very lucky. As my dad would say, "That's the breaks. That's the way the cookie crumbles. Life isn't fair. The sun will still rise tomorrow."

You have heard me say before that I don't know who the lucky ones are—the ones who get in or the ones who get turned down. Those who get their first choice sometimes find the reality quite a come-down. On the other hand, I have seen many a boy turned down at his first-choice college, who then digs deep, discovers deeper reasons for having a healthy self-respect, and ends up loving and doing well at the college he does attend. Countless young men have told me, "One of the best things that ever happened to me was not getting into Brand X College." It is, I submit, arguable that those whose dreams do not come true regarding college are better prepared for life than those whose dreams do come true.

"The Moral of the Story"

So what do these illustrations add up to?

First, we all need to keep some sense of perspective. These teenage tragedies—being cut from a team, not playing as much as you'd like, getting a low grade after much effort, not getting into your first-choice college—are not really tragedies. Disappointments, yes. Tragedies, no.

Tragedy is millions of young men your age who right now are starving to death, who are homeless, who have none of the opportunities you have. That's tragedy.

It is an obscenity to confuse disappointment with tragedy. It is an obscenity to regard being cut or not getting enough playing time or not getting a good grade or not making your dream college as tragedies. Disappointments, yes. Tragedies, no.

Second, life is not fair. You can attempt something with all your might and still not succeed. All of us—adolescents and adults—cry out at times: "It's not fair!" but only fools believe that if you want something badly enough and work hard for it, you will always get it. Good is not always rewarded. We complain about good not being rewarded when we think we deserve something we don't get. But—and this happens just as often—when we get something we don't deserve and didn't earn, we don't complain about life's injustice!

Mature, thoughtful people do not live in the foolish expectation that everything will go their way if they just work hard. Mature, thoughtful people are strong enough, however, not to give up when things don't go their way. They don't waste their energy lamenting their defeats, whimpering about life's unfairness. They get up and try again.

Third, every disappointment, every setback you will have in life is an opportunity for growth. The great Viennese psychiatrist Viktor Frankl, who survived years in a Nazi concentration camp, said over and over, "That which does not kill me makes me stronger." Expect to suffer in life, because you most assuredly will. You will be very lucky indeed if the worst thing that ever happens to you is being cut from a team or getting a low grade on a paper you slaved over, or not being admitted to your heart's-desire college. Accept such setbacks as opportunities to dig deep within yourself to find out who you really are and to discover inner strengths you didn't know you had. Use such disappointments as opportunities to grow stronger.

I talked recently with a boy who was denied admission to Roxbury Latin six years ago. I have followed his career with some interest, and he called to tell me he had been admitted early to Princeton. He said, "The best thing that ever happened to me was to be rejected by Roxbury Latin. My parents were crying and everything, as if my life were over. I knew right then that I'd prove to you you were wrong not to take me at Roxbury Latin." If we had accepted this boy, I doubt very much that he would have done anything like the soul-searching he did as the result of being rejected; I doubt very much he would have approached his high school days with anything like the same determination. Every setback is an opportunity for deepening self-knowledge and for rethinking one's goals. When suffering comes your way—and it will!—determine to use it. "That which does not kill me makes me stronger."

Listen to this summary of Abraham Lincoln's personal life and public career: He had an impoverished and difficult childhood; he failed in business when he was twenty-two; he was defeated when he ran for the state legislature; he failed in business again; he tried again for the state legislature and was elected. His fiancée died when he was twenty-six; he was defeated when he ran for speaker three years later. He was married at thirty-one, but only one of his four sons lived past eighteen. He was defeated when he ran for the U.S. Congress at thirty-two, but elected when he ran again at thirty-five. He was defeated when he ran for the U.S. Senate at age forty-six, defeated when he ran for vice president a year later, and defeated three years after that when he ran again for the Senate.

His experience of setback and loss and defeat, the deepening he underwent because of his suffering, is undoubtedly what enabled Lincoln to lead the nation through the most tragic and perilous years of its history. Without the experience of setback and defeat, without the experience of personal and political suffering, he could never have achieved the greatness of character that make him one of the towering figures of history.

When you suffer setback and defeat, remember Lincoln. Use your suffering to dig more deeply into yourself, to grow, to become stronger.

Fourth, don't look back with bitterness. Let go of your setbacks and defeats. Don't torture yourself with what might have been, if only . . . if only . . . if only. . . . If only I'd stayed at my old school, I would be under much less pressure, I could hang out with my old friends. . . . If only . . .

I wasted a lot of time when I was your age on regret: if only I'd stayed in public school, if only I'd made the team, if only I had so-and-so's brains or looks. That tendency to look back still afflicted me even after I was a priest in my twenties. I looked on my contemporaries with envy: they were piling up fortunes as lawyers and businessmen, they were getting married and having families. (Have you ever noticed how we always compare ourselves up and not down? We rarely compare ourselves to those who are less fortunate than ourselves.)

Yet, even in my twenties as I was comparing myself up to contemporaries who'd gone into business and were raising families, they were coming to me for counseling as they looked back with regret at the choices they'd made. I wish I had a dollar for every well-to-do person who's said to me over the years: "You're so lucky. I wish I had a sense I was doing something worthwhile with my life."

Every time you make a choice in life, you necessarily rule out other choices you might have made. Every time you make one choice, you give up other choices. Every choice involves pain. That's the way life is.

Finally, there is a great tendency to focus on our problems. So here is a final great saying (one my grandmother repeated endlessly): "Count your blessings." We spend too much time focusing on our problems and not enough time focusing on our blessings. Very few people on earth your age have as much to be thankful for as you: health, loving families and teachers, amazing opportunities. When you say your prayers each night, by all means offer up your brokenness and disappointment, but do not forget to thank God for all the good things.

10

In Praise of Martin Buber

 WANT TO SPEAK WITH YOU this morning about Martin Buber. At the time of his death in the mid-sixties, the *New York Times* called Buber "the foremost Jewish religious thinker of our time and one of the world's most influential philosophers." Of his many books, the most famous, *I and Thou*, has never been out of print since he wrote it in 1923 and has been translated into all the major languages.

Martin Buber was born in Vienna and was brought up by his grandparents, following the divorce of his parents. His grandfather was a successful businessman who gradually turned the running of the family business over to his wife—a woman generations ahead of her time who ran the business even more successfully than her husband and who was widely acclaimed for her enlightened treatment of her workers. The grandfather then devoted his attention to the passion of his life, Judaism, and became a noted rabbinic scholar. Martin Buber grew up in an atmosphere, then, of both liberal (so-called enlightened) Judaism on the one hand and religious (so-called traditional) Judaism on the other. By the time of his Bar Mitzvah he was already thinking for himself, asking deep questions, and rebelling. For the rest of his life, in fact, he lived in a state of tension: he was inexorably and inescapably drawn to Judaism and yet simultaneously he often found himself fighting it, resisting it.

After graduating from the University of Vienna he went to Berlin. Taking after his grandmother, he established a successful publishing firm for Jewish literature, and taking after his grandfather he became a scholar of Hasidic texts and a lecturer and writer. In 1923 he became professor of Jewish history at Frankfurt University in Germany. Ten years later he was deprived of this post when the Nazis came to power; he then moved to the countryside where he worked quietly at his studies. As the danger increased, he fled Germany in 1938 to take up the post of professor of sociology at the University of Jerusalem. Here he remained for the rest of his life.

Since this academic year marks the fiftieth anniversary of that move and since Martin Buber has been a major influence on my own view of the world, I want to share with you some of his insights that have affected me. Most of them are found in *I and Thou*.

Openness the Key

You cannot understand anything of Martin Buber unless you are willing to acknowledge that there is a great deal more to life than meets the eye and ear. Let me use music as an analogy. When I was twelve I had to take the same music class our seventh graders have to take. My attitude was: I like my own music; this stuff is bor-ring! We were taken to hear the Cleveland Orchestra. I remember sitting there in Severance Hall for what seemed an eternity defiantly saying to myself and others: This is just noise. It's absolutely meaningless. Nobody could like this stuff; these people are just pretending they like it. Several years later, of course, someone helped me to hear classical music. Suddenly what had been ugly became beautiful. It had been there the whole time; I had heard it, yet I had not really heard it.

I was lucky to be able to spend two hours this vacation at the Metropolitan Museum in New York seeing the stunning new exhibition of art from Siena. I found myself at one point next to a husband and wife and two children. The teenage boy was saying, "These pictures are really stupid. They all look the same. Why do you have to drag us here?" I was just like that: closed to many of life's possibilities, not open to understanding things more deeply, convinced there was nothing there.

Martin Buber says that if you do want to go deeper, there are three gates to a fulfilling life. "True life," as Buber calls it, is found only beyond ourselves, in relation to something beyond ourselves. The three gates to true life are found in deep relationship with nature, with man, and with God. We are able, says Buber, to enter into deep and intimate relationships—to enter what he calls the I-Thou relationship—through all three gates. "Thou" is an awkward English translation of the German word "*du*," the intimate and yet elevated German word for you. Buber calls our deepest and most intimate meeting with nature, with man, and with God, the I-Thou relationship.

I want to look briefly at each of these I-Thou relationships, at each of these gates through which we can pass to the abundant life.

The I-Thou Relationship with Nature

The first gate to the abundant life is in and through our relationship with nature.

You and I live most of the time in what Buber calls the I-It relationship: Most of the time we're not in a deep relationship with the people and things around us. When I was thirteen my whole family drove across the country (your classic middle-class American educational family trip). I was in the ho-hum, "Big deal" phase of my development, and I recall finally igniting my long-suffering father as he rhapsodized over the beauty of Crater Lake: "Big deal," I said, "Big deal—blue water and more mountains." In retrospect I don't know why my father didn't drown me in Crater Lake. He must have wanted to. I was completely closed to the beauty of a place that almost defines natural beauty.

Years later, when I was a student at Cambridge, which is—I say with some objectivity—the most beautiful university on earth, I took an American friend of mine on a walking tour of the buildings and gardens of Cambridge after dinner. He smoked, so he smelled nothing. He talked incessantly, so he heard nothing. And he looked at me as he talked, so he saw nothing. As I pointed out one beautiful sight after another, he said, "Yeah. Right," and went right on talking. I'm sure he told others that he "saw" Cambridge, but Cambridge remained for him an It, not a Thou. He never saw it at all. It was all there for him, but he could not enter the gate into a relationship with it.

Nature becomes a Thou to us when—somehow—we are open to a deeper relationship with it. What occurs then is a "mountaintop experience." My father entered into an I-Thou relationship with Crater Lake: its beauty enveloped him, moved him, transformed him. I—on the other hand—entered into no such relationship; I saw but did not perceive, and I went away empty. I entered into an I-Thou relationship with Cambridge: its beauty enveloped me, moved me, transformed me. My American friend—on the other hand—avoided and refused such a relationship; he saw but did not perceive, and he went away empty.

A physicist friend of mine once said to me, "I'll tell you what Buber meant. Most of the time in my research I see a jumble of data. Every now and then, everything comes together and all of a sudden—in an utterly transforming split second—I see the whole majestic structure of things, the amazing beauty of the natural order. I have gone from the normal I-It relationship we all have with nature to an intimate—now I see it—I-Thou relationship with nature."

We describe that relationship in many ways. In comic books the artist draws a light bulb ("a moment of enlightenment"). We talk about being inspired or transformed. We have in that moment entered into a profoundly deep relationship with nature—we have passed through one of the gates to the abundant life. Wordsworth describes this experience as being "surprised by joy." It is the joy of seeing what is beautiful, of knowing what is true. In such moments we experience the joy of what Buber calls "true life."

The I-Thou Relationship with Others

The second gate to true life is our relationship with our fellow humans.

Most of the time this relationship remains at the I-It level. Most of the time we see people in terms of their function. We don't relate to the bus driver as a full, rich human being. He remains for us an It—a bus driver. Most of the time you don't relate to your teachers as full, rich human beings. They conduct classes, correct errors, give grades; you perceive them in terms of their function. This point was driven home to me twenty years ago when I was a young teacher in Cleveland. I taught a class of juniors and in it I had a boy named Tom. He was in an automobile accident and was still unconscious when I went to see him in the hospital. There he was—lying there. And there were his parents—across the room—by now very anxious that he had not "come out of it." I talked with them a while, and before I went I said, "I'm just going to say goodbye to Tom, even though he probably can't hear me." So I grasped his hand and quietly said something inspiring like, "Hang in there, Tom, we're all pulling for you." The second I spoke his eyes flickered open and he rubbed them and said, "Mr. Jarvis. . . . Oh, I'm glad you woke me up. I've got to get to work on my paper." At that moment both his parents leaped up and said, "Tommy, you're OK." His mother went gushing on till Tom said to her, "Mom, what are you doing here?" She said: "Tom, I'm your mother!" "I know," said Tom, "but how come you're at school?" "This isn't school," she said. "Oh yes it is," said Tom. "Mr. Jarvis is here." Tom's total picture of me was as a teacher. He responded to me as a student. If we were talking, it must be school. The student-teacher I-It relationship is the sort of relationship in which humans normally interact with one another.

In our I-It relationships we use one another. Buber says, "I-It can never be spoken with the whole being." In the I-Thou relationship we meet one another. "The I-Thou can only be spoken with our whole being."

Many people are fearful of risking their whole being. They hide behind their function: They remain a teacher or a student. They remain a doctor or priest. They remain a husband or a father. They may be very good in these functions (and it is often appropriate that we remain in our functions), but some never dare go beyond them. I had a conversation recently with a married couple in which the man for an hour and a half repeatedly referred to his wife as "my wife." Never once did he use her name, never once did he truly see her in any other function than as his wife. One could quickly guess (and guess accurately) that he had never in their marriage related to his wife as anything other than as a wife. He had never "spoken to her with his whole being" nor ever seen her as a "whole being." They had never passed from the I-It to the I-Thou. I pester you to call me and one another by name because to call a person by name is to take a significant step to recognizing his totality, his rich wholeness. Those of you who have studied Hebrew Scripture are aware of the overwhelming importance the Jews place on names—just for that reason.

It never ceases to amaze me—even in a school as small and intimate as ours—how often boys hide full time behind the image they want to convey. We package ourselves to be a salable product and we relate to others who are packaging themselves to be attractive products. We are packages relating to packages. As we hide behind the image we're trying to convey we encounter others hiding behind the image they're trying to convey. Mask encounters mask. As a result we pigeonhole one another, classifying each other as types, putting those around us in categories. We are afraid to risk our real I in relation to others. Buber says, "This is the risk: the [I-Thou] can only be spoken with the whole being. He who gives himself to it may withhold nothing of himself."

Only to those who find the courage to risk themselves will come those occasional moments in which we suddenly find ourselves in full relationship with another—in which I experience you as Thou. Buber is quick to point out that such moments are not to be confused with erotic or sexual infatuation or with physical attraction. Physical expressions—a pat on the shoulder or a kiss or embrace—may occasionally accompany such moments, but not usually. Such moments are beyond sensual feeling and physical expression. A Roxbury Latin boy in college said to me this past vacation, "Do you remember one day in my junior year when we talked on the sidelines of a soccer game? I'd never thought of you before that time as anything more than a teacher." As he groped for words, I responded: "I remember that moment very clearly. I know just what you mean. I never saw you as anything more than another student until that moment." In such moments we are surprised by joy. For a fleeting moment we relate fully with our whole being to another person. We are no longer categorizing, we are no longer standing aside and observing, we are no longer using others or seeing them in terms of their function. We have gone beyond the I-It relationship. We actually meet, we actually enter briefly into the I-Thou relationship—one of the gates to "true life."

The I-Thou Relationship with God

The third gate to true life is our relationship with God.

Some years ago, when the Russians orbited a space craft, the Soviet astronaut spoke on TV from outer space and said, "Well I'm way up here and I don't see anything that looks like God. Ha. Ha. Ha." If there is a God, of course, He is utterly beyond all the confining attributes of time and space. He cannot be seen or touched or heard in the normal sense in which we use those words.

Right now through this room are flying radio and TV signals. We can't see them or hear them; I can't take a jar with a lid and catch or bottle those waves the way I would a butterfly. We're not thinking about those radio and TV waves right now because we're not even aware of their presence. Yet—if we had a radio or TV here—if we had something that could receive those signals—we would discover they are there.

Some of you have had the experience of standing by a dog whose ears are suddenly pricked up by hearing some high-pitched sound that remains absolutely inaudible to you. It is there, but you can't hear it.

If you want to know God, the first step has to be suspension of disbelief, the first step has to be the admission of the possibility that something real is there, even if it cannot be literally seen or heard.

People sometimes say to me, "You can't talk about God to adolescents. They're not interested. They can't relate to that." But that is not my experience. I have a much harder time talking with adults about God because most adults have settled on some very small and confined picture of God. To many adults God is only an It, a list of attributes— "almighty, eternal," etc. Many adults live their whole lives rejecting a picture of God they were given in the sixth grade. And many also live their whole lives accepting such a picture of God as the whole story.

Many adults have settled on some picture of God and entered into an I-It relationship with that picture. Go to mass, makes the kids go to mass, get the kids confirmed. Get the boys bar mitzvahed, go to temple on the high holy days, do the table rituals. Such adults may be practicing a religion, but they are not meeting God. They're not entering into an I-Thou relationship with God.

I would rather talk with adolescents about God than with adults because, in my experience, adolescents are much more open to the possibility of a real, vital, living relationship with God. Buber says (and he wants to offend by overstating), "It is not necessary to know something about God in order to believe in Him." To "know something about" God is to categorize him and pigeonhole him as an It, the same way we categorize and pigeonhole people. I know people who can talk you to death telling you God is this and God is that. They have God all neatly packaged and labeled. They can tell you all about God. Buber tells us to beware of such people.

Buber goes back to the Exodus story of Moses at the burning bush. Moses, you recall, is tending his flock in the desert, going about the business of everyday life, when suddenly he sees a burning bush, a bush that—though it is aflame with fire—is not consumed by the fire. Moses approaches it—transfixed. Out of the bush comes a voice: "Moses, Moses." "Yes. I am here," says Moses. The voice speaks again: "Come no nearer; take off your sandals; the place where you are standing is holy ground. I am the God of your forefathers, the God of Abraham, the God of Isaac, the God of Jacob." God then calls Moses to lead the Israelites out of captivity in Egypt. "Then," the account continues, "Moses said to God, 'If I go to the Israelites and tell them that the God of their forefathers has sent me to them, and they ask me his name, what shall I say?' God answers, 'I AM, that is who I am. Tell them that I AM has sent you to them.'"

I AM: The great insight of biblical Judaism is that God cannot be defined. His very name—I AM—shows us that we can only meet him as Being Itself, vibrant, throbbing, vital Reality that cannot be packaged or controlled or neatly understood. We do not know God by understanding him as a package of attributes—an It. We know God only if we meet him in the I-Thou relationship in which we encounter him as I AM, vibrant Being, uncontrollable Reality.

I have at several points in my life come in this way into the presence of God. Many others have as well. Some of you have. No words are adequate to describe such a meeting. It is an experience, as Buber says, that is "beyond words." Such an experience brings—as it did to Moses and the prophets and Paul and the apostles—an awesome sense of the overwhelming majesty and mystery of God as well as a sense of our own smallness and unworthiness. "I am a man of unclean lips," whispers Isaiah. "I repent in sackcloth and ashes," whispers Job. Such a meeting brings not a glib serenity, but rather (as it did to Moses) the troubling awareness that one must give up one's former life and undertake obligations that will be onerous and costly.

Buber writes, "The God of Abraham, the God in whom Abraham had believed [entrusted everything] and whom Abraham had loved is not susceptible of being [contained in] some system of thought precisely because he is God." God is I AM, Being Itself beyond our comprehension and control. We can define him and define him and define him, but we can only know him by meeting Him as awesome indefinable Being.

This God—says the religion of Jews and Christians—seeks us out. Right here now—invisibly, inaudibly—in this room in this moment. Pascal puts it this way, "The entire religion of the Jews [and we could add, the entire religion of the Christians] consists only of the love of God." God loves us and seeks us for his own. "The very hairs on your head are numbered," so infinite is his knowledge of us, so infinite is his love for us. He seeks to meet us, but it is up to us to decide whether or not we will seek to meet Him.

Conclusion

Aubrey Hodes, in his biography of Martin Buber says, "I recall what [Buber] said about the true prophet: [the true prophet is a] quivering magnet needle, pointing the way to God."

If you've ever used a compass you know that the needle quivers as it points the way. The path to the abundant life, my dear children, is not simple or easy or exact. "We work out our salvation," as St. Paul says, "with fear and trembling."

We cannot experience life in any depth, we cannot hear the music of life to which we have previously been deaf, unless we seek that experience, unless we risk that experience, unless we are open to that possibility.

Another great Jew said to his contemporaries, "You see, but you do not perceive; you hear, but you do not understand." He also said, "Ask and you shall receive, seek and you shall find, knock and it shall be opened unto you."

Aubrey Hodes notes that the border—the border that divides states and people and classes and races and families and even brothers may be the truest symbol of our century. Buber both recognized life's borders—"the barbed wire fences of the heart"—and "taught us the way to bridge [those borders]." As we today begin together a whole new year, I rise—on this fiftieth anniversary of his flight from darkness and evil— to bless the name of Martin Buber who with his quivering compass gives us hope that we can cross the "barbed wire fences of the heart," that we can move from mere existence to abundant life.

11

The Spiritual Dimension

S I APPROACH the new school year, I find myself still mulling over two conversations I had this summer.

The first conversation was with the parents of a student at another school whose son had not gotten into the college they wanted him to get into. I have to assume that the boy was dying to go there from what they said, but I quickly realized it was the parents' hearts that were broken. The minute the father stopped ranting about how his son's school had "failed him" by the lousy job it had done on getting him into college, the mother started in, her complaints soon dissolving into sobs. I had a hard time sympathizing because it seemed to me their son was going to a very good college.

The second conversation occurred on my trip to Greece in July. I was with a small group of fellow Hellenophiles, and we had just spent our second day at Delphi. At the evening meal I was—as a single traveler—placed at a table for four with a mother, father, and son. The son turned out to be a junior—soon-to-be senior—at a fine public high school in the suburbs of Baltimore. They must have been bored with each other because all three focused their attentions and questions on me. The parents seemed rather like the parents I'd talked with early in the summer, but I quite liked the boy. When they found out I was a high school principal (as I put it to them) they immediately obsessed about college. Both parents and boy had their heart set on Princeton, and it was clear that there was nothing in their lives more important than his admission there. As the conversation developed, they grilled me with questions about myself. With some reluctance, I responded. When I answered their questions about where I'd gone to college and graduate school, the son lighted up: "Wow. That's some resumé you have! That's really great." I realized—from this and his subsequent remarks—that he saw people as resumés and that he was himself in search of a resumé. Underlying everything he said was an overwhelming belief—a profound faith, I'd have to call it—that happiness was somehow assured if you collected a resumé that had Princeton on it. He had a deep belief that if he was admitted to Princeton, all the rest of life would be one big happy and successful resumé.

In my first conversation, with the disappointed mother and father who came to see me, I began by trying to tell them, as sweetly as I could, that they had things out of proportion, that their son's rejection by their number one choice college was not really a tragedy. But I got nowhere and eventually lost patience. I found my voice rising as I told the mother that this was not a tragedy, that if she wanted tragedy I'd take her on a tour of a children's cancer ward; I found myself telling her that tragedy was Darryl Braithwaite, a boy in my parish in Dorchester, with a bullet through his head; I found myself telling her that her sobbing would be appropriate if she had a son who was a helpless drug addict. I finally also lost it with the father and told him that his anger would be better directed at conditions of injustice that prevented many boys his son's age from finishing high school, much less aspiring to college and to all the opportunities he assumed were his son's right. This couple later told friends of mine that I was unsympathetic. They were right.

In Greece, I also found myself losing patience and finally snapping at the resumé-obsessed senior-to-be, telling him there were plenty of Harvard and Cambridge graduates I knew who were unhappy—whatever their material success—and that it didn't much matter whether he went to Princeton or his local community college.

Looking at the propaganda I receive from other secondary schools, it is clear that for many of them college admission is the number one priority. When a school defines itself as a "college preparatory school" it automatically asserts that getting kids into college is the be-all and end-all of its existence. Many a school thus reinforces the kind of obsessiveness I observed in my conversations with parents and students this summer.

Let me tell you again. Roxbury Latin does not call itself a college preparatory school—and never has—because no one in 350-plus years has ever been willing to settle for so debased and diminished a statement of the School's purpose. When John Eliot founded Roxbury Latin he didn't say the School's purpose was "to get boys into prestigious colleges." He said its purpose was "to fit students for public service." Its purpose was, in short, to prepare them for life—and only, very incidentally, for college.

A school that prepares students for life has, I believe, a twofold mission: first, to remind students of the stark reality that life is short and ends in death; and second, to help students gain some insight into the meaning and purpose of their short and fleeting earthly lives.

Life Is Short

The farther along I get in my own journey through life on earth, the more convinced I become that only those who have the courage to see life in the perspective of death—only those who understand that life is short—can be truly happy.

Let me pause to say here that over the years many adults have said to me, "You can't talk to teenagers about death. They have no concept of death. They think they're Teflon-covered. They think they can drive fast, do drugs, have sex, and that nothing bad can happen to them. They're oblivious to danger and to death." But that has not been my experience with Roxbury Latin boys. First, some of you sitting here have a profound understanding of death—you have lost a mother or father or sibling or close friend. You have a deeper understanding of the reality of death—of how life ends for all of us—than many adults I know.

There are a number of studies now of those who came of age in the 1960s—a generation that idolized youth and that never expected to grow old. Some members of this generation are afflicted with what's called the Mick Jagger Syndrome: you've all seen this fifty-something-year-old man, his sagging body corsetted in tight fitting clothes, his face lined with age, gyrating on stage as if he were sixteen. Others are afflicted with the Teeny Bopper Mom Syndrome: middle-aged women striving to dress and talk like their teenage daughters. The common bond is an adulation of youth and a fear of growing old and dying.

The realization that life is short comes in many ways. We have a wonderful superintendent of construction for our new science building, John Adams. Ten days ago his fifteen-year-old son was killed jet skiing. His parents and friends were, of course, stunned by his sudden and horrible death. One minute he was a lively, irrepressible teenager, the next moment he was dead of a ruptured aorta. Some of you have watched a parent or a grandparent or sibling die gradually and inexorably. Others of you have had little or no experience of death. Men and women who came of age in the 1940s watched men die beside them in battle—as most of you have seen in the film *Saving Private Ryan*. Some of my earliest memories are of the World War II map of the Pacific my mother put on the kitchen wall—plotting the putative movements of her Marine brother (my Uncle George) and the prayers she and my father taught me to say every night for my two uncles and two aunts who were serving in the armed forces. To the renowned Russian novelist Fyodor Dostoyevsky, the profound awareness of death came when he was blindfolded and placed before a firing squad. Though he was reprieved at the last second, the experience brought him to a shattering awareness and acceptance of his mortality—one that affected every minute of the rest of his life and every word he wrote.

Every great school in every age has always regarded the awareness of death as the foundation stone of education. A realistic perception of human life begins with the awareness of the stark reality that life is short and ends in death.

The celebrated headmaster of Eton College, Cyril Alington, was once importuned by an aggressive mother. He did not suffer fools gladly.

"Are you preparing Henry for a political career?" she asked Alington.

"No," he said.

"Well, for a professional career?"

"No," he replied.

"For a business career, then?"

"No," he repeated.

"Well, in a word, Dr. Alington, what are you here at Eton preparing Henry for?"

"In a word, madam? Death."

Roxbury Latin is only incidentally preparing you for college. Its principal mission is to prepare you for life. And the starting point of that preparation is the reality that life is short and ends in death.

We Reach Out for What Lasts

When you finally face with courage the reality that nothing in this world endures, you instinctively reach out for what does endure and for what provides meaning, for the reality beyond what can be seen and heard and felt and smelled.

This grasping for what is eternal and lasting, this longing for what provides purpose and meaning, takes many different forms. I saw it this summer in Greece. I felt that longing on the slopes of Mount Parnassus at the Shrine at Delphi. I felt it in the stratospheric monasteries built at the top of volcanic rocks high in the sky at Meteora—reachable only by hours and hours of perilous climbing. I felt it at the home of Mary at Ephesus, the tiny, tiny stone shack (we'd call it) where she died, today a place of pilgrimage for thousands daily.

These places, and countless places like them, are testimony to man's instinctive reaching out for what Plato called the realm of Reality beyond everything earthly, beyond what we can see and feel and touch and smell.

We'd all like to reduce this realm beyond to something we can fully grasp and understand and control. I remember Woody Allen once saying (in so many words), "If only God would give me some clear sign of his presence—like making a large deposit in my name to a Swiss bank account." But, we are earthbound and such indications of what we're looking for are few.

But the longing persists—revealed most clearly in our instinctive need to pray. For many that desire remains dormant until a time of crisis. How often I have been told as a priest words to the effect: "I never really prayed until my daughter was gravely ill"; "I never really prayed until my husband got caught up in alcoholism"; "I never really prayed till my son started messing up his life with drugs." It is in such crises—both great crises and comparatively trivial crises—that we instinctively pray.

You are familiar with the aphorism, "There are no atheists in foxholes," a reference to the fact that soldiers—taking cover in foxholes when they're being shot at—tend to pray. An acquaintance of mine—a highly regarded professor and author—contracted cancer a year ago. He is a lifelong atheist but he nevertheless wanted to talk with me about his situation. I mentioned to him something about prayer. He said, "I'm the exception to the statement that there are no atheists in foxholes. I'm in the foxhole about to die and I'm not praying. I'm not turning to God—no pie in the sky for me." I quietly told him that I and many others were praying for him, but I added that it was possible that God might actually admire him for trying to tough it out and die an atheist. When I was visiting with him recently in the hospital, his doctor arrived and I, naturally, quickly said goodbye to get out of the way. At the end of my previous visits I'd always said that I—and others—were praying for him. I didn't repeat these predictable words on this visit because I was trying to get away quickly. But as I left, he called out to me, "Are you still praying for me?"

Blaise Pascal observed, "In the heart of every soul is a God-shaped vacuum."

Not Self but Others

Eric Anderson pointed out, in his address here last spring, the false promises of the countless self-fulfillment books that spew forth from every publisher: ten steps to personal happiness, how to get ahead in business, how to be successful, how to win friends and influence people.

Most of them share a basic me-me-me orientation: if I get this or that prize or success or conquest, then I'll be happy.

But the insight of the best and most profound minds—in every culture and every generation—has been that happiness comes not by focusing on yourself, your needs, your rights, your advancement, but on the needs of others. The words of Jesus encapsulate and typify this insight: "It is more blessed," says Jesus, "to give than to receive." The Greek original really means: happiness (that's a better translation than blessed); happiness comes not from getting but from giving. Unlike prayer, this orientation toward others rather than toward yourself is not instinctive, not natural. It is wisdom learned and acquired by practice and determination.

Schools not only fail young people when they deny the spiritual dimension of life, but they also fail their students when they neglect to teach the other most important insight into life: that happiness is the product of giving, not of getting. As a result, students often live in a desert of arid materialism, starving and thirsting for what will sustain them.

When the soldiers in the film *Saving Private Ryan* finally find Private Ryan—the only one of his parents' four sons not yet killed in the war—he refuses to leave the battlefield. He points to his fellow soldiers defending the bridge and says, "These are now my only brothers, and I'm not leaving them." The soldiers who've been searching for him instinctively know he's right, and they join him in risking their lives in the terrible battle that ensues. "Greater love hath no man than this: that a man lay down his life for his friends."

How often, in small ways, I've seen that self-sacrificing commitment to others here at Roxbury Latin. The lineman who practically has to be carried off the field after a football game; the Model U.N. delegate or the debater staying up late, late hours to advance the team; the boy who spends hours helping another boy with his studies. These actions—which are a denial of self—are the actions that ironically bring us the greatest happiness and fulfillment in life. They echo Private Ryan: "These are my brothers and I'm staying with them no matter what."

Dag Hammarskjöld, secretary general of the United Nations until he was killed on a peacekeeping mission, summarized this great insight in these words: "The only value my life has is the value it has for others."

Those of you who have taken Western Civ have seen the film in which Malcolm Muggeridge remarks to Mother Teresa that she and her fellow nuns in the slums of Calcutta seem to be working not for a cause, but for someone. Yes, says Mother Teresa, we are working for someone. We're trying to do "something beautiful for God." You do something beautiful for God by loving and sacrificing yourself for His children—your brothers and sisters—around you.

Be a Rebel

Only a few in every generation have insight and courage enough to see that life is short, that what is Eternal and Enduring lies beyond all the things that we can see and feel and smell and touch in our short sojourn on this planet. Only a few in every generation overcome the self-centered orientation that dominates every age and come to see those around them as their brothers and sisters.

You won't find this concern for others in most of your contemporaries, any more than I find it in most of my contemporaries. Most of our contemporaries think happiness is wrapped up in admission to a certain kind of college, that happiness is wrapped up in a certain kind of success, in popularity, in money. Happiness, to most in every age, is wrapped up in getting. I heard a teenager say, after seeing *Saving Private Ryan*, "I liked the movie, but that's not how people act in real life. Nobody would stay on a battlefield if he didn't have to. I'd have gone home. Why would anyone risk his life when he doesn't have to? You gotta be kidding. I don't know anybody stupid enough to do that."

I think that boy probably speaks for the majority of people his age. But I also know that there are other boys his age who would stay, as Private Ryan did. I think most of you would stay. Roxbury Latin boys have always been different. For twenty-five years, I've heard from people outside Roxbury Latin: "Your school may be small and it doesn't recruit athletes, but you have the toughest kids." I've seen that toughness—that difference—in every aspect of school life over the years.

You are different. You are, many of you, rebels against the spirit of your age. The best people in every generation always have been. They're a minority, but they change the world and they have the happiest, most fulfilling, and most exciting lives. Roxbury Latin boys have always dared to be different, to go against the pack.

I saw a snippet on public television in July about a summer camp that had these words written over its entrance—words that sum up my hopes and prayers for all of you, words that sum up everything I've been trying to say. The words are these: "God first, others second, myself last." That is the formula for the best of lives.

12

Suspending Disbelief

MY BOYHOOD HOME in Ohio was just about exactly one hundred miles from the home of my maternal grandparents in western New York state. My grandparents lived in Westfield, in the so-called grape belt along Lake Erie. I frequently visited them, taking the New York Central Railroad from Painesville to Westfield.

When I was about ten I was staying with them—alone—in midwinter. Perhaps it was on one of the presidents' birthdays still separately celebrated then in February. My visit, whenever it was, coincided with the funeral of Nan Johnson. Nan and Fred Johnson were old and dear friends of my grandparents. Fred was a farmer and the Johnsons lived in a farmhouse outside of town. My grandparents and I drove out there on what must have been the day before the funeral. The scene was one of all-pervasive bleakness: the snow lay on the ground, the trees were leafless, the skies leaden gray. It was the landscape of death.

The farmhouse loomed in the distance and, when my grandfather turned off the ignition, the silence was overpowering. We entered the backdoor into the kitchen, the equivalent, I suppose, of the modern family room. It was where you lived in the winter. My grandparents spoke to Fred. They were closest of friends, but there was no hugging, no kissing, no tears as there would be today. Hugging, kissing, crying were regarded as inappropriate. After we had spoken with Fred, we went into the dining room. It was cold. Nan was laid out in her coffin on the dining room table, as was the custom. We "paid our respects," as was the custom, and returned to the kitchen.

It was my first real experience of death, the first time the finality, the bleakness of death had hit me. I was the only child there and I stood alone gazing out the kitchen window at the bleak landscape of death, the snow-covered fields in the dead of winter as the darkness coldly, sadly descended. I felt devastated, empty, bereft. "If people can just die," I said to myself, "what's the point of anything?" That stark question is one that I would bet most of you have at some point asked yourselves: "What's the point of it all?"

There are people, of course, who never ask any profound questions about the meaning of things. I was talking recently with a Roxbury Latin mother who had taken a temporary job in which she was supervising women in their twenties at very low-level clerical work. She said that most of them talked all week about what they'd buy on Friday when they got their paychecks. They never went any deeper. They had no goals, no aspirations beyond what they'd buy and what party they'd go to. A Roxbury Latin graduate home from college this vacation was telling me about an evening he spent with some childhood friends from his neighborhood. "All they care about is the Patriots and the Bruins. They don't have any long-range goals at all. They just exist."

But most of you are not like that. Most of you have had some encounter with death and most of you are asking deep questions about the meaning of life.

Now to a nihilist, who asserts that life has no meaning, to a nihilist, death, if you look it straight in the face, is the ultimate demonstration that life has no meaning. There have been nihilists in every generation: some nihilists are sad and view life as a long and harrowing drowning in meaninglessness. Other nihilists are proudly militant and proclaim, "You see, it all adds up to nothing!"

Nihilism is, of course, a self-fulfilling prophecy. If you don't believe there's any meaning to life, you will never find any. As a boy I fought all efforts of my parents and teachers to initiate me into the beauty of classical music. I steadfastly maintained: "There's nothing there. It's horrible. I hate it." So, of course, I never heard it. Then at St. Mark's I had to take a course in music listening and for the first time I heard it, and my life was changed. My unwillingness to suspend disbelief deprived me of the beauty of classical music. I was a smug nihilist proudly asserting: "There's nothing there." If you begin with the assumption that there is no meaning, you will find none.

Thoughtful people down the ages have suspended disbelief and looked and listened for clues that life has meaning. We see such longing and seeking in the three wise men, the three privileged, affluent, well-educated Roxbury Latin graduates of the ancient world, who left all the luxury and security of their homes to follow a star that led them to the baby Jesus at Bethlehem. T. S. Eliot writes of their journey:

> 'A cold time we had of it,
> Just the worst time of year
> For a journey, and such a long journey:
> The ways deep and the weather sharp,
> The very dead of winter.'
> And the camels galled, sore-footed, refractory,
> Lying down in the melting snow.
> There were times we regretted [leaving]
> The summer palaces on slopes, the terraces,
> And the silken girls bringing sherbet.
> Then the camel men cursing and grumbling
> And running away, and wanting their liquor and women,
> And the night-fires going out, and the lack of shelters,
> And the cities hostile and the towns unfriendly
> And the villages dirty and charging high prices:
> A hard time we had of it.
> At the end we preferred to travel all night,
> Sleeping in snatches,
> With the voices singing in our ears, saying
> That this was all folly.

The search for meaning in life is often difficult, costly, and discouraging. And there will always be a nihilist to tell you that the journey is "folly." And yet, somehow the three wise men persisted in their search, continued their arduous journey believing, in spite of all the hardships, in spite of the cynics who told them "This was all folly," that they would find something worth finding. And what did they find? A baby. Not at all what they expected, not at all what they thought they would find. They presented their gifts to the Object of their search, and then they went home. They returned to ordinary life. But St. Matthew's Gospel concludes his account of the three wise men by telling us that they returned home "by a different route." That is, they saw a new path for their lives, a new direction, a new and different route to take in life, even as they returned—as we always have to do—to ordinary life. The journey, the search for new meaning, had been worth it.

I remind you of this story of the three wise men because its subject is man's deepest longing: the longing for meaning. You cannot even begin to search for life's meaning unless you hope and believe there is something to find. You cannot even begin to search for life's meaning unless you suspend disbelief.

In another poem, "East Coker," Eliot says,

> *We must be still and still moving*
> *Into another intensity*
> *For a deeper union, a deeper communion. . . .*

That is what we are all seeking, whether we know it or not: "a deeper union, a deeper communion" with something beyond all the passing things of life: beyond grades, beyond college admission, beyond even a good job or a good wife. St. Augustine puts it this way: "Thou, O Lord, didst create us for Thyself, and our hearts are restless until they find their peace in Thee."

In his recent encyclical, Pope John Paul II says, "The search for truth is so rooted in the human heart that to be obliged to ignore it would be to cast our very existence into jeopardy. . . . [M]en and women are on a journey of discovery which is humanly unstoppable, a search for the truth and a search for a person to whom they might entrust themselves." We are all looking, all the time, to find persons right here at Roxbury Latin to whom we can entrust ourselves. Usually we find a person or persons with whom we dare to share something of our real selves; usually we find someone with whom we can—at least at times—remove our mask, and dare to share who we really are. Someday most of you will find a partner to whom you will entrust yourselves. But even the deepest and most satisfying human relationships leave us still longing for something more: "For a deeper union, for a deeper communion" with a Person beyond all the fragile and incomplete relationships here on earth, with a Person, beyond death, to whom we can totally entrust ourselves.

Death is the only certainty in life; each of our journeys leads to death. "Here [on earth]," says the author of the Epistle to the Hebrews, "Here we have no continuing city, but we seek for one to come." When you go to college, you will frequently fill in forms on which you are asked to record your "permanent residence," and you will put down your parents' address. But in actuality, that is not your "permanent residence." We are not permanent residents of this planet. "Here we have no continuing city." Pope John XXIII put it this way, "We must live with our bags always packed." John Eliot's favorite Scripture passage was Psalm 90 of Israel. The Puritan paraphrase of Psalm 90 is engraved on the wall behind me: "O God our help in ages past, our hope for years to come." The next two lines go this way: "Our shelter from the stormy blast and our eternal home." The earth is not our eternal home; the earth is not our "permanent residence." We are passing through, our bags packed for the journey to something beyond this life, to an "eternal home" beyond.

For twenty-five years I lectured in Western Civ, here and in Cleveland, on *Victory Unloosing Her Sandal,* a relief from the parapet of the Temple of Athena Nike now in the Acropolis Museum in Athens. As all of you who have taken Western Civ know, I regard this relief as the greatest single achievement of Greek civilization. But I had never actually seen *Victory Unloosing Her Sandal* (except in photographs) until it was brought from Greece to New York as part of an exhibit at the Metropolitan Museum a few years ago. When I saw it there, I found it even more compelling than I had imagined, and I stood transfixed, gazing at it in silent awe. After some time had elapsed and I regained consciousness of the world around me, I realized that most of the thousands of people at the exhibition were stopping for a moment or two, reading (or glancing at) the label, and moving on. I wanted to shout, "Stop, shut up, and look at the beauty here." (I'm sure I miss a good deal of beauty myself in other areas.) You can never see or hear anything beautiful if you don't suspend disbelief, stop, look, and listen.

The philosopher Friedrich von Hügel wrote these words to his niece: "Be silent about great things; let them grow inside you. Never discuss them: discussion is so limiting and distracting. It makes things grow smaller. You think you swallow things when they ought to swallow you. Before all greatness, be silent—in art, in music, in religion: silence."

As we embark on our journey through this new year, let us suspend disbelief, let us believe that if we look and listen intensely we shall find intimations, hints, of a Beauty and Truth beyond our temporary homes here on earth, "a deeper union, a deeper communion" with the Person to whom we can entrust our lives.

LET ME CONCLUDE with the sequel to the story of my first encounter with the reality of death. As I stared out Nan Johnson's kitchen window into the bleak midwinter, my grandfather came up behind me and put both his hands on my shoulders. "Tony, look out there at that field," he said. "Everything is cold, everything is dead. But when we come out here next summer, it will all be lush and green: the trees in full leaf, grapes ripening on the vines. You have to wait, but then God brings back life from death. Winter can be long and dark, but—in God's good time—it always gives way to spring."

When I was writing the School's history, I did a lot of reading about the English settlers of New England. A huge number of them perished in their first New World winter. They lost hope that spring would come and they gave up. Still others barely held on—starving and freezing in their meager shelters. Those who managed to hold on owed their survival more to spiritual than to physical strength. They believed there was a reason to live despite of the apparent hopelessness of their lives, and they held on.

Your own life, like everybody else's, will have troubles, bleak periods when the landscape of death seems to destroy the hope that spring will ever come. I recall one such period in my early years at Roxbury Latin when all my efforts seemed in vain, when the landscape seemed totally bleak and I lost hope that spring would ever come. In the midst of this bleak winter of my life, Mr. Chauncey said to me in his quiet and wise way, "Tony, sometimes in life you just have to hold on." Thanks to him, I did. I give you the same advice for enduring the dark moments on your journey to discover meaning. Do not despair. The journey may seem hopeless at times, as it did to the three wise men. Persist, as they did, through all the difficulties. "Sometimes in life you just have to hold on." Ignore those who tell you "This is all folly," and you will find the Object of your longing. Then you can return home, to the rest of your life, by a different route.

That, I believe, is what T. S. Eliot meant when he wrote, in "Little Gidding":

> *We shall not cease from exploration*
> *And the end of our exploring*
> *Will be to arrive where we started*
> *And know the place for the first time . . .*
> *And all shall be well*
> *And all manner of thing shall be well. . . .*

13

David and Goliath

ECENTLY I was introduced to someone as the headmaster of Roxbury Latin. He immediately asked, "What can you possibly say to young people as they look to the future?" He didn't really want my answer, and he launched more salvos of pessimistic, gloom-doom rhetorical questions before walking away.

I actually thought a good deal about his first question—"What can you possibly say to young people as they look to the future?" Since you can't walk away, I'll share my answer with you. It is, simply, the biblical story of David and Goliath.

Scene I

At the battlefront. All Israel despairs. Its king and army are arrayed on one side of the abyss. The giant Goliath, with the army of the Philistines, mocks the Israelites from the other side of the abyss. He struts back and forth, the epitome of power: Rambo, the Refrigerator, the A Team all rolled into one. "Why are you even here?" he shouts at the Israelites across the chasm. "I represent the Philistines. Choose one of your so-called men to come and fight me. If he can kill me in a fair fight, we will submit ourselves to you. But if I kill your man, you will submit yourselves to us. Here and now I draw the line; I call your bluff. Give me a man and we shall fight it out."

The account continues: "When Saul and the Israelites heard what the Philistine said, they were shaken and dismayed." No one dared to tackle this giant problem. No Israelite was strong enough—either in bodily strength or weapon. This giant problem overwhelmed them, undermined their confidence. They did not know how to face a future whose problems were beyond their power to control, beyond their ability to solve. They were dismayed, afraid, despairing, and hopeless as they stood on the edge of the abyss.

Scene II

Back in Bethlehem. Jesse summons his younger son, David, a boy old enough to tend the sheep in the faraway fields but not old enough yet to join his brothers at the front as a soldier. "Take these ten loaves of bread to your brothers," said Jesse, "and these ten cream cheeses to their commanding officer. See if your brothers are well and bring me back some token from them."

The account tells us specifically that "David left someone in charge of the sheep" and early next morning set out on the errand exactly as his father had directed.

Just as David arrived at the front and located his brothers, Goliath shouted one of his periodic challenges across the abyss. As usual the Israelites cowered and ran, and one said to David, "This man comes out every day to insult Israel. The king would give his daughter in marriage and a rich reward to anyone who could get rid of him."

David was there to do what his father had told him to do—deliver the food from home and come back as quickly as possible to tend his sheep. He was only an errand boy. No one expected or wanted David to be anything other than an errand boy. He was not called upon to do anything else; he was not called upon to say anything else.

Doubtless, as a boy of fourteen, he had imagined the battlefield to be a stirring place of adventure and heroism. He must have been astounded to find it a place of despair and cowardice. He blurted out his dismay. He turned to his brothers and their fellow soldiers and asked a simple question: "Who is this uncircumcised Philistine to defy the army of the Living God?"

His older brother Elias was furious. "What are you doing here anyway? And who have you left to look after our family's sheep in the wilderness? I know why you're here, you little brat. You came out here to see the fighting."

David replied, "What have I done this time? You're always putting me down. I only asked a question."

David, the ruddy-cheeked, bright-eyed boy, was out of place among his bitter, angry brothers and their fellow disillusioned soldiers. His question aggravated them and they told him to shut up and go home.

Scene III

But David was not about to shut up and he was not about to go home. He found his way into the presence of the king, Saul, where no one was saying much of anything and where he was even more out of place. And he addressed the king: "Do not lose heart, sir. I shall go and fight this Philistine!"

"You?" said the king. "You cannot fight this Philistine. You're only a boy. He's been a fighting man for years."

The world is not waiting for fresh ideas, for creative solutions. The world is not waiting for heroes. All things considered, Saul was remarkably patient and gentle: he quietly pointed out how preposterously unrealistic David was being. David was obviously too young, he had no experience in warfare, and it was ludicrous for him to offer his services against the strongest fighting man in the world. "Now trot along home before we run out of patience with you."

Any but the most brash and impertinent adolescent would have made a discreet exit. He had taxed his brothers' patience and taken up the king's time by half-wittedly offering his puny services.

But David did not discreetly exit. Instead he went on to make his case to the king: "Sir," he replied, "I am my father's shepherd. When a wild animal comes and tries to carry off a sheep from the flock, I go after him, attack him, and rescue the sheep from his jaws. If the animal turns on me, I struggle with him and if necessary kill him. I have killed a number of these animals and this uncircumcised Philistine will fare no better than they. He has dared to defy the army of the Living God. The Lord who saved me from the wild animals will also save me from this Philistine."

The speech appears to the brothers, their fellow soldiers, and the king—to everyone, in other words—as the ravings of an adolescent caught up in a dream-of-glory fantasy. This boy has no realistic help to offer, and his fantasies to them seem utterly inappropriate in this dismal scene where real solutions (and not childish dreams of glory) are so desperately needed.

Since we have the advantage of 20/20 hindsight, we see what David said to Saul in a different light. We see that what David says is a statement about the future that is based on his experience in the past.

He tells first about his experience with God in the past: "I am a shepherd. When a wild animal comes and tries to carry off a sheep from the flock, I go after him, attack him, and rescue the sheep from his jaws. If the beast turns on me, I fight with him, and if necessary I kill him." So far we might say: This kid seems a bit of an egotist bragging about how tough he is. But David then adds: "The Lord has always saved me from these wild beasts." David does not say, "You're looking here, Your Majesty, at the toughest kid in Israel. Let me flex for you. See my biceps ripple!" He says instead, "The Lord has delivered me from these wild beasts."

On the basis of his experience in the past, David then goes on to make a statement about the future: a statement of faith, a statement of hope. He says to the king, "The Lord who has saved me from the wild animals will save me from this Philistine. God is not dead. He is the Living God who has saved us in the past and who will save us in the here and now."

Scene IV

Saul, of course, was not endowed with our 20/20 hindsight. For him and his soldiers, David's words remain just the fantastic rantings of a youthful imagination.

But Saul, of course, has no solution himself, nor do any of his soldiers—no realistic alternatives to propose. He therefore gives David his despairing permission: "Go then," says Saul, "and the Lord go with you."

Saul knows David is going to his doom, and feeling perhaps sad or guilty, he makes a rather tender gesture: "Saul placed his own tunic and coat of armor on David and gave him his own sword." Saul could think only in the narrowest, most conventional frame of reference. Such old weapons were obviously no longer of use in the new circumstances Goliath had brought into being. But Saul could think only in terms of tunic and armor and sword and, with a kindly motive, he thrust these upon the boy.

David hesitated. They were not familiar to him; he had no experience using them; they weighed him down. And he said to the king: "I can't go out with all these things. I've never used them before." So he took all of them off; he cast aside all the weapons of the past.

If God wished to use David here, God would find a way that would make use of David's own particular experience. At this point all David had was faith, his belief that the God who had delivered him from danger in the past would show him a way now in the present.

Scene V

Then, the Bible continues, he picked up his stick, chose five smooth stones from the brook, put them in his shepherd's pouch, and walked out with his sling in his hand to meet the Philistine.

Goliath advanced—with his shield-bearer preceding him. As the boy approached him, Goliath looked him up and down and poured contempt on him: "What am I, a dog, that you come at me with only a stick in your hand. Come and fight me and I'll feed the birds and beasts with your pathetic little body."

David knew that he had only his pathetic little body and that he was in no position to match Goliath with any macho statements about his own strength (which was nothing compared to Goliath's).

David, rather, replied: "I come towards you in the name of the Lord of Hosts, the God of Israel whom you defy. The Lord will put you into my hands this very hour. Everyone gathered here shall see that the Lord saves neither by sword nor by spear. Everyone shall see that there is a Living God in Israel—and that the battle is his."

David then ran towards Goliath, and twirling his sling around his head, he hurled the first stone at Goliath and struck him on the forehead and the giant fell dead before the gasping armies of Israel and Philistia.

The Triumph of Weakness

So often in the face of life's giant problems—and God knows there are what appear to be unsolvable giant problems in the world we live in—so often in the face of such problems we are tempted to say, "What can I do? I am not brilliant or handsome or powerful. I don't have the necessary training. This problem is bigger than all of us. If the experts—the government, the armed forces, the diplomats—can't solve these problems, what can I be expected to do?" Like the Israelites we are faithless, despairing. We overlook the small talents we *do have*, the unspectacular small things we *can do*.

Saul (and his whole army on the edge of the abyss) could only think in narrowly military terms, and in those terms there was no solution. There was only despair and hopelessness.

David asked them a simple question: "Who is this Philistine to dare defy the Living God?" The question only made his brothers and the king and his soldiers angrier in their despair. His brother withered David with his contempt: "Go back where you belong, you little brat." The king discounted him: "You are only a boy—this giant Goliath is the strongest and most powerful man in the world." And finally David had to face Goliath's contempt.

But with quiet and abiding trust in God, David persisted in the face of this universal contempt. He put his very small talents, his very limited experience, in the service of the God of Israel, confident that the Living God would use him to overcome evil with good.

One of the giant problems our country has faced in our century has been racism—a blatant racism that was still legalized and institutionalized in our country a mere twenty-five years ago. Who killed that giant? Was it soldiers and armies? No. Was it, in the first instance, legislators and laws? No. Was it the vision and courage of rich and powerful men and women who had the influence to make big changes? No. It was, in the first instance, a black seamstress who quietly said, "No, I won't move to the back of the bus."

What killed the giant of institutionalized and legalized racism in our country was the quiet witness of folks from Duluth, Minnesota, and Gary, Indiana, and Columbus, Ohio—who were willing to invest their time and risk their lives in joining peaceful marches throughout the country. These folks were not powerful or rich or influential or brilliant or eloquent or charismatic. But they knew what was right and what was wrong, and they quietly invested the small talents they had on the side of what was right.

Sheriff Bull Connors—with his guns and his dogs—told the unarmed marchers that he had power and that they had better not dare to defy him. When he threatened them with dogs, they said, "Go ahead, let them loose on us." When he threatened them with guns, they said, "Go ahead, shoot us." They were not terrorized by the giant. They were not threatened by his weapons. They dared to be "unrealistic." They dared to be "naive." They dared to face the contempt heaped on them. They dared trust that the Living God could use their apparently insignificant lives to overcome the strutting and powerful giant. And it turned out that they were the realistic ones, and it was they who prevailed.

Men of Faith

When Moses led the Israelites across the Red Sea—where God delivered them from Pharaoh and their Egyptian captors, the Israelites (who had been so eager to escape Egypt) immediately started to complain: "We had it made back in the fleshpots of Egypt and you have brought us out here into this wilderness to die." But Moses was a man of faith. He said, "God has not (in the past) delivered us from Pharaoh to let us die here in this wilderness." And instead of joining the bitchers, instead of wringing his hands, he focused his energies on seeking a solution: he found an herb that made the water drinkable; he found food to eat.

The world is filled with people like the army of Saul and the Israelites in the wilderness who stand around wringing their hands in despair and assuring everyone that nothing can be done. It is rare that a Moses or a David stands out of the whining crowd—and with daring faith believes that even his tiny talents in the service of truth can become powerful and efficacious.

Jesus of Nazareth commanded no army, held no public office, knew none of the influential people of his time, never even went to college or achieved success in business. He was put to death, silenced as a nuisance. His few followers scattered in fear and despair. And yet this single person has had a more powerful impact than anyone in all of history. He was armed only with a single weapon: love. And yet long after all the supposedly powerful people of his time are dead and forgotton—the influence of this Jewish peasant persists. That is why a Bishop Desmond Tutu—the tiny man who owns no gun and holds no political or military office—can stand up to the South African racist regime (with its tanks and guns) and say, "I come to you armed only with a single weapon: the power of love. Kill me if you will, but I tell you—my brothers and sisters—this love shall prevail, this love shall overcome all your weapons of repression, this love shall triumph."

I do not feel sorry for you, I do not despair about the future that you have to face. I do not wring my hands in dismay about what lies ahead for you. In all of history, there has never been a more thrilling time to be alive than this moment. Humanity faces the greatest crisis it has ever faced. Nothing less than the survival of the human race is at stake.

For most, it will be a time of whining, of complaining. The vast majority of your contemporaries will stand around wringing their hands in despair asking, "What can I do? Little me." When you look at the world's problems and consider the very meager talents you have, you will be tempted to join in their despair.

In that moment of temptation, remember David. Remember David's faith—ridiculed as naive and unrealistic by everyone from his brothers to the king. Remember Moses and Jesus. Remember the Davids of every generation: Rosa Parks and Desmond Tutu—the few in every generation who believed that the Living God could use even their pathetically tiny talents to challenge the giant evils of their time.

I do not despair for you. I rather rejoice. Times of maximum danger provide maximum opportunity. If our time is the most dangerous time in all of history, it is also the most sublime. Some of you who are sitting here this morning will find the faith and courage to place your lives in the service of the Living God confident that He can use what little you have in his great purpose. And like David, in His service you shall prevail.

14

Coping with Pressure

LMOST DAILY we are reminded sententiously in the media that: "We live in an era of great stress." And everywhere you look you can find a seminar on "stress management."

Doubtless every other era has flattered itself by thinking that it was a time of great stress. Actually, our claim to live with the most stress is nothing like as strong as the claim of those who lived in the South in the Civil War, or Europe in the world wars, or in the war-torn Middle East or famine-ravaged parts of Africa today. We in this room are not victims of war, nor are we hungry or homeless. We have been given all the necessities of life and, on top of these necessities, lavish opportunities that few on earth enjoy or can ever aspire to.

Once we acknowledge these blessings, however, it is not, I believe, inappropriate for us to consider the pressures that also are ours (in part because of those very opportunities). Because there is considerable stress in our lives.

Alumni of Roxbury Latin talk often about the pressures they experienced here. One prominent alumnus said in the *Globe*, "After Roxbury Latin everything in my life has seemed easy." We somehow get the impression that Roxbury Latin boys worked much harder in the tough old days than they do now.

When I was in elementary school my father used to tell my sister and me every September how far he had to walk to school when he was a boy. The distance increased by roughly a mile a year; by the time I was in the sixth grade, his walk to school was six miles. That year I said something to my grandmother about the hardships of my father's childhood. "What nonsense," she replied. "He rolled out of bed into school. I could walk that distance today with my cane in five minutes!"

So much for the myth of "how hard it used to be." The same is true for students at Roxbury Latin. People tell me that the atmosphere of the School today is much more supportive and encouraging than it was in times past. But we know from course descriptions in old catalogues and from old final exams, that students are pushed much farther and faster today than they were twenty or forty or sixty years ago. Roxbury Latin students have never been under greater pressure than they are today.

And that pressure will not end with graduation. Recently employed young alumni tell me they're working long hours. One said to me the other day that he routinely worked a ninety-hour week. So it's a safe bet that the pressure is going to continue in your lives after you leave here.

What I want to talk about this morning is the ongoing, inescapable reality of pressure—and how to live with it.

Accepting What You Cannot Change

I think one of the biggest causes of stress is our unwillingness to accept the simple reality that there are things about our lives we cannot change.

I grew up with a farm boy who loved horses. We had the county fair grounds in our town and on those grounds was a track (with grandstand) for horse racing. This kid liked horses better than people, and all he wanted to do in life was to be a jockey and race horses. By the time he was ten he could stay on the back of the friskiest racehorse. Alas, by the time he was twelve he was almost six feet tall. He starved himself and he smoked cigarettes to stunt his growth. But nothing availed. By high school he was 6'3" and weighed 180 pounds. All hopes of being a jockey were gone. He was angry, bitter, resentful. He never made peace with the unalterable reality that he was big. He never used his size to advantage by involving himself in alternative pursuits, such as football or basketball. All his energy was put into backward-looking regret.

In my early years of teaching, I talked a number of times with a 5'4" high school junior. His great ambition was to be a world-class basketball player, and he had been cut from the team. He seethed at every kid in the school who was taller than he. All his energy was invested in resentment. "Look back in anger" became the theme of his life.

There are things in life you cannot change—and not just physical attributes. I can't tell you how many Roxbury Latin boys have said to me over the years, "My father isn't a typical father. He never takes me to hockey games," or "He's wrapped up in his own life, he's not interested in mine." "My father never hugs me," a boy said to me recently. "Never hugs you?" I asked. "You know," he said, "like on TV—on *Growing Pains.*" But fathers in the real world are not like TV sitcom fathers. Real fathers have real long-standing imperfections. And every son must come to grips with the reality of his parents—something he can do almost nothing to change, something he must learn to live with and then adjust to.

There are certain realities about this place that you cannot change and that you have to accept and adjust to if you're going to be happy. You have to get up early in the morning in order to get to school, for instance. When I was your age, that was the cruelest reality for me, the one I bitterly refused to adjust to. I had to be pried out of bed. One time when I stayed overnight with a classmate, he tried to get me out of bed to go to school and I rolled over. He was one of those bright-eyed, bushy-tailed kids who love school and who leap out of bed every morning eager for more of it. And he finally yelled at me—lying there in bed—"Get up! What's the matter with you?" "What's the matter with you?" I growled back. I made myself miserable for years by never making peace with the reality that you have to get up in the morning to go to school. That is a reality I couldn't change. And instead of facing that reality and dealing with it, I expended enormous energy (and experienced enormous anger) fighting it.

It is always a losing battle to fight against things you cannot change.

Hopeful Pessimism

Another cause of stress is optimism. In my experience it is foolish to expect things to go well. New boys, when they arrive here, are optimists. They work hard on a paper or test and they therefore expect to do well. Then they get back a low grade and are devastated. Anger follows at life's injustice, and tears flow. Older students have begun to learn not to be optimistic: they have begun to accept the fact that hard work is not always rewarded. They have learned to be pessimists: they expect that things may not go as well as they hope.

Any remaining optimism in a Roxbury Latin boy is usually crushed in Class I. "Don't get your heart set on Brand X college. You might not get it." That's the advice we give seniors all fall. The wise pessimists expect the worst. The foolish optimists, however, do get their hearts set on Brand X college, and the end result is devastation when they don't get in.

Every year in this first week of January disappointed boys come in to talk about what happened at home over the holidays. They had approached the vacation with high expectations. It was going to be a happy and fulfilling family time. But, alas, the high expectations had not come true. The holidays had not turned out like the TV sitcom in which all the family conflicts and misunderstandings are resolved in twenty-two-and-a-half minutes with happy hugs. These boys were optimists. They had expected things to go well, and they were bitterly disappointed when they didn't.

"In the world," said Jesus, "you shall have tribulation." Or, as the late Senator Green put it, "Life is just one damned thing after another." It is stupid to be optimistic.

I had the misfortune to drive with someone to Logan Airport recently. I said, "Let's go by train and subway." "I always drive," he said. "I never run into traffic." Perhaps I jinxed him, because we were stuck in traffic for over an hour and the person we were to meet had already left the airport when we finally got there. What struck me, though, was the towering rage the man who was driving worked himself into. He was honking, shaking his fists, cursing. He was a foolish optimist. He expected he'd whiz right through to the airport. Anyone dumb enough to drive to Logan should expect that there will be a traffic jam. Anyone taking an exam should expect that there may be difficult questions.

Anyone applying to college should expect that justice will not be done and that he will not be admitted.

Nothing could be crueler than what some parents say to their teenage children: "These are the best years of your life." For one thing, it's a lie. I had, I think, an extremely happy adolescence, and yet my teenage years have not been the best years of my life—nor are they for most people. To tell a teenager that these are the best years is tantamount to telling him that there's something wrong with him if he's not happy all the time. But no teenager is happy all—or even most—of the time. The statement is cruel because it leads teenagers to a foolish optimism: to expect happiness.

The happy adolescent, the happy adult, is pessimistic: he expects that things will not turn out as he hopes.

There is a big difference between hope and optimism. When you hope, you aspire to something worthwhile. When you are an optimist, you expect that what you hope for will happen. If you're an optimist, you will be bitterly disappointed over and over in life when your hopes are not realized. Optimism is foolish. Optimism is dangerous. Optimism is bad for your mental health.

I urge you to hold onto high hopes—to aspire to great things. But I also urge you to be pessimists: to expect things to go badly, to go wrong; to expect that many of your hopes will not be realized. Much of the immense happiness I feel in my own life comes from being a hopeful pessimist. If you're a hopeful pessimist, you will again and again be surprised by joy when some of your hopes are, in fact, realized.

Inventory Your Worries

To these first two pieces of advice: accept what you can't change and expect the worst, let me add a third: Inventory your worries.

A few years ago I was talking with a boy who, when he got home at night from Roxbury Latin, would beat up his little brother. At the same time he was verbally abusive of his mother. "Why are you so awful?" I asked him. "I don't know," he said. "I just feel angry with all the pressures, and I want to let it out on someone." Most of you have experienced that anger, that frustration, that jangling anxiety of being trapped by life's demands and pressures and expectations.

The first step toward maturity is to recognize that anxiety—even if you can't get it under control.

The second step is to try to analyze what it is that's causing you to become upset and enraged. If you can recognize that you're upset, you can sometimes sit yourself down and figure out what it is that's bothering you (and what's really bothering you is not your little brother or your mother).

A year or so ago I was dealing with a senior who—in the face of all the pressures on him for college, grades, extracurriculars—was simply shutting down, paralyzed by the seeming impossibility of doing all the things that were expected of him.

"You're just spinning, aren't you?" I said. "Yes," he said. "That's exactly what I'm doing, and I can't stop spinning."

But he did. By a simple device. He made an inventory of all the things he had to do. He wrote out a list of all the things he had to do—of all the responsibilities that were pressuring him.

The very act of transferring to a piece of paper all these pressures spinning around in one's head is excellent therapy. There is something immensely relieving about transferring them all from your brain onto a piece of paper. They seem much more under control that way. You can then quietly decide from your list: (A) what items on the list you can't change and must adjust to, (B) what items on the list you need to deal with first, and (C) what items on the list you will address if you have time or which you will let go of if you simply can't do them.

Making lists has been an enormously helpful tactic to me in dealing with pressure. For years—especially as a parish priest—I made commitments and promises that I could fulfill only by never sleeping or relaxing. Now I keep a list—a perpetual ongoing list—of all the things I have to do. As a result, I am now able to be much more realistic about the commitments and promises I make. And sometimes now, I have the wisdom to say, "No. I can't do that. I can't add that to my list."

Offering up Our Concerns

My final suggestion for dealing with stress—the most important suggestion—is prayer, real prayer, not the going-through-the-motions, listening-to-someone-else-pray sort of prayer you are perhaps familiar with from church or synagogue. I'm talking about prayer from the heart, prayer that is often beyond words, prayer that is offered with our whole being.

Studies show that people who attempt spectacular things, people who undertake spectacular responsibilities—pray much more than others. Big-time college and professional athletes pray more than any other element of the population. Presidents have a way of becoming more and more prayerful. The more you attempt in life, the more you undertake in life, the more you realize your own weaknesses and vulnerabilities, the more you realize how many things there are in the universe that affect you—that you cannot control.

The foolish go through life expecting nothing but good. They never dream that their son could be killed in an automobile accident, that their father could die of cancer, that they could lose their job, that their wife could go off with another man. The wise realize that all these things could happen. They know how vulnerable they are. They know they're not self-sufficient. They know they're not in control.

I've prayed more or less all my life, as many of you have. When I was your age, I prayed in order that I could achieve what I wanted to achieve for myself (and I certainly don't mean to imply that there's anything wrong with that).

When you become older, you discover that there are people you care more about even than you care about yourself. This usually happens when you have children of your own. You realize that there are times when they are away from your presence and beyond your control—and all you can do is to hope and pray they will be safe. Wait till the day when your own daughter goes off with a sixteen-year-old boy with a new driver's license.

I began to have some clue what prayer was about when—as a young parish priest—I realized that, even with my infinite wisdom, there were people I couldn't help no matter how hard I tried.

For example, a boy's parents and his psychiatrist asked me to talk with a boy I vaguely knew who had tried to commit suicide. I went to the psychiatric ward of the hospital. The boy was strapped down. As I entered the room, he said, "The minute I'm out of here I'm going to do it again. And there's nothing you can say that will change my mind." I had plenty of hubris and I felt there were things I could say, and I tried—foolishly. But the boy was right. All my wisdom and persuasiveness failed to make the smallest dent. As I left—in despair at my own inadequacy—I said, "Peter, you're drowning. God's up there and he's throwing you a life preserver. Try to grab onto it. Reach out. Pray." When I got home an hour later, the phone was ringing. It was the psychiatrist. He said, "Peter wants to talk with you. Can you come down right away?" When I walked into the room, Peter said, very calmly, "Show me how to pray."

Sadly, we are often brought to the very dregs of life before we reach out in prayer, before we reach—out of our weakness—for a strength beyond us.

Prayer always begins with a recognition of our weakness. When we pray we offer up all the things we cannot change, and we ask for the strength to live gracefully with our own limitations and with the things about others that disappoint us. When we pray we offer up our whole list of anxieties—all the burdens and responsibilities and aspirations and hopes—that are ours, and we ask for the courage to bear those burdens and to cling to those aspirations. When we pray we offer up those we love (those we love more than ourselves) whom we cannot protect from every danger.

Happiness in life is not the absence of pressure and stress. Happiness in life is finding a way to deal with the inevitable pressure and stress of life. We can deal with stress by accepting gracefully the things we cannot change, by expecting the worst (even as we hope for the best), by taking inventory of our anxieties. But ultimately we must look beyond our own limited and feeble resources. Ultimately we are drawn to prayer. That is why the psalmist writes [in Psalm 84]:

> *Happy are those whose refuge is in Thee, [O Lord,]*
> *Whose hearts are set, as pilgrims, on searching for Thy way.*
> *As they pass thirsty through [life's] dry valleys*
> *They will find water from a spring.*
> *For the Lord provides, even to those who lose their way,*
> *pools of water to quench their thirst.*
> *O Lord of Hosts, happy is the man who trusts in Thee!*

15

Standing on Our Own Two Feet

OU HAVE TO LEARN to stand on your own two feet. I don't know if parents still say that to their children, but my parents said it to me over and over when I was growing up. "Nobody's going to take care of you in life. You have to do things for yourself. You have to learn to stand on your own two feet."

It's excellent advice and I pass it along every year to the parents of new boys when I meet with them in early September. I tell your parents that we are trying to help you to fend for yourselves, to take responsibility for your lives, to fight your own battles, to stand on your own two feet. It's a tough world out there, and to live in that tough world a boy needs to gain the self-confidence that he can face up to burdensome responsibilities on his own. He needs to realize that he is tough enough to handle his own problems, to survive on his own.

All this I say to your parents. Some of them have a tendency to indulge you or baby you. My hope is that they will step aside, at least a bit, so that you can have the space to become self-reliant: to become tough enough to sort out your own life, tough enough to survive in a tough world, tough enough to stand on your own two feet.

Acknowledging Our Weakness

Paradoxically, I want to start by talking about our weakness as human beings. Let me begin right where we are this very morning. Almost all of you have returned to school full of fresh resolve.

The rustle of new leaves being turned over at this time of year is deafening. Several of you have already said to me, "This is going to be my best year. I'm really going to do it this year." The rest of you may not say it publicly; nonetheless, you secretly nourish exalted ambitions for the new year. But almost all of you have made resolutions as you approach the start of school.

As all of you know—and as some of you are honest enough to admit to yourselves right now—somehow the willpower to keep noble resolutions often fades away. As early as next Tuesday or Wednesday some of you will begin to lose the high resolve you now feel. By mid-September some of you will have tossed in the towel. I say this not to demoralize you; I say it because it's a reality and we need to base our lives on reality.

Why does this happen? Why do we lose our resolve? New boys—or younger boys—sometimes lose their resolve because they become intimidated. They sometimes conclude that they're not as smart as all the others here, that the work at Roxbury Latin is just too hard for them. Sometimes that causes a new boy to lose his resolve and decide there's little point in trying.

Older boys have long since recognized that they are capable of doing the work, so they place the blame on external forces, or external circumstances. They blame the teacher ("I can't figure out what he wants," "He just doesn't like me," "We're not on the same wave length," "He's an idiot," "He's prejudiced," "He's unfair," whatever). Or, they blame the subject or the course ("If I'd known it was going to be like this, I would never have taken this course"). Or they blame the School ("I'd be fine anywhere else. But at Roxbury Latin the workload is absurd"). What comes next—as night follows day—is a bleating reference to how happy life might have been if only you had gone to the local high school. "If only I were there I'd be doing no work and getting all A's—like all my friends." (I said that every fall of my own high school years—comparing myself always to the least ambitious and the least able of my public school friends, refusing to admit that many of my brighter friends were working very hard for their good grades in the high school in my town.)

Most of you, however, are mature enough to recognize that you cannot spend your life trying to find someone or something to blame for your problems. The more mature among you have also come to discover and to admit weaknesses within yourselves. When I was your age, I would again and again promise myself that I'd be tough, and then time and again, I'd be distracted by a magazine or my radio or the telephone, and there were times when I'd just bag it all and sleep. You've all experienced such times of paralysis, loss of desire, what the French call ennui, the empty feeling that it's not worth it, or, worse, that sense that you're just not strong enough to do it. St. Paul put it best when he said "The good that I wanted to do, the good that I set out to do, I just couldn't do."

And all the exhortations to stand on our own two feet and to be tough, all the exhortations by our well-intentioned parents and teachers only make things worse.

The beginning of human wisdom, perhaps, is not the knowledge that we are strong, but the realization that we are weak. We hate to admit our weakness, our fragility. I've had boys in my office crying disconsolately that they weren't invited to a certain party and then walk out of my office conveying to all that they couldn't care less. I talked this summer in England with a schoolteacher who has spent his life criticizing how parents bring up their children. Now his own children are adolescents, and he feels humiliated by the difficult (and in one case cruel) behavior of his own children. Life goes on inflicting hurts, constantly bringing new humiliations, new suffering, constantly showing us new ways in which we are weak and vulnerable.

"I'm so down," a boy said to me last year, "I can't even ask for help."

Accepting Our Frail Humanity

When I was little, my mother and father used to compare (or rather contrast) me with the kid down the street. "Why can't you be more like Dicky Schaeffer? Dicky comes home for lunch on time. Dicky's so nice to his mother. Dicky vacuums the living room every day." My friends and I periodically plotted the murder of this little saint.

When I was older—when I was the age of most of you and people like Jarvis and my teachers and my parents were always urging me to stand on my own two feet—the most discouraging thing of all was that, when I looked around me, I saw kids who actually looked as if they were standing on their own two feet: who were models of consistent hard work and success, who never seemed to waste or misuse a minute of their lives. However, every time I actually got to know one of these apparent paragons of virtue, I would always discover that he also—like the rest of us—had weaknesses.

As a young clergyman I was sent to a large and eminent parish in Cleveland, and I looked around and said to myself, "These people are all rich, they all have lovely homes and good jobs, they are all good looking and successful. They don't need me; they don't even need God." But by the time I left that parish I realized there was not a single family— not one—that hadn't had to deal with significant problems and heartache, that there was not a single person without weaknesses. Life spares no one. Every one of us has weaknesses. Every one of us is vulnerable and has to deal with lack of drive and failure and disappointment.

People ask, "How could Vincent Foster, President Clinton's boyhood friend, be so unhappy as to kill himself? He had everything: great family, office in the White House, friendship with the president. What more could you want?" But as we know, despite all his credentials of success, despite all the indications of his strength and power, he too was weak and vulnerable.

Our capacity for denial, however, is immeasurable, and some people get far into adulthood denying their weakness and vulnerability.

From the Book of *Job* on through *Jurassic Park*, history records a parade of what David Halberstam (describing the arrogance of Ivy League grads in the White House in the sixties) called (sarcastically) "the best and the brightest"—people, men and women, unaware of their own human weakness and vulnerability, who played God. Such people—as *Jurassic Park* aptly demonstrates—often end up damaging others as well as themselves.

But we all have this urge to play God—to be in control. We want to be invincibly strong, invulnerable. We want never to have to ask anyone for help.

But I submit to you this morning that the acceptance of our humanity—of our impermanence and of our frailty—is the beginning of wisdom. Throughout the literature of Israel runs the theme: "The fear of the Lord is the beginning of wisdom." These ancient wise men offer us the single most important truth for living in the modern world: that making peace with life begins with the recognition that we are mortal, frail, human beings.

Kneeling on Our Own Two Knees

Last year a Roxbury Latin mother who'd been through a terrible professional and personal crisis wrote me that it was as if she'd known nothing about life before she went through the suffering she'd just endured. "Never before," she wrote, "had I been forced to come to grips with the fact that—like everyone else—I am a mortal human being on a very short journey through life." Some people get well into adulthood before they come to grips with the fact that they are frail and impermanent human beings. The longer you put it off, the harder it is.

And it comes in strange ways. A Roxbury Latin boy said to me this summer, "I thought once I got into Harvard that I'd never be worried or anxious or unhappy again. Now, if anything, the stress and grind of life is worse!" When I was in my twenties an old priest said to me, "Be careful what you pray for. You might get it." The trophies we long to win often turn to dust even as we clasp them in triumph. A few years ago, a wise boy said to me, "More than anything I wanted to win the Graves-Kelsey Wrestling Tournament and I did. I thought if I could do that I'd be really happy. It's several months later now, but everything's still the same. I find myself wanting to win something else, hoping that will change things. And I suppose I'll go through life chasing one trophy after another."

Even when you get all A's, set athletic records, and break the bank in college admissions; even if you are the best looking and best built and smartest, there still remains a restlessness, a longing, something no earthly prize can satisfy.

Just a few days ago I had a conversation with a Roxbury Latin grad entering his senior year in college. He is brilliant, good-looking, has everything going for him, and he said to me: "Everybody always tells you how to live—you should do this or do that. But nobody ever tells you why you should live—whether there's any meaning or purpose to it all."

He talked at length about his inner restlessness. He had come to realize that no earthly success, no fabulous grades or trophies or money or glory could satisfy that inner restlessness. "I've been brought to my knees," he concluded.

This kid—and I mean this in the best sense—is one of the toughest kids I've ever known—the model of the kid who could stand on his own two feet. And if I may paraphrase him, what he was telling me was that in the process of standing on his own two feet he had been driven to kneeling on his own two knees.

I greatly treasure in each of you the ability to stand on your own two feet, to be tough, to be self-sufficient. But the highest form of toughness, the truest self-sufficiency, comes only from the realization—as with this kid—that we are not tough, not self-sufficient. Socrates said the wisest man is the one who realizes how little he knows. I submit that the strongest and toughest and most self-sufficient man is the one who realizes how vulnerable and frail he is.

Every one of us is on a journey—we each have one and only one life, and in the perspective of all things, our own life is remarkably short. We are not gods who are invulnerable and immortal. In our fleeting and temporary existences, as we realize that all our trophies are so much tinsel and frippery, we instinctively reach out for what is lasting and permanent. The psalmist of Israel sings, "As the deer pants for the pool of clear water to quench his thirst, so longs my soul, God, for You." Or as the old Bible sublimely puts it, "Like as a hart desireth the water-brook, so longeth my soul after Thee, O God." St. Augustine expresses this same restless yearning: "You, God, have created us for Yourself and our hearts are restless until they find their peace in You."

The beginning of wisdom is the realization that, if you want to stand on your own two feet, you must learn to kneel on your own two knees. To be strong and tough you must acknowledge your humanity, your temporariness, and your weakness, and have the courage to ask for help—from your fellow human beings (who are on the same journey as you are) and from God—who alone endures, who alone can give you ultimate peace.

In St. George's Chapel at Windsor Castle is a small chapel in which is buried King George VI, the father of the present queen. On the gate of that chapel are engraved the words the king addressed to the British people in his Christmas broadcast in 1940—when Britain stood alone against the Nazis and when few thought she would survive. These are the words he spoke to his battered and beleaguered people in their darkest hour: "I said to the man who stood at the gate of the Year, 'Give me a light that I may travel safely into the unknown.' And he replied, 'Go out into the darkness and put your hand into the hand of God. That shall be to you better than light and safer than a known way.'"

If you are honest with yourself, as you feel your way along the human journey, you will experience times when you lose the vision, times of discouragement, times of loneliness, times when you feel powerless or lost, times of suffering and despair and emptiness. In all these darkest moments you are never, ever separated from the love of God—no matter how insignificant or worthless you feel. You need not wait until the darkest hour to place your hand in the hand of God. The truly strong man—the man who can stand on his own two feet—is the one who realizes his own weakness, his own limits. The truly strong man knows that he needs to ask for help from his companions on life's journey and from God.

16

Sometimes I Get Discouraged

OST PEOPLE don't set great goals for their lives. Matthew Arnold remarks, "Most men eddy about here and there, striving blindly, achieving nothing." Most men aspire only to comfort and security — that is enough for most.

It is my hope and, from what I hear in my talks with alumni of this school, it is my belief that most of you have set great goals for your lives. Those goals may not yet be specific for all of you, but most of you know, at least in a general way, that you want to do something great with your lives. My remarks this morning are addressed to you, and they have to do with the greatest problem we face if we set high goals for our lives, namely: discouragement. "Sometimes," the old gospel hymn reminds us, "I get discouraged."

The World Is Not Waiting to Acclaim You

The youngest among you has already discovered the elemental truth that life on earth is not just. He works five times as hard preparing for a test as a classmate and then discovers that the classmate gets a better grade; or he goes all out in athletic practices—comes out early, goes in late—and then a boy with half his commitment starts in games and gets all the glory. I'd be a millionaire if I had a dollar for every time a student told me how "unfair" it is that his efforts have not been rewarded by a grade or by a starting position.

If we set high goals for ourselves we begin by having to face the cruel reality that our noble motives and our all-out effort may well not achieve the goals we hope for, that we may well not be rewarded.

Another unpleasant discovery we make when we set high goals is that we are not as tough as we thought we were. We set out with high resolves about doing homework, for example, and then discover that our willpower gives out on the third night and our minds and bodies wander. Our resolutions go down the tubes. And we are faced, if we're honest, with a depressing truth about ourselves: that we are weak. We somehow lack inner strength.

So we are disillusioned both about the unfairness of life and about our own lack of willpower.

And then there are certain "friends"—friends who tell us that we were crazy to set high goals in the first place. Several years ago a Roxbury Latin boy who lived in a city housing project called me on a Sunday afternoon, and I went over to his apartment. He had been worked over by friends all the previous day. They told him he was stupid to go to Roxbury Latin, that he couldn't hang around at night any more because he had homework, that they all had fun while he slaved over his books, that he was missing out on life. When I left my hometown in Ohio to go to St. Mark's I heard those same comments every vacation from my friends. They often devastated me. How easily we believe that the grass is greener on the other side. How quick we are to leap to the conclusion that everybody else's life is one endless joy, while we— almost alone—are left out of life's fulfillment and fun.

If we do decide to persist in striving for the high goals we've set, still another devastation awaits us. Lurking in each of us is the desire for recognition, the hope that people will notice what we do and thank us for doing it. Sadly, however, the more "successful" we are in life, the higher we climb on the ladder of achievement, the more problems we discover, the more enemies we collect, the more people there are to criticize the decisions we make. This is true not only in commerce and industry but even in the so-called service professions. The dean of American university presidents, President Theodore Hesburgh of

Notre Dame, once said, "If you want appreciation in this business, go out and buy a dog."

If we set out to follow the Founder's goal of service-to-others, we discover, to our surprise, that the world provides us with no standing ovations for our efforts, often not even a smattering of applause. As a young parish priest, I was charged to take the Sacrament twice a year to elderly and infirm shut-ins of the parish in their homes. One old lady that first Christmas said to me, "Well I suppose I won't see you again until Easter. I'm sure you find it an unpleasant chore to visit me." "No, I don't find it a chore," said I, the bright-eyed bushy-tailed young priest. "I enjoy it. Tell you what, I'll come and see you once a month from now on." So I went in January and, as I tried to make my exit, the lady said to me, "Well, I suppose I won't see you for another month. You must hate having to come and visit me." "Tell you what," said I, the sophomoric priest. "I'll come to see you once a week." You can guess what all this leads to! I could have visited her every hour and she'd have concluded by saying, "I suppose I won't see you for another hour."

Suffice to say, people quickly take us for granted, people are usually not grateful. St. Mark tells us that Jesus cured ten lepers on one occasion, but that only one of the ten returned to give thanks. If you set out upon a life of public service, the world is not going to line up to cheer your goodness, to recognize your generosity. That is a depressing reality. If you set out to do great things with your life, you will soon come to understand and share the age-old experience of that Gospel song, "Some times I get discouraged."

Anger—Bitterness—Despair

Discouragement can easily lead to disillusionment, anger, bitterness, and even to immobilization.

"I hate this place," we say. This "place" may be our school, our job, or our marriage. "I was a fool to come to this school, I was a fool to take this job, I was a fool to marry this woman."

We spend enormous energy on backward-looking regrets: that we ever came to this school, that we ever took this job, that we ever married this woman. And how facile our minds are at imagining what might have been! If only I'd stayed in public school I'd be getting all A's and be surrounded by adoring females. If only I'd taken that job I'd be making five times as much money as I make now. If only I'd married that other woman. In my former school there was a young teacher who depressed us all by every day telling us how much more money people in other professions made, how rewarded they were. And this vacation, again, a highly successful young businessman told me at length how much he hated business, how unrewarding it was, and how he really wanted to teach. It is especially easy to wallow in regret when we imagine the grass on the other side to be so much greener.

When we're discouraged, we are also tempted to run. Inside each of our adult bodies is the little kid who ran away from home when he didn't like the reality of something his parents insisted on. In my first year at St. Mark's I had a recurring fantasy of walking to Framingham, jumping a Boston & Albany freight train, and heading west for home. (Why it had to be a freight train, I don't know—more melodramatic, I guess.) In my senior year at St. Mark's I had a recurring fantasy of shouting at one of my teachers whom I particularly disliked: "That's a stupid assignment, you jerk, and I won't do it." As an adult I've worked for two bosses—both men whom in retrospect I'm glad I worked for—but how often (and for what reasons I mostly cannot now remember) I fantasized marching into their offices and saying, "I quit, that's it, I'm not taking any more of this." When we're discouraged, running is a natural instinct. Related to it is the instinct to find someone or something to blame our unhappiness on: this school, or this job, or this boss, or this wife is the cause of it all. Scapegoating goes all the way back to Adam blaming his mistake on Eve and Eve blaming the serpent.

Another response when we're discouraged can be to blot out our discouragement by drugs or drink or pleasure. The unhappy middle-aged husband tries to run away from his life with another woman, or he tries to blot out his problems with alcohol. But drugs and drink and sex don't alter or help our situation; they only provide a temporary escape from it. And, far from being a real solution to our problems, they often end up compounding our difficulties. The little boy who runs away inevitably returns. Just as inevitably, we cannot keep running from, we cannot escape from, the realities of adult life.

And so we are left to face the reality of our discouragement. For some, that facing up is bitter: "I expected a lot more from my school, from my job, from my wife. I expected a lot more from life." Anger, regret, disappointment are the primary emotions for some. For others, despair is primary. Winston Churchill called it his "black cat," that depressing sense that life is not worth it, that sense of ennui, of emptiness, that makes the whole landscape of our lives a bleak midwinter.

Endurance and Faith

If we set no great goals for our lives, we will encounter little discouragement. But if, like Churchill, we do set out to do something great with our lives, then we must expect the disillusionment that comes from being treated unfairly. If we set out to serve others—whether in business or commerce or the professions—we must be realistic about the cost. We must expect that we will not be adequately thanked or rewarded, that we will be assailed by the temptation to quit, to run, to abandon our goals, to give in to despair.

We must accept the reality that every decision we make rules out other choices for us. When we choose one woman to marry, we exclude others. When we take one job—with all its joys and sorrows—we rule out other jobs. Much unhappiness in life seems to me to stem from the unwillingness of people to live with their decisions. So many people live backward-glancing lives consumed with thoughts of "what might have been," consumed with the jealous imagining of how happy everyone else is who's not stuck in his life. If we really have made a wrong decision and are realistic about the opportunities a change might bring us, then we should correct our decision. But it is my observation that many people are unrealistic about the opportunities another choice offers them, and they leap into a change that brings as much misery as the life they've fled—or sometimes more misery. Much of life's unhappiness is caused by our unwillingness to face up to the inevitable discouragements entailed in any one of the lives we might choose.

When we face the fact that every life worth living has its discouragements, its own "unfairness" if you like, we have then taken a giant step towards happiness.

We are then no longer crushed or consumed by the injustices and discouragements of life. We expect them. We learn not to let those discouragements distract us from focusing on the great goals we have set for our lives. When I asked a varsity football player this fall if he was discouraged by a nagging injury, he said to me, "Yes, sometimes it gets to me. Then I think, well, this is football, you have to expect that you'll be hurting a lot of the season, and then I think about getting up for next Saturday's game and it really doesn't bother me that much." In any life worth living, we will be hurting much of the time. But as we mature, we acquire the faith, the perspective, that the discouragements, the injuries, cannot break us, cannot make us lose sight of the great things we are determined to achieve. With our minds on the goal of winning Saturday's game, we are able to endure the injury. That faith grows stronger and stronger every time we overcome discouragement and pick ourselves up, dust ourselves off, and go on. That's why Sanderson could write at the end of his time as headmaster of Oundle School: "Faith is the belief in the ultimate triumph of right-doing, [faith is] not a formal assent, but a living belief acquired by endurance, by 'hardness' of life. It is belief which is forced slowly upon the individual; it is the result of experience, of actions tested in the past. It becomes the basis of his future."

Such faith gives us a new perspective about discouragement—each discouragement is a test, each discouragement overcome is a victory. Viktor Frankl, the great Viennese psychiatrist who was incarcerated in a concentration camp by the Nazis because he was a Jew, could therefore think of each ghastly moment of suffering this way: "That which does not kill me makes me stronger." We grow through our discouragement, we grow through our suffering. St. James writes in his brief epistle: "Blessed is the man who falls into divers kinds of trials, knowing that the testing of his faith will produce the spirit of endurance and endurance will enlarge and confirm his faith."

How alone we sometimes feel—like Elijah under the tree—"I only am left . . ." And sometimes we are virtually alone in our discouragement. In *Paradise Lost*, Milton writes of the single angel who alone refuses to support Satan:

> *So spake the seraph Abdiel, faithful found;*
> *Among the faithless faithful only he;*
> *Among innumerable false unmoved,*
> *Unshaken, unseduced, unterrified,*
> *His loyalty he kept, his love, his zeal;*
> *Nor number nor example with him wrought*
> *To swerve from truth, or change his constant mind,*
> *Though single.*

If we set out as pilgrims—often seemingly alone—to live such a life, we will surely encounter discouragements along the way. However, if we keep our eyes on the great goals of our lives—on our "first avowed intent"—we shall not, Bunyan assures us, be overwhelmed by those discouragements:

> *There's no discouragement*
> *Can make him once relent*
> *His first avowed intent: To be a pilgrim.*

In January 1945, shortly before he was executed, the German Protestant pastor, Dietrich Bonhoeffer, imprisoned by the Nazis, wrote his parents a poem-prayer from prison. It says everything we need to know about the confident faith and courageous hope of the true pilgrim, about the pilgrim's "first avowed intent" that enables him to overcome all the inevitable discouragements that assail him on the journey of life.

Let us take Bonhoeffer's prayer as our theme as we embark upon a new year.

With every power of good to stay and guide me,
Comforted and inspired beyond all fear,
I'll live these days with you in thought beside me,
And pass, with you, into the coming year.
The old year still torments our hearts, unhastening;
The long days of our sorrow still endure;
Father, grant to the souls Thou hast been chastening
What Thou hast promised, the healing and the cure.
Should it be ours to drain the cup of grieving
Even to the dregs of pain, at Thy command,
We will not falter, thankfully receiving
All that is given by Thy loving hand.
Today, let candles shed their radiant greeting;
Lo, on our darkness are they not Thy light
Leading us, haply, to our longed-for meeting?
Thou canst illumine even our darkest night.

17

Through the Valley of the Shadow

EN DAYS AGO in Virginia I visited Appomattox where—you will recall—Robert E. Lee surrendered to Ulysses S. Grant, on April 9, 1865, thereby ending the War between the States.

Appomattox—or Appomattox Court House, as the little village was called at the time—has been restored to its Civil War appearance. The interiors of the McLean House (where the surrender occurred) and other buildings now look the way they did in 1865. The interior of the courthouse, however, has been transformed into a museum where photographs and memorabilia are displayed.

I've noticed, over the years, that when I see such a display, I almost always remember vividly one or two seemingly insignificant items. After I left Appomattox, I realized that one photograph had seared itself on my consciousness: a photograph of General Lee just after the surrender. He is on horseback, his head downcast, surrounded by the beaten and bedraggled men of his Army of Northern Virginia. His face is the picture—the definition—of abject defeat and utter despair. Four years of unrelenting, exhausting endeavor, four years of staggering loss and appalling sacrifice, had now ended in this godforsaken place. Everything to which he had devoted himself for four years had been lost. The photograph captures it all: inconsolable grief, total desolation.

My visit to Appomattox was purely last-minute and incidental to my reason for being in central Virginia. I went there to see William Collar Holbrook, grandson of the School's greatest headmaster, William Coe

Collar—whose career here lasted fifty years, from 1857 (before the Civil War) to 1907. William Collar Holbrook is a retired professor at Hampden-Sydney College. He graduated from Roxbury Latin in 1916 and is now in his nineties—and I spent two days with him recording his remembrances of the School and of his grandfather.

The School archives contain some of William Coe Collar's letters to his wife and children, but, unbeknownst to me, Professor Holbrook had in his possession a diary kept by Collar in his fifties. Much of it, frankly, is dull: the weather, how well he slept, his health. But there are several remarkable passages that make the time spent reading it worthwhile. I want to share with you just one passage. Collar was in Germany at the time, visiting the schools there and trying to learn the language. He was now fifty-six years old. He was happily married and had four thriving children. He had taken the two-room schoolhouse in Roxbury and transformed it into a nationally renowned educational institution. His Greek and Latin textbooks were used by all the best American schools (and his first-year German text would soon be highly successful as well). And he had been given honorary degrees by his own college (Amherst) and by Harvard. But this is what he wrote in his diary on December 30, 1889:

> *If I am with my family [at home] I am perpetually interrupted, and cannot be by myself; if I am alone, I am almost always depressed in spirits. Age is rapidly advancing upon me, and I am daily conscious of my feeble powers. My life has been one of dreary monotony. I have been all my life struggling to get knowledge, and alas how pitiful is the outcome! I shall never know any language well, and what do I know besides? Pitiful is the state of one whose youth and young manhood have passed without getting a good education, and [who] then finds himself launched upon life in a situation where education is by everyone assumed. What then am I to do? I can do nothing but what I have done and am doing. The weary struggle will be over by and by.*

It is easy for us to understand the despair of Robert E. Lee—after all, the cause to which he has sacrificed everything for four years had been brought to total defeat. But it is not as easy to understand the desolation of Collar—who from every outward appearance—had proceeded from one success to another, one triumph to the next, throughout his long and fruitful career.

A Common Experience

It is Collar's despair that I want to focus on this morning. A year ago today I had just returned from two weeks at Eton, and I began the term with an upbeat description of my experience there. Later that morning one of the boys in Class I stopped by my office. I greeted him rather shallowly: "How're you doing?" And, as kids sometimes do, he answered unshallowly: "I thought you were going to talk about something important this morning, like the meaning of life. But instead, you just gave a happy little travelogue." It was easy to tell that he was angry and hurting, and so I said to him, "What's the matter?" He replied, "That's what bothers me. I don't know." He then listed his successes. He had been admitted early to his first-choice college, he'd had one triumph after another inside and outside the classroom. I knew he was popular and respected. "What really depresses me," he concluded, "is that I've got everything I want, but I'm not happy." The Collar diary passage made me think of this boy.

Winston Churchill—perhaps the most famous man of this century, a universal hero—had recurring experiences of depression in which he lost almost all sense of purpose and enjoyment in life. He called these periods of depression "my black cat." If you read the lives of the saints (you won't, so I'll tell you!), you discover at least one period of despair in the life of virtually every one of them. These periods of despair are so common they are called by a generic name, "the dark night of the soul." It is these periods of depression that I want to talk about, and I use the word depression not in its clinical definition, but as it is popularly used to describe those times in life when—often for no apparent reason—we feel downhearted or empty, when we lose our sense of the meaning and purpose of our lives.

I bet most of you have had such periods. I bet most of you can identify with Churchill and with Collar. I bet most of you have had some
experience like that of the boy who came to see me last April who said,
"I've got everything I want, but I'm still not happy."

I'll give you two examples from my own life of this experience:

The first is from June of my junior year in high school. Final exams
loomed. We were told repeatedly how important they were, how critical it was for us to do well. All through the pressure-packed hours of
study, I kept thinking of the thousand and one fun things I was going to
do when exams were over: I want to go there or do that. I even made a
list of all the delights I was anticipating so rapturously. Then—suddenly—exams were over. I looked at the list and there was nothing on
the list I wanted to do. Now that I could do anything I wanted, I didn't
want to do anything.

The second example is the publication of my first book—one of the
few books I've written that you don't have to read. It is not one of the
great tomes in the history of human literature, but it was an instant success. By good fortune it appeared at exactly the right time, and had
three huge printings in the first five months, and I was called to come to
New York for a party in my honor. "You are not only our youngest
author," said the publisher on the phone. "You are—at least for this
brief moment—our best selling author." I didn't go. One of my more
searing memories is finding the publisher's copies of the book at my
mailbox—sent from New York on the first day of publication. I rushed
up the stairs to my apartment and breathlessly opened the box. It was
the supreme moment of anticipation. But as I pulled the top book out of
the box and fondled it, it figuratively turned to dust in my hands. I was
overcome by a completely unexpected, yet vivid sense of despair. What
was so great about writing a book? Millions of books are published. All
the fruits of my labor, all that I had strained to produce, seemed worthless. I felt empty, depressed, crippled with ennui.

I know exactly how Collar—and the boy in my office—felt because,
from time to time, I have glimpsed into the abyss, experienced reason-
less emptiness and despair. I think many of you have, as well.

My tutor at Cambridge, J. S. Bezzant, said the most reassuring possible thing to me about this experience when I was in my early twenties, and I pass it on to you: "From time to time, almost every thoughtful and reflective person walks through life's valleys. Such experiences of depression and despair are natural to people who labor strenuously to achieve something important. The issue is not so much that you are depressed as what you're going to do about being depressed."

His insight—that times of depression are natural and normal for a bright, sensitive, and ambitious person—is the most important thought I have to share with you this morning. Because if you know that you will, from time to time, feel depressed, you will not be surprised, or overcome, or undone by it. You will even learn how best to avoid it and, when you can't avoid it, how best to deal with it.

Let me share three tactics I have found useful in dealing with depression. I share these with you because I think it is neither necessary nor desirable simply to wallow helplessly and impotently in depression.

Don't Run

Not long ago I called a boy into my office after his grades had dropped. He said (and I've heard boys say these words many times before): "I don't know what it is, but lately I just haven't been able to get down to work, to do my homework. I've been bagging it for several weeks now. I just can't seem to face up to it. I've lost my willpower." I quote this boy not in order to make the point that we sometimes don't want to do our work. (The loss of "willpower" is something almost all of us have experienced.) I quote this boy in order to call your attention to his statement that he had been (to put it a bit too strongly) paralyzed for several weeks: "I've been bagging it for several weeks now." Rather than dealing with his loss of desire and energy, he had been passively wallowing in it.

The first piece of advice I have, then, is to be honest with yourself. Don't run away, don't pretend, don't wait for it to pass, don't wallow. Don't be passive!

Our first instinct when we're "down" is cowardly: take something to kill the pain. A boy this winter told me that he secretly watched television all evening night after night for several weeks when he should have been doing homework. Others bury themselves in magazines, some attempt to numb their brains with acid rock. The most pathetic—those who are running away in terror—seek to blot out the pain of depression with drugs or with drink.

Still others—less pathetic, because less passive—deal with depression by striking out in anger: it makes us feel better to blame someone. I'll blame the school—or my parents. I'll beat up my little brother.

These methods of dealing with depression—trying to deny it or blot it out, or blaming someone else for our own bad feelings—are essentially cowardly and pathetic.

The first step in coping with depression is to admit honestly that we are downhearted—to admit it to ourselves first, and then to share it with others.

There is a great saint's day hymn that says, "They [the saints] wrestled hard, as we do now, with sins, and doubts, and fears." But that is exactly what we often do not do. We do not wrestle hard.

"Wrestling hard" begins with admitting to ourselves that we are in one of life's valleys, one of life's depressions. Admitting it early, not two or three weeks into the paralysis. Once we've honestly and quickly faced up to how we feel, the next step is turning to others for help. It takes no courage to run away into television or drugs or drink. That is the way of the cowardly and the pathetic. It takes courage to admit to ourselves that we need to share our pain, our hurt, our emptiness, our ennui with others. The macho Marlboro cowboy, in my experience, does not have the guts to do that. He's too much into preserving his tough-guy image. He's more likely to run, to head for the bottle. The real man, however, has the courage to admit to himself and to others that he needs help. The real man does not run, he dares to share his vulnerability with those who can help him.

Take One Step at a Time

If the first tactic is to be honest with ourselves, to admit that we are depressed and to reach out for help, the second, I suggest, is to take life one step, one day, at a time.

One evening last term the phone rang and it was a Roxbury Latin student. He was nearly incoherent, his nerve ends jangling. I soon gathered that he had tests, lab reports, papers—all due the next day. He was just reeling. With my usual amazing wisdom, I said to him, "Let's make a list." "I don't have time," he said. "Well," I said, "we have to get you to stop spinning. Let's get everything onto a piece of paper." We did— pretty quickly and easily, actually—and he soon calmed down and began to set priorities among all the conflicting demands.

Other people can be astonishingly objective and helpful about our lives. When I got back from the South last week, I had mounds of mail (most of which required an answer), a bunch of phone messages to return (half of them marked urgent), two reports to get written, thank you letters to send, and mounds of material on the school history to sort out. I sat in the midst of these literal piles of responsibility and spun for about an hour till the phone rang. By good fortune, it was an old friend. I started in on all I had to do, how impossible my job is, how overburdened my life is, how I couldn't possibly do all that everybody expected me to do. Jangling nerve ends. The friend replied, "Might I suggest something?" "Anything," I responded. "Why don't you make a list?" he said. I was lucky that this man called me. Clergy—especially those who are headmasters—are great at imparting wisdom, at telling other people how to run their lives. But they all too infrequently listen to or take the advice they're dishing out.

When we are overcome with responsibilities, when we are inclined to wallow in impotent despair at the impossibility of meeting these seemingly overwhelming demands, we need to make a list, break things down into single steps, and then take the first step.

When we are overcome with a sense of the futility or difficulty of life, our natural inclination is a bad one: to give up, throw up our hands in despair, to run, to surrender, to wallow in our impotence, and find something to blot out the pain. It is exactly at that point that we need to have the guts to reach out for help and to try with all the courage we can muster to take one small step out of the quagmire.

The most frightening thing about being depressed is the loss of desire to help ourselves. This was put most poignantly to me, years ago when I was a parish priest, by a recovering alcoholic who had fallen off the wagon and gotten drunk. He sobbed and sobbed and repeated over and over, "I don't care, I don't care, I just want to drink, I don't ever want to stop." He *did* want to stop—he d*esperately* wanted to stop. What he was sobbing about was his lack of willpower. He knew he could have called a fellow member of Alcoholics Anonymous, but he didn't. "I couldn't even dial the phone," he said.

When you're pulled down by life's demands, you sometimes don't even know whether you can reach out for a life preserver. That's when you need all the courage you can muster.

I admire those who can find this courage on their own. I'm not sure I could find it on my own, and, like many of you in such straits, I cry out for help in prayer. "Help me," I pray with my whole being. "I'm paralyzed." With God's help I somehow find the courage to take the first step.

Find and Keep the Vision

Finally, we need to try as best we can to turn the bad experience of depression into something good. We need to try to turn the negative into a positive. Viktor Frankl, the Viennese psychiatrist imprisoned in a Nazi concentration camp, wrote, "That which does not kill me makes me stronger."

Being depressed is almost always a sign that our life is out of control, that we've lost our balance. Depression is the blinking red light that tells us that something's wrong. As we work our way out from under the dark cloud, we need to figure out what's wrong.

We need to make it our first priority to find a time to be quiet, to take our pulse, to rethink and revisit the goals of our life, to reorder our priorities.

In fact, finding moments of quiet in the midst of our often frantically busy lives—moments in which to regain our focus, regain some overall vision of our lives—finding such moments is the principal formula for preventing depression in the first place.

The prophet Isaiah writes, "They that wait upon the Lord shall renew their strength." It is, I submit, "renewal of strength" that we are all seeking: "renewal of strength" certainly when we are paralyzed by depression, "renewal of strength" certainly when we try to get ourselves in good spiritual condition so we can avoid depression.

We "wait upon the Lord" by finding the time and being quiet enough to contemplate the goals of our lives.

The former Archbishop of Canterbury, Arthur Michael Ramsey, was interviewed once when visiting the United States. A bright young reporter asked him, "Archbishop, what have you been doing so far today?" "Right up till now I've been saying my prayers," he replied. "What were you seeking to accomplish when you said your prayers?" she asked. "I was trying to talk with God." "Did you talk with God?" she asked. "Yes," he said. "For how long?" was her next question. "For about thirty seconds," he answered, "but it took me nearly thirty minutes to get there." We have to quiet down and listen if we are to find the center of our lives. That is why Isaiah says, "They that wait upon the Lord shall renew their strength."

If you read that great insight into the human experience—the Psalms of Israel—you will see there that depression is assumed as part of the human experience: "Yea though I walk through the valley (the depression) of the shadow of death. . . ."

Do not be terrified when you come to life's valleys. Almost all bright and sensitive people experience such clouded, visionless depressions. Face them squarely when they come, reach out to others to help you, ask them to walk with you, to help you take one step—one step at a time—out of the valley.

And remember—when things are going pretty well—to wait upon

the Lord, to take stock of your life. For if we wait upon the Lord in the high places—in what Churchill called "the broad, sunlit uplands" of life—He shall also be with us, to help us, when, inevitably we find ourselves walking "through the valley of the shadow of death," through the visionless, darkened, clouded depressions of life. Then you can say, with the psalmist: "Yea, though I walk through the valley of the shadow of death I will fear no evil, for Thou art with me."

18

The Journey of the Magi

ODAY, January 6, is the last day of Christmas, the Feast of the Epiphany, the day on which is commemorated the visit of the wise men from the East to the baby Jesus in the stable at Bethlehem.

You all know the story—three wise men journey from the Far East, guided by a star, first to Jerusalem, where they talk with King Herod, and finally to Bethlehem, where they present their costly gifts: gold and frankincense and myrrh.

When I was in college and knew everything, I wrote a paper on T. S. Eliot's poem "The Journey of the Magi" which is based on this story. I began the paper with several pages of withering contempt for the biblical account concluding with the words, "If you believe this story is historical, you can believe anything." I didn't have much good to say about the poem either. Now that I'm older, I know a lot less. In Western Civ you all have the opportunity to read the last word on the historical background of this story by a brilliant, handsome, and charismatic educator and clergyman whose book I hope you all buy new and treasure forever. That book sets out some of the evidence for and against the historicity of the story. It discusses whether the story is literally true, whether it actually happened or not. I don't really think it matters. Whether it actually happened or whether it is a myth—a myth like the story of Adam and Eve or the Tower of Babel or the Aeneid—it has, I now think in my old age, the ring of truth about it. Mythical stories, as you all know, are often greater conveyers of the truth than documented accounts of historical events.

I've preached sermons on this story in the context of Christian worship. I know that only a relatively small minority of you are believing Christians, and I'm not going to talk about the story the way I would in that context. It is the story's universal truth—as opposed to its specific meaning for Christians—that I'd like to explore with you this morning.

The story is told in twelve short verses in St. Matthew's Gospel. I see the story as a play in five acts:

Act I

St. Matthew begins: Now when Jesus was born in Bethlehem of Judea in the days of Herod the King, behold there came wise men from the East to Jerusalem, saying, "Where is he that is born? For we have seen his star in the East and are come to worship him."

Now these three wise men—variously called astrologers, magi, kings, wise men—were obviously men of considerable affluence and position. As all these descriptions indicate, they were highly educated. Not only were they wise, however; they were also rich. They could afford to leave home for a long period, they had the leisure and where-withal to travel—to take a long trip, by camel, with their retinues, usu-ally staying in the best hotels, and carrying cumbersome and costly presents. The fact that they are often called kings—"we three kings of orient are, bearing gifts we traverse afar"—indicates they were not only well educated and rich, but also men of consequence and power. Some think they were sultans or sheiks of minor Middle Eastern states.

Why, then, did they leave their comfortable lives behind, the secu-rity of their own families, the warmth of their own homes, the conve-nience of their own community? They had everything anybody could want without leaving home.

And, yet, apparently they didn't. Apparently, something was miss-ing. Apparently, amid all their affluence, all their comfort, all their sta-tus, there was something lacking. There was at the heart of all their glittering well-being a gnawing emptiness. And so they left it all behind—at least for a while, driven by this emptiness to look for some-thing that would fulfill them. They longed for something beyond what they had.

Moral of Act I: The search for truth, the search for the meaning of life, begins with the experience of emptiness.

Some of you know that emptiness. Some of you've lain on the top of your bed in the summer or in a vacation and known the ennui, the debilitating boredom of it all, the lack of desire to do anything. If you have not experienced that basic emptiness, then there won't be anything for you in all the rest I'm going to say this morning and you need listen no further. The search for the meaning of life begins with emptiness.

Act II

Jerusalem. The Court of Herod. Matthew continues: When Herod the King had heard all these things, he was troubled. And he gathered all the chief priests and scribes together and demanded of them where this child was supposed to be born. "At Bethlehem in Judea," they replied, and they referred him to the prophecy. Then Herod, when he had called the wise men to meet with him privately, inquired of them diligently when it was that the star appeared. And he sent them to Bethlehem and said, "Go and search diligently for this child. When you have found him, bring me word again, that I may come and do him homage also."

We know quite a lot about Herod from historical sources outside the New Testament: He was the puppet king of Palestine under the Roman rule, a terrible man. He murdered many people, including his own wife and three of his sons. The Bible tells us that when Herod realized the wise men were not going to report back to him, he killed all the children in Bethlehem who were two years of age or younger—the "Slaughter" or "Massacre" of the Holy Innocents.

Obviously the wise men had realized that Herod was a liar—that he did not want to pay homage to this child but that he wanted to kill him.

Moral of Act II: The world contains people—some of them very powerful—who, far from seeking the truth, want to obliterate whatever is true and beautiful and good. Herod is such a killer. Evil is grippingly real in some people. I have seen killers like Herod—pretending to do good while actually seeking to destroy: I have seen a drug pusher lure an eleven-year-old into drug use by glittering promises of the kick he'll get. I've counseled a twelve-year-old girl whose "loving" father importuned her repeatedly into sexual encounters. I've watched a middle-aged woman try to tempt a reformed alcoholic friend of hers back into drinking. These people—like Herod—are liars and murderers.

The irony of this scene, though, is that the wise men hear the truth about how to find Jesus from the liar Herod. In our own search for what is good we, like the wise men, will often encounter evil. But, like the wise men, we may possibly discover even in the very heart of evil some valuable insight. When we encounter evil we can learn from it, provided we are not sucked into it. The wise men were not sucked in by Herod. They took their leave of Herod and never went back to him.

Act III

Back on the trail. St. Matthew continues: Lo the star that they had seen in the east went before them until it came and stood over the place where the child was. When they saw the star they rejoiced with exceeding great joy.

I don't know what the wise men expected when they set out on their journey, but I bet they imagined that it would be rather like a *National Geographic* expedition—waterfalls and wildlife, interesting encounters with exotic people, the stimulation of new foods and smells, and finally—at the end of this fascinating and triumphal progress the goal of the expedition—the child the prophet had long foretold who was born to be king, messiah, savior. That's what I bet these guys expected. It's what we all expect.

But it wasn't like that. If the search for what is good and true and beautiful begins with emptiness, it continues to be a hard journey, a long and arduous search, through encounters not only with the Herods of this world, but even worse, with our own inward sense of despair, that terrible sense that the whole journey is not worth it.

T. S. Eliot's reflective wise man says:

'A cold coming we had of it,
Just the worst time of year
For a journey, and such a long journey:
The ways deep and the weather sharp,
The very dead of winter.'
And the camels galled, sorefooted, refractory,
Lying down in the melting snow.
There were times we regretted
[What we'd left behind,]
The summer palaces on slopes, the terraces,
And the silken girls bringing sherbet.
Then the camel men cursing and grumbling
And running away, and wanting their liquor and women,
And the night-fires going out, and the lack of shelters,
And the cities hostile and the towns unfriendly
And the villages dirty and charging high prices:
A hard time we had of it.
At the end we preferred to travel all night
Sleeping in snatches,
With the voices singing in our ears, saying
That this was all folly.

The star, lost sight of. The initial enthusiasm of the search gone. The clinging to hope. The bare warding-off of despair.

Somehow they continued. And then they saw it. The star, glimpsed, lost, glimpsed, lost again and again and again and again, and finally glimpsed right over the place. "And they rejoiced with exceeding great joy."

Moral of Act III: If we are somehow able to leave behind what is known and comfortable, and undertake the journey in search of life's meaning, we must realize that the journey will be arduous, filled with discouragement and despair, filled with the voices singing in our ears, saying that the search is folly. We must somehow sustain hope, as the wise men did, when in the depths we lose all sight of the star. And we must expect, like the wise men, that we shall never experience great joy until we have suffered many sorrows.

Act IV

Bethlehem. The Stable. St. Matthew continues: And when they were come into the stable, they saw the child with Mary his mother, and they knelt down and did him homage; and when they had opened their treasures they presented him with gifts: gold and frankincense and myrrh.

Again—I don't know what they expected to find after their discouraging journey. I know what I'd expect. At least one of those signs you see outside of motels: "Welcome to Boston, Jerry and Sue from Duluth!" Or "Welcome Shriners' Convention!" Or some such. A brass band, the mayor of Bethlehem with the key to the city: "Sure glad to welcome you distinguished visitors to our historic town—here to see the child born to be king picturesquely lying in the manger of a stable." Like Ed McMahon on the Johnny Carson Show. Here's ——————. Jesus!

Seriously, they must have imagined that at this point there'd be some big slam-banging climax, some grand finale. They were wise men, educated men seeking for truth. Surely at long last they would learn the answers to their questions: perhaps some satisfying slogans to live by, three quick and easy ways to happiness and fulfillment. Surely at last there'd be some reward for their efforts, surely at last after all the emptiness and despair and all the hardness of the journey, they were entitled finally to reward and satisfaction.

And what did they find? No neon signs of welcome. No brass band. No mayor. No silken clothes and palaces. An ordinary looking baby in a cattle shed with a poor Jewish refugee peasant couple who'd had a baby in a cattle shed because there was no room for them to stay in the local inn, and a bunch of cattle. Was this the child born to be king? It was hard to imagine. It would be hard to imagine a child less likely to have any future significance. And yet these men of wealth and stature took out their costly treasures—gold and frankincense and myrrh—and lavished them on the baby in a manger as they knelt in homage before him.

Have you ever thought how utterly incongruous their presents were? Here was this couple who didn't have a bed, or running water, or heat, or anything except a baby? What on earth were they supposed to do with gold and frankincense and myrrh? What bizarre, inappropriate gifts. What do you suppose Mary and Joseph made of these weird visitors and their even weirder presents?

For years I thought how disappointed these three men must have been. After all their costly searching to arrive at this: a peasant baby in a stable.

An old priest told me—when I raised this question in seminary— that he didn't think the wise men were disappointed because, he said, they found a baby. Nobody ever sees, or touches, or feels a baby and goes away unmoved. Bring a baby into a room and he or she immediately becomes the center of attention. Middle-aged men in grey flannel suits are suddenly cooing and dangling toys and holding its hands and kissing and cuddling it. A baby brings us into touch with the most elementary and elemental truths of human experience. We are suddenly and mysteriously face-to-face with the very process of creation. The sight, sound, smell, and feel of a baby bring out in all of us the basic, primal instincts that otherwise lie dormant and atrophied. What else, the old priest asked me, could you imagine at the end of their journey that would give them a better insight into life than a baby?

Years later when I was a parish priest in Cleveland, along with several other city clergy, I worked with boys in the Juvenile Detention Center downtown. The delinquents—aged twelve through sixteen— who were detained here were supposed to be the toughest and most dangerous and were therefore kept behind bars. When you got to know them, of course, they turned out to be as vulnerable as all the rest of us. I was telling one of the old ladies in my parish about playing checkers with these boys one day and she said, "Well I can do that—I'd like to go down there," and despite my discouragement she did and so did her friends, and these tough kids found in these old ladies a tenderness most of them had never known. Their visit on Thursday nights to play cards and other games became a highlight of the boys' week.

The other clergy and I started a weekend visitation program on which we'd take a kid from Friday night through Sunday night into our homes—one boy at a time. I always warned the kids that I had to be at church all day Sunday from 7 A.M. to 7 P.M. and that they'd have to come with me. Most were so eager to get out that even the thought of a day at church didn't bother them. And each week they conducted a contest to decide the order in which they'd get to go to a clergyman's home for the weekend. The biggest and physically toughest kid on the two floors was a sixteen-year-old who could have passed for twenty. A huge muscular kid who was in for assault and rape. The state had sought to try him as an adult.

Every week, while the kids were deciding who would get to go for the weekend, this kid would come over to me and say, "I don't want to go to your G.D. house and I'd never go in any G.D. church." I always said, "Nobody's making you go. If you decide you'd like to do it sometime later, you can pick a number in the contest." "I'll never do that," he said. I said, "I think you'll do it when you're ready." Months went by and one day he just sat on his bed. Didn't come over and tell me he'd never go for the weekend. So I went over to his bed and said, "I guess you must be ready." He said, "Maybe." And a few weeks later he won the contest and as agreed, he shaved, cleaned up, and put on his best clothes. We went out to a movie on Friday, and a basketball game on Saturday, and had pizzas and did the other little things we all take for granted. This kid was one big kid—probably 6'1" or 6'2", 185 pounds—but, unlike all the others I'd had, he didn't open up at all. There was no change at all in the tough-guy exterior. No progress. He remained tense and angry and bottled up. On the way to church on Sunday morning I said, "I bet you're not looking forward to going to church." He said, "I hate this. I wish I'd never come out here for the weekend." (I said to myself, "Who needs this?") As we arrived at the church up walked a fifteen-year-old girl, one of the girls in our youth group who took care of the babies while their parents were in church. I introduced her to this kid and she said to me, "Two of the volunteers are sick, so there's only Sue and me in the nursery today." I said to this kid, "Maybe you'd rather help out there than sit through church." "I don't want to do either," he said. So I sent him off with the girl.

Then, when I was in church, in the middle of the service, I suddenly realized what I'd done! "Jarvis, you idiot, what have you done? Left this hulking convicted rapist all alone with two little fifteen-year-old girls and a bunch of infants!" By the time the service was over I was sweating from head to toe and ran to the nursery. When I got there I saw the kid sitting in a rocking chair with a baby in his arms, softly talking, slowly rocking him. I said to one of the girls, "Is everything okay?" "He's really terrific," she said. "He's the best boy who's ever helped out. He really understands babies." (My God—I thought—if they could hear that at the Detention Center!) It was all I could do to drag the kid away for lunch, even after all the parents had picked up their babies. He saw his counselor on Monday and talked of nothing else but the babies. To tele-scope events, when he finally left they got him a job in the children's ward of a big Cleveland hospital.

There is something about a baby that just knocks down the impreg-nable walls of defense we build around ourselves. We are brought back into touch with our deepest feelings and emotions. We become loving and gentle and tender and protective. Like the boy, we are changed.

When something touches us—when for a moment we come into touch with what we've been looking for, we do all sorts of ridiculous things. The gifts of these rich Gentile wise men from afar were prepos-terously inappropriate presents for a Jewish peasant baby. A few years ago I baptized a baby girl in Dorchester and there was a little party at her parents' house afterwards. One of our choirboys who was about ten knew the mother and father, and they invited him to the christening and the party. I said to him the week before, "Tommy, you know you're supposed to take a little present for the baby." He looked at me in com-plete disgust and said, "It's already wrapped." And he told me that he had bought her a copy of his favorite book. At the party the mother unwrapped each little toy or blanket or one of the other fripperous things people give babies. Then she got to Tommy's present and unwrapped this large tome entitled, *The Celtics—Basketball's Best.* One old lady looking on said, "What a present for a three-month-old girl. She wouldn't care about basketball even if she could read!" The mother said, quick as a flash, "Tommy, this is the nicest present of all; it'll last the longest because I'll put it away until she's grown up like you and can read it. Thank you."

Without a doubt, the old lady was right. It was a preposterous present for a baby girl. But the mother understood that the boy had given (by his own lights) the gift of what he treasured most. I think Mary understood what was in the wise men's hearts. What matters—the only thing that matters—is that their instinct to open themselves, their instinct to give, so long dormant and atrophied, was brought to life again by the baby. Just as it was for the detention-home boy.

And that's the end of the story. Almost.

Act V

Matthew has only one more sentence: They departed to their own country another way.

The wise men went back to the life they'd left for a time—to their normal life in their normal homes. But Matthew says, "They departed to their own country another way." That may mean nothing more than the literal fact that they went home by a different route to avoid Herod in Jerusalem. But it also may mean that for the rest of their lives there was a difference; that somehow, their lives had been changed forever— the way the detention-home boy's life was changed forever—by their contact with the baby; that the rest of their lives would be lived "another way."

I don't know. But that's my hope. And that's my hope for you and for me, that we shall return to our lives here this term—back to the same old thing—a different way. That we shall commit ourselves to the arduous journey in search of the truth, that we shall endure the hardships and find the goal of our searching, that we shall be changed—that we shall return to the rest of our lives by a different route, that there will be a new gentleness and sweetness that others will see in us.

PART II
Values to Live By

19

A Memory of My Father

Y FATHER'S DEATH in January and the months of sickness that led up to it evoked (as death and dying always do) a flood of memories. I found myself recalling incidents from early childhood that had been absent from my conscious memory for many years. I'd like to share with you one such memory.

It was the summer of 1948, shortly after my ninth birthday. We lived in a small Midwestern town. Our street—Cadle Avenue—had perhaps fifty homes on it: sturdy, respectable middle-class two-story six-room houses. Each house had a small front lawn and a long backyard, but there was not much space between the houses. I could communicate with my best friend next door, from my bedroom window to his, in a low voice. Family squabbles in summer were always overheard by the neighbors on either side.

It was a summer morning, mid-July. In small-town America in those days there were no organized activities—no one went to summer camp, there was no swimming pool, no basketball court, no Little League, no television. We were left to our own devices from morning to night. And we lived by our imaginations. At the back of all our backyards, my buddies and I had dug elaborate trenches. (This was just after the war, you have to remember.) Truth to tell, we were disappointed the war was over. But every other day another story would appear in the papers saying Hitler was alive and had been seen in South America or Switzerland or wherever, and we therefore fantasized his return and the renewal of war. Day by day we played for hours in our trenches, preparing for Hitler's impending attack on Cadle Avenue.

But even the most imaginative little boys could sustain such a fantasy only so long each day and then we'd turn to other amusements. That was how it was on that fateful summer day—we had finished with war about an hour before lunch. I was standing in my backyard with two friends—both ten-year-olds, a grade ahead of me in school—Rusty Stewart and J. C. Daly. I tell you their names so that they will live in infamy. Suddenly they dared me: "Bet you don't have the guts to go into Old Lady Harriger's garden and pull out her vegetables." Old Lady Harriger's garden—which she still called a Victory Garden—was the biggest and best on the street: it took up her whole backyard except for the chicken coop at the very back that our trenches protected from enemy attack.

As a boy I could never resist a dare—never. And within seconds I had crept through the grapevine that served as a fence and was crawling on my stomach—just as our brave G.I.s did when they stormed the beaches in the newsreels. I imagined the bullets whizzing overhead as I advanced on my strategic objective—several freshly weeded rows of vegetables. With all the dispatch and skill of a highly trained commando, I pulled up one carrot after another, one onion after another, one radish after another. Never before had I felt such delight, the delight of sheer glorious destruction, of unrestrained, utterly satisfying vandalism. So delighted and fulfilled was I, so caught up in the thrill of destruction was I, that I did not notice the presence of the enemy. My first awareness came when a shadow cast itself across my advance. I looked instinctively to the sky for enemy aircraft. But by then the entire horizon was blotted out by the looming figure of Old Lady Harriger.

Here I must pause to add a footnote. I suppose that almost every family on the street had a least one grandparent living with them. There was no old folks home in our town. The old and even the dying lived with their children and their children's children. Most of you are deprived of the daily presence of old people in your lives. You therefore miss seeing the whole human picture: you have little experience of old age and dying, the ultimate realities of our human condition. Old Lady

Harriger lived next door to us with her son, his wife, and their son. You must not be offended by the term "Old Lady"; "Old Lady" was a standard Midwestern term—its connotations were affectionate. My own grandmother was called "Old Lady Jarvis," and we all referred to our fathers as "My Old Man."

Meanwhile, back in the victory garden—in the shadow of Old Lady Harriger who had sighted me from her kitchen window. She also spied Rusty and J.C. on the other side of the grapevine, and when they started to run away, she summoned them. "Where do you think you're going?" she asked them. "We didn't do it, we didn't do it," they said about four hundred times in perfect machine gun staccato. Then when that salvo was exhausted, they renewed fire with: "We told him not to do it, we told him not to do it." My friends! My buddies! "OK, run along," she said, and they escaped.

And I was alone. Alone in the dirt, alone amid the corpses of the fallen vegetables, alone in the shadow of an enemy with distinctly superior forces.

The captor escorted her prisoner of war to the adjoining yard and house. I was delivered into the hands of my mortified mother—who apologized abjectly to Old Lady Harriger not only for my actions but practically for my very existence. Then my mother turned to me, "Go to your room. Your father will deal with you when he gets home."

I don't suppose mothers nowadays would handle matters that way. But that's how it was done in Ohio in the 1940s—the father handled the discipline. And there was not a boy on Cadle Avenue who didn't cringe at the dreaded words, "Wait till your father gets home!"

Maybe there's something to be said for such a practice. There is certainly nothing more agonizing in life than waiting, especially if one is waiting for certain doom. And wait I did—alone in my bedroom. Wait I did—through each hour-long minute of that afternoon.

Finally—as always—at exactly 5:14 came the sound of my father's arrival home in the family car. Muffled voices. The slamming of the screen door into the backyard. They were touring the battlefield. The corpses were being viewed; my mother had specifically asked Old Lady

Harriger to leave things the way they were "so that Frank [that's my father] can see for himself."

He saw. The backdoor screen slammed again. The steps sounded on the stairs. As the Bible says, "The earth trembled."

He spoke in a low, constricted voice. "Why did you do this?" At age nine one is not entirely witless, and I allowed myself to think for a few seconds that there might yet be a way out of all this. And so I began my answer, "Rusty and J.C. dared me. . . ." I hardly got these words out when my father cut me off, "You did this. Nobody else. You pulled the vegetables out of the garden. Why did you do it?" There was a terrible silence. I had no idea why I'd done it—aside from the dare. That line of argument having been ruled out, there was nothing I could say. I have never known such stillness uninterrupted by a single sound. Unendurable silence. For a billionth of a second I glimpsed my father's face. It was the face of Moses just as he has descended from Mount Sinai to discover the Israelites worshiping the Golden Calf. It was Moses' face of sheer rage the second before he smashed the tablets of the law.

"Why did you do this?" I could think of nothing I could say by way of explanation for my heinous crime. I was unable to answer.

At length my father asked in the same constricted voice—"What are you going to do about this?" Again—I could think of nothing. I wondered pathetically to myself if I could put all the vegetables back in the ground, but something inside warned me not to suggest that. What could I possibly do? At length my father said, "For starters, you will give Mrs. Harriger every penny you have." "My piggy bank?" I said, eagerly grasping at the possibility that I might still have the power of speech. "My piggy bank?" Mine was ceramic. I took it off the table, and turning it upside down and shaking it, I said—with incredible stupidity—"But the money won't come out." "Oh yes it will," replied my father. He seized the piggy bank, raised it high in the air, and brought it crashing down onto the floor where it shattered in a million pieces, coins flying in all directions. "Get every penny of this and take it to Mrs. Harriger. Tell her you are sorry. Tell her you will work for her every day in the garden for the remainder of the summer."

So I gathered together all my earthly riches, about $7.00 in coins (equivalent to maybe $35 today): a lot of money, long saved. Every penny. It was exactly 6:00 P.M. I can see the windup clock by my bed. Supper was over on our street. No one ate dinner after 5:30. Old Lady Harriger would be coming out to sit on her front porch. All the neighbors would be coming out to sit on their front porches. I would be the lead story on the Cadle Avenue evening news that traveled from front porch to front porch starting right about six. "Think of it," I could hear them saying. "Right here on Cadle Avenue, the crime of the century."

I gathered my vast wealth in a tin can and walked—alone—next door to the Harrigers'. I put my face close to the screen door on the porch. There she was: Old Lady Harriger in her chair awaiting the criminal. I knocked. "Come in." On the porch beside her stood her son, Mr. Harriger, and her grandson John who was five years older than I was—an enormous, elderly fourteen-year-old. They looked down at me as spectators might view a two-headed human freak in the sideshow of a circus: I was deformed humanity and they gazed upon me with silent fascination as I stumbled through my presentation. As my father had directed, I offered up my money (all of it), I offered up my apology, and I promised a summer of servitude in her garden. She received these offerings in silence. Her only words were those of dismissal: "You may go home now."

As I opened the screen door to leave, I felt the gaze of a thousand front-porch eyes. The progress of human history paused as I stepped off that porch. All the people of the earth looked upon me with loathing. My own eyes focused intently on the ground, I returned to my house and went to my bedroom; I knew there would be no supper. It was hot and I lay alone on top of my bed—sweating, despised, rejected, impoverished, desolate, my life in ruins.

At about 8:30 my father came up as always to hear my prayers. He sat as always at the foot of the bed. As always I rendered my prayers to God and my father. At the end there was a short silence—which I, pathetic and pitiable, broke by saying, "I'm sorry, Daddy." "I know," he said, and ran his fingers through my hair. And then he arose and returned down the stairs.

The power that two little words can have: "I know," he said. What more do any of us want in life than to be understood? Those two small words conveyed to me that he somehow understood how I could do something so terrible. That he understood that I was sorry. I was no longer alone.

And the power of a tiny gesture—his fingers through my hair. Despite my crime, I was not only understood, I was loved.

Two small words and one small gesture and the whole universe was again set right. I lay back upon my pillow and slept the profound sleep of one who is at peace.

WHEN I STARTED TEACHING in the sixties, guilt was out of favor. There was nothing worse you could do to someone than to "lay a guilt trip" on him. Had I remembered and told this story back then, my father would have come in for a great deal of criticism. For, make no mistake, he was "laying a guilt trip" on me.

I have told you this story because I think he was right to do so, because I believe that there are things in life that people should feel guilty about. There have, perhaps, been eras in human history when people had too keen a sense of guilt. That is not the case in our time. Psychiatrists, as well as moralists, are concerned, in fact, that in our era there is not enough sense of guilt, not enough sense of obligation.

There are actions that are wrong, that we should feel guilty about. It is wrong to abuse the property of others. It is wrong to take pleasure in destruction. It is wrong to try to evade responsibility for one's own actions. My father was rightly outraged by my destruction of a beautifully tended garden, by my vandalism of someone else's property, by my cowardly attempt to blame my actions on the other two boys. His terrible wrath (and it was terrible) was absolutely appropriate.

How deprived I would have been—deprived for life—if my father had let me blame my actions in any way on the other two boys, if he had let me weasel out of the consequences of what I had done, or if he had let me get away without making restitution.

I submit that there has to be regret, remorse, and restitution before there can be true forgiveness. I had to put things right before everything else could be put right. There was to be no cheap forgiveness, no overlooking, no shoving under the rug.

My father's righteous indignation at my wrongdoing forced me to face myself squarely, to face up to my misdeeds and their consequences fully, and to make restitution. It was extremely painful for me to be forced to take responsibility for my actions and deal with the consequences of my misdeeds. But, as so often in life: no pain, no gain.

It has been my subsequent experience that most of the time when people have made the effort and taken the risk to correct or rebuke me, they have done so because they cared about me. People who don't care about you don't take the trouble to rebuke you. Most people avoid such confrontations. They simply don't give you the raise or the promotion, and you never find out why. So if I could give you any advice from this story it would be to try hard to understand what someone is getting at when he rebukes you. It may well be that he cares about you. It is always painful to be criticized, but it may well be that you can gain from the pain.

And now we come, as Ecclesiasticus says, "to the conclusion of the matter," to the last chapter of the story. I worked for Old Lady Harriger every day for the rest of the summer. The punishment was not reduced. The hours were not shortened. Not a penny of my money was returned. I was not "let off easy." And for that I'm glad because I felt by summer's end that I had paid for my sins. And that's a great feeling.

In retrospect, however, what amazes me most is the fact that neither my father nor my mother ever—ever once—referred again to what happened that summer day in 1948. They didn't drag it up and hurl it at me in the future whenever they were annoyed at me. My father's punishment had been very hard and very swift, and then it was over. Several months before my father died, I tried to remind him of this incident. He had absolutely no recollection of it. Once he had made me face up to what I had done, once I had expressed genuine sorrow and set about making restitution, the incident, as far as he was concerned, was over—completely closed and finished.

Now that he is gone and I can't thank him, I thank God that my father loved me so much that he did not spare me the pain—the loneliness, the desolation—by which alone I could grow to become a better and stronger person.

20

Faith

N HIS FIRST LETTER to the Corinthians, St. Paul identifies three great virtues: faith, hope, and charity. I want to speak today about faith, the virtue St. Paul—not by accident—puts first.

We All Believe in Something

Faith is what we believe. We all have it; we are all believers. We all have faith in someone or something; we all believe in something or someone. When I say I have faith in my doctor, I mean I trust him. When I say I believe in democracy, I mean that I trust it is the best form of government. I can't prove my doctor is trustworthy, I can't even prove democracy is the best form of government. Almost nothing of great importance can be proven. That's why we all have to believe in something, that's why we all have to put our faith—our trust—in something. When I punish a boy, I cannot prove to him that I'm punishing him in order to help him. So when a boy gets punished, I almost always ask him, "Do you believe we care about you, that we are trying—by this punishment—to help you?" Because, if a boy doesn't have faith in us, if he can't see that our punishment is motivated by love, if he can't believe in us, if he can't trust us, he will probably not learn from the punishment.

As I talk with former students, I often try to figure out what it is they believe in, what they put their trust in. Some put their faith in success: "I'll work hard, get a good job, have the money I need to buy things, gain a sense of fulfillment from my success. . . ." Such men believed as boys that getting into a good school would help them, if they worked hard, to get into a good college which would help them, if they worked hard, to get a good job which would help them, if they worked hard, to get a better job and more money and therefore happiness and peace of mind. They held this belief with deep conviction, and they pursued it with devout hard work. They have faith in this promise of fulfillment; they believe that security and peace of mind will be their final reward.

This is the faith of many, many a successful young man in his twenties or thirties. It is, unfortunately, a naive faith, and most people who hold it discover eventually that it cannot sustain them.

I've told you about the conversation I had with a Roxbury Latin graduate as we came out together on the last train, the 10:30 P.M. from South Station a year or so ago. [See Chapter 1.] This former student—now is his early thirties—won all the "glittering prizes" as a boy at Roxbury Latin. His career ever since has made his contemporaries green with envy. After some chit-chat, which included his complaints that the train "left so early," his tone of voice suddenly changed and he said, "Recently, more and more I've been asking myself, Why am I working so hard? Is this all there is to life—hard work to win the next prize? I've been asking myself whether there's any purpose and meaning to things, whether all this hard work adds up to anything real, whether life is worth living."

What he was really saying was that he was losing his faith in the formula for happiness that he'd believed in since he was a boy. That formula—hard work and success—had not brought the happiness he believed it would bring. Even sadder than this young man are men in their forties and fifties, men who are eminent professionals, who define "brightest and best," who discover—as they reach the peak of their profession—the shallowness of this faith in success. I think of an eminent lawyer who has suddenly this year collapsed into depression, I think of an eminent scientist who this year has lost all zest for his work, of a doctor this year who said to me, "I've come to hate all this. I can hardly get out of bed in the morning." The more successful these men have been, the more devastating is their loss of this shallow faith. The bigger they are, the harder they fall.

Last fall I told you about the young man who jumped down off the parapet of the Harvard Square subway kiosk and stopped me in my tracks: "I have AIDS," he said. "How old are you?" I asked him. "Twenty-two," he replied and immediately added, "I'm going to die. When I tell people that, they all say, 'Oh, you'll beat it, you won't die.' But I know I'm dying. I never thought I'd die in my twenties. Nobody will talk to me about it!"

When he was your age, he put his faith in the belief that you get a job so that you have the money to spend your leisure time having fun, finding pleasure. That is the philosophy of many people—regardless of their sexual orientation. Work on the weekdays. Then enjoy your earnings. What this young man never asked was whether any real or lasting satisfaction could come from such a life? Now, dying at age twenty-two, he had discovered that his belief—his faith that happiness came from pleasure—was not adequate to face or cope with life's inevitable reality: death. He had put his faith in an inadequate belief whose promises had turned out to be a lie. "I never thought I'd die in my twenties. Nobody will talk to me about it." He was searching for an adequate faith.

Some of those who have been to the best schools and the best colleges (such as the one you all attend) carefully dress themselves in the garments of modesty. Underneath, however, they really regard themselves as the brightest and best, as urbane sophisticates who are too wise to share the unsophisticated religious beliefs of common people. And yet perhaps no group has been more credulous, more naively taken in by preposterous beliefs than these well educated and privileged young people who regard themselves as the brightest and best. Arguably, no group has put its faith so naively—trusted so credulously—in inadequate beliefs.

When I was a young priest in Cleveland, Lyndon Johnson declared the great War on Poverty. The premise underlying this ill-fated, ruinously costly, and risibly unsuccessful "war" was the touching belief that poverty, indeed that just about everything that was wrong with society, could be cured by huge expenditures of money. I was running a citywide youth program in my parish on a budget of about $1200 a year; so I was keenly interested in how the War on Poverty would affect teenagers. I went to meet the well-paid people who came to Cleveland—with their millions—to work with young people as part of the War on Poverty. They were supplied with expensive steel desks and push-button phones and bookcases stacked with professional psychological journals. They had tons of money at their disposal, and I naively believed they were going to transform the youth scene in Cleveland. Extravagant sums were expended, programs were planned that sounded wonderful. But in the end almost nothing happened. Very few actual, live adolescents were affected. The crime rate among young people actually increased. All the highly paid experts sent by Washington talked to each other on their phones, and only a tiny fraction of them ever had contact with young people. Hardly a single life was changed or touched for the better. And, no. I am not exaggerating.

I am not advocating the abolition of government programs, but I am telling you that the belief that people are transformed by money or by government bureaucrats is naive.

I am also telling you that the brilliantly successful young man I sat with on the train had placed his faith in an inadequate belief that couldn't withstand the reality of life. I am also telling you that the twenty-two-year-old dying of AIDS in Harvard Square had no belief adequate to sustain him in the face of the reality of his own death.

That's what I mean by the credulity of "enlightened" modern man, that's why I say that perhaps no age has believed so naively in inadequate faiths: the faith that promotion and success bring real happiness, the faith that pleasure brings real happiness, the faith that government money will solve the problems of society.

Maimonides, the Talmudist, spoke of such credulity in the twelfth century when he said this to the young men who were his pupils:

> *Awake from your slumbers, you who have fallen asleep in life, and reflect on your deeds. Remember your Creator. Be not of those who miss reality in the pursuit of shadows, who waste their years seeking vain things that neither profit nor deliver. . . . (Repentance, Code of Law 3,4)*

Faith in God

In every age and in every culture, life has driven many of the deepest people to put their faith in God. God is called by many names and approached by many different pathways. We tend to think of the late twentieth century as an unreligious time, something (by the way) the statistics do not bear out. Every age thinks it is less religious than previous ages. The Book of Samuel (from the Hebrew Scriptures), written nearly three thousand years ago, says, in recounting the story of the boy Samuel: "The word of God was rare in those days; few people had vision." G. K. Chesterton characterized every age when he spoke of "the idolatry of the immediate to the exclusion of the ultimate." People in every age are so preoccupied with immediate demands that they neglect to deal with the ultimate issues of life.

It is therefore, not surprising, that many of us become aware of God only when other beliefs fail us, only when we recognize a deep need, an unfulfilled longing within ourselves. In all the great religions, as far as I can tell, God comes to those who recognize they are in need, who experience a yearning for something more. In Christianity, for instance, when (as Christians believe) God became a human being, he was not born in a palace in Alexandria or Rome to very busy and successful "brightest-and-best parents," but to a peasant couple who were Jews—a race despised by the rulers of the Roman Empire—in a cattle shed in a remote province called Palestine. The guests in the inn— which had no room for Mary and Joseph—didn't know anything special had happened that night. The emperor in Rome died without ever knowing anything about this baby. Only the shepherds—regarded as the lowest class of society because their work prevented them from keeping all the rituals of Judaism—only the shepherds were aware that something significant had occurred. They were watching their flocks in the quiet of the night. They were listening. While the brightest and best, the important people, slept, it was the shepherds who heard the angels sing. A few days later, the magi (variously three kings or three wise men) arrived at the cattle shed following a long journey from the

Orient. They were following a star, searching for something, seeking a deeper understanding of reality. They were rich (as we can tell from their gifts) and they were leaders of their society—they were, like the Roxbury Latin boy on the train, successful—they were "the brightest and best" in their society. But somehow their faith in success had let them down. Even though they had wealth and power, they were nonetheless in need; they longed for something more than they had; they went in search of something distant, something beyond the confines of their lives.

Those who recognize their need, who are honest enough to see the emptiness and inadequacy of their lives, those who search for God in their need, always find him. The magi found the baby in the manger.

The Hebrew Scripture records how Jacob fled from his angry brother Esau (whose birthright he stole) and from his mother and father. Alone, homeless under the stars, with a stone for his pillow, Jacob dreamed of a ladder reaching up to God who told him: "I am the Lord, the God of your father Abraham, the God of Isaac." When Jacob woke he said, "Surely the Lord is in this place and I did not know it. How awesome this place is. This is none other than the house of God. This is the gate of Heaven." Unexpectedly, when Jacob was alone, broken, when he was bereft of all the false faith in career or money or status, God came to him in his need.

"The Lord was always in this place, and I didn't realize it. I didn't recognize him—until now," says Jacob. My best course at St. Mark's was music with a man we called "Doc" Sheppard. He taught us to hear things in music we didn't know were there. I remember protesting, "I don't hear what you're talking about." A friend of mine joined in, shouting angrily, "There's nothing there!" But we all—eventually—heard. It had always been there, but we didn't hear it at first.

That's what happened to Jacob. He suddenly "heard" God. He suddenly became aware of the God who was always there. Since God is God (and infinitely beyond our understanding as mortals)—since God is what Rudolph Otto calls "the utterly Other"—we get only hints of God's presence, intimations of the Divine in the midst of our human lives. That's what Jacob felt. Alone, acutely aware of his human frailty, he was (as Wordsworth put it) "surprised by joy."

These hints or intimations of God come in moments when we experience what is beautiful and good and true. We hear and are lifted beyond ourselves by a moment of surpassingly beautiful music. Then it is gone. Even if we play it over and over, it cannot be grasped and held onto. Walter Oakeshott wrote of looking at great works of art: "The statue, even if it is a statue by Michelangelo himself, the painting, even if by Leonardo, is not beauty itself, but a sort of ghost of the real beauty. In time, the stone is broken, the colours fade; the canvas or the wood perishes." The real beauty is beyond all its earthly imitations and representations, beyond all the earthly intimations and hints. It is at the top of Jacob's ladder. It is above the passing things of earth; it transcends time.

At Greg Elinson's Bar Mitzvah last month, I was struck again by one expression of this aboveness, this beyondness, in the service. The Torah scroll is brought from the ark and read. Then it is carried through the congregation. People reach out (their hand covered with their prayer shawl) to touch the scroll. That scroll is regarded as sacred because it is a visible representation of the eternal law of the invisible God who was there long before we were born and who will be there long after we are forgotten. We reach out in the midst of our lives for what is lasting and eternal.

At my church in Dorchester this Christmas, a woman I've never seen before came to the altar rail and knelt to receive the Blessed Sacrament—her hands held out, seeking the eternal in the midst of the transitory—her eyes filled with longing. It was one of those sudden arresting moments in which time stands still. My grandmother used to tell me about an odd thing that happened to her during World War II. With many others, she was standing on Fifth Avenue in New York City, watching a contingent of young men in the army march to the Queen Mary to sail to England to fight in the war. One young man completely unknown to her—out of the thousands marching by—gazed deeply into my grandmother's eyes and she into his. It was only for a fleeting second, but she referred to him often: I wonder if he lived, she'd say. I wonder if he died. That's how I felt with this woman at the altar rail. Our eyes connected for a split second that lasted an eternity. As I placed the Sacrament in her outstretched hands, she whispered, "Thank you, padre." (I looked for her when the mass had ended, but she had vanished and I had to ask myself if she had been there at all.) God always nourishes those who stretch out their hands to him in longing hope. Such yearning always finds what it seeks.

Some years ago I shared with my section of senior English some thoughts similar to these I'm sharing with you now. A highly successful senior, one of the brightest and best—recently admitted to the college of his choice—rejected my thoughts. In essence what he said was: "I've got what I want. I'm not in need and don't expect to be. I'm sorry if others are needy, but I'm not. They may need God, but I don't." He was right to this extent: if you think you have the world pretty much by the tail, if you think you have pretty much everything you need, you will in all likelihood not meet God. God doesn't usually burst into people's lives. Jesus says, "Behold I stand at the door and knock." God comes into your life only if you open the door. Recently that boy—now very much a man—reminded me of the class discussion that day. I only vaguely recalled it. "It took me a long time," he told me, "and my life was nearly destroyed, before I was able to hear God knocking at the door to my life, and open it to him."

Faith As a Virtue

St. Paul calls faith a virtue. For many years, that stuck me as odd. I suppose there is a virtue of sorts in recognizing one's humanity, one's mortality, one's need. "I know I am only a man," says Sophocles' hero—King Theseus—in *Oedipus at Colonus*. That recognition—"I know I am only a man"—is the perfect expression of the humility that Sophocles regards as the starting point of true piety, as the recognition of our true place in the scheme of things.

But faith, I now realize, is a virtue in another way as well. Faith is not just that momentary realization of the God who is beyond us—that glimpse of reality, that intimation of beauty and truth—faith also involves holding on to that vision.

Only rarely in life are we on the mountaintop—with a momentary glorious vision. More frequently, we are plodding our way through the valley—sometimes even through the valley of the shadow of death. That is when faith becomes, as St. Paul says, a virtue, when we plod on, clinging to the vision we once had on the mountaintop. Faith is a virtue because it takes courage. Jesus says, "He who endures to the end shall be saved." Life has terrible disappointments. Disease and death strike randomly and unfairly. What we hope and slave for is denied us. Even worse, in a way, is what Frances Cornford called "the long littleness of life," getting up on a cold January morning, getting here, grinding out the homework, going hard in the practice, getting home, sitting down to more work, finally staggering to bed. All that requires us to hold onto the vision—to keep the faith—that the effort is somehow worth it.

One January, when I was a parish priest in Cleveland, I got a call to go down to St. Vincent Charity Hospital to see a teenager who had been arrested for, among other things, drug abuse. The phone rang while it was still dark—maybe 4:30 or 5 A.M. It was about ten below zero. Even though I was often called to get up in the night, I was at low ebb; I barely pulled myself together to get dressed and go out into the cold. I have never again been as cold as I was that morning in my car on my way to the hospital. Shortly after I arrived at the emergency room, one of the night cleaners said to me, "Cheer up, Father, you're lucky to be here where it's warm." He was a much better Christian than I. While I (who was so fortunate) was cursing the darkness (wondering if it all was worth it), he (who was far less fortunate), was lighting a candle to enable me to count my many blessings. Faith is a virtue because you have to have the guts to cling to it when you are in the valley and you lose the vision. It may cheer you to know that I have found that, for particularly uncourageous people like myself, God often sends in reinforcements to help just at the right moment.

Some of you—a large number of you (I know because you have told me)—have already recognized how needy you are, have already reached beyond all the passing things of this life (even beyond the glittering prizes you have won) to enter into a relationship with God. One of you said to me recently, "I finally surrendered." Another told me, "I finally said yes." For others of you, the moment will come later—to some dramatically, to some almost imperceptibly. "I know I am only a man," you will say. "Please take my small life—I give it to you, for what it's worth. Perhaps you can help me make something of it."

My final words this morning are inscribed on a plaque in the chapel of Balliol College at Oxford, a plaque in memory of one of the college tutors who died in an accident on Mount Blanc. It summarizes much of what I've been trying so inadequately to convey to you this morning. These are the words on the plaque: "He loved great things and thought little of himself."

21

Hope

 WANT TO TALK this morning about hope. St. Paul calls hope one of the three great virtues: "And now abide faith, hope, charity, these three. . . ."

Hope Is Not Optimism

Let me begin by saying what hope is not. Hope is not optimism. My grandfather was a banker in a tiny town in western New York. Once a year he and his fellow small-town bankers gathered in Buffalo. In 1931—in the depths of the depression—when most bankers were barely holding on, a big-time banker came from New York City and addressed this gathering. He made two pronouncements: "Things aren't that bad" and "Things are going to be a lot better soon." My grandfather—and all the other bankers there—knew that things were very bad, and they also knew that things were going to get even worse. Nearly forty years later I could feel the palpable rage in my grandfather's voice when he talked about this optimistic fool.

Hope is not optimism. Hope is not a put-on-a-happy-smile, every-thing-will-be-all-right attitude. Hope is not glib cheerfulness; it has nothing to do with pie in the sky. Hope begins with a stark analysis of how things really are.

Hope starts with the realization that life is filled with tribulations, that things go wrong. I'm amazed by the number of people my age who have not yet accepted that reality—that life is filled with tribulation and that things go wrong. Recently I was on Storrow Drive in rush hour. The car I was in was being driven by a man the age of most of your parents. Evidently this guy expected the rush hour traffic on Storrow

Drive to go sailing along without a hitch. So the minute traffic came to a standstill the guy went berserk: banging the steering wheel, blowing the horn, cursing everybody on the road. He was beside himself.

How much grief we cause ourselves in life by assuming that everything will always go smoothly. How absurd to drive in rush hour traffic and assume there will be no bottlenecks. But we keep making the foolish assumption that life should go smoothly.

Ten days ago I was in London in a taxi at five in the afternoon. I was going from central London to St. Paul's School to have dinner with the high master. It's a twenty-minute journey at worst and—being super-cautious—I allowed thirty-five. The minute I got in the taxi, traffic came to a halt. When it finally moved, it did so at a snail's pace. I soon found myself exclaiming: "This is ridiculous!" "What the hell is going on?" and phrases of a similar nature that I'd rather not repeat. My first fantasies were quite positive: "Spread your wings!" I said to the driver. But it was not long before my fantasies became violent. I pictured myself as James Bond's 007 obliterating the cars ahead—driving right over them. I was not the picture of calm maturity accepting the reality that life is full of tribulation.

Not only is life filled with tribulation, it is unfair and unjust. Waiting for me when I got back to Boston were three letters from parents of boys we'd rejected for admission. The most strident of the three wrote: "You've done my son a grave injustice; you've probably ruined his life!" Soon some of you in Class I will experience—as others have every year—a huge sense of injustice, of unfairness, as some classmates luck out in the college admissions sweepstakes while you lose out. But a college-admissions injustice is trivial when set beside life's real injustices: real injustice is what happened to a nineteen-year-old boy in my parish in Dorchester. Six months ago, trying to break up a fight, he was shot through the head. He is now a vegetable, and yet the wonders of modern medicine will probably keep him alive for decades. Trying to do good by breaking up a fight, your whole future is taken away. *That's* injustice. Let me tell you, don't try any glib, put-on-a-happy-smile optimism on Darryl's family.

"In the world," says Jesus, "ye shall have tribulation." Life is not fair, not just. And in the end you die. If you're Billy McDonald, at 6'2", 200 pounds of vital good health and captain of the Roxbury Latin football team, you die of cancer when you're eighteen years old. If you're the 102-year-old deaf and nearly blind lady to whom I take Communion, you may linger to 105. But the reality is that—sooner or later—we all die.

Our own lives, then, are filled with tribulation—and, beyond our own selfish concerns, when we look out on the world, we find little to be cheerful about. My early years at Roxbury Latin were spent fretting about the very real prospect of nuclear holocaust. As the threat of nuclear annihilation recedes, in its place come terrorism and violence: a bomb in Jerusalem, a bomb in London, sixteen innocent children killed in their school in Scotland, Darryl Braithwaite in Dorchester. You can all furnish your own examples.

Hope then should not be confused with optimism. Optimism denies reality and strives for pie in the sky. Hope begins by accepting the cruel realities of human existence—tribulation, injustice, danger, and death—and strives to find meaning in the face of these realities.

Hope Finds a Reason to Live

Educational researchers now estimate that only about twenty percent of our total intelligence is measured by current I.Q. tests. The I.Q.—intelligence quotient—test was invented by a Roxbury Latin alumnus, Edward Lee Thorndike, Class of 1891, professor of psychology at Columbia. It measures only the intellectual aspect of our intelligence. And we all know—know from Roxbury Latin and universal experience—that many people with very high I.Q.'s are tremendous failures in life. That's why people are now talking about emotional I.Q. as being more important. Motivation—what one psychologist insists on calling a "can-do attitude"—seems more crucial to success in life than the narrow kind of intelligence measured by the I.Q. test. Mr. Chauncey knew all this before it was discovered by the researchers. He has, for years, said an applicant's "I will" is more important than his I.Q.

That "I will," that "can do" attitude, that inner motivation that enables you to accomplish something is founded upon hope. Real hope finds a purpose amid the cruel realities of life. That purpose provides motivation.

As I was flying back from London a week ago today, I read *The Imaginary Girlfriend*, the new memoir of John Irving, one of the great contemporary American writers. It's only about 130 pages and I read it straight through on the plane. As a boy, Irving was dyslexic; he was admitted to Phillips Exeter Academy only because his father was a faculty member. To survive he had to spend at least twice as long on any assignment as his classmates. He knew—realistically—that the odds were against him. But the hope of survival motivated him to superhuman hard work in the classroom. Outside the classroom his wrestling coach told him that he was not a great athlete but that with hard work he could become "a halfway decent" wrestler. Irving was realistic about his abilities, and the hope of becoming "halfway decent" motivated him to put forth a huge effort. He goes on to claim that he is not a naturally talented writer, but that he is a great reviser. Wrestling, he says, requires you to practice a hold over and over and over. Great writing requires revision and revision and revision. This dyslexic student who ranked at the bottom of his class, this modestly successful wrestler who won no tournaments, is now the most famously successful Exerter graduate of his era.

Hope comes from the gut. Hope gives you the motivation to endure the hard work, the pain, the exhaustion that are part of any worthwhile endeavor. That's why hope is a virtue. All of you have experienced discouragement, and most of you have proven you can overcome discouragement to fight through the pain, do the assignment, get the work done, learn the hold.

A boy in the Class of 1991 went on to Harvard where he was wrestling captain his senior year. As many of you know, he has been teaching and coaching wrestling at another school in our league this year. I was talking with him when he came here with his wrestlers in January. Commenting on them he said, "Our kids are extremely well coached, they're physically in superb condition, and they're better athletes across the board than the Roxbury Latin wrestlers." "Well," I interrupted. "Sounds like you're announcing a win." "No," he replied. "We'll probably lose. The Roxbury Latin boys have an inner strength—they'll win on toughness, mental, maybe it's spiritual, toughness." He was right.

That toughness defines what St. Paul means by hope: setting a goal, realizing the huge odds against you, and fighting all-out to achieve it nonetheless. I went with Bill Oates, one of our life trustees (a Groton School graduate), to raise money from a prospective donor. The donor asked him, "What's special about Roxbury Latin boys?" Quick as a flash, Mr. Oates replied, "They're hungry." By hungry, he meant that Roxbury Latin boys are motivated, ambitious; they possess an inner strength and determination that does not give up in the face of exhaustion, discouragement, setback. They have what the modern educational researchers call "long-range motivation." They have what St. Paul calls hope: in the face of heavy odds they will battle on—not in optimism, but in hope.

In the *Inferno* Dante describes the entrance to Hell—over which the famous words are written: "All hope abandon, ye who enter here." In addition to describing the real Hell, Dante was describing hell on earth: We experience hell on earth when we lose our motivation, when we lose the hope we've just been talking about. From time to time, we've all experienced that kind of paralysis, that kind of ennui, that loss of hope and motivation. We've all asked in mid-February or early April, "Is it worth it?" And we've all struggled to regain the hope that will enable us to go on.

Our Hope for Years to Come

And that struggle brings me to my final point: If you are struggling to live in hope, to cling in hope to a motivating sense of purpose, you will in all likelihood turn to God. Almost all men and women involved in a great cause turn to God. It is frequently noted that "there are no atheists in foxholes." When you're being shot at and your life is on the line, you turn instinctively to God. It is also frequently noted that virtually everyone elected to the presidency becomes more religious (I don't mean makes more of a show of his religion—some do and some don't do that for political purposes. I mean in the privacy of his own heart, every president comes into a deeper relationship with God.) Likewise, I have known no parent with a very sick child who doesn't pray.

Like many of you, I was a very successful teenager—pretty much everything went my way and I got more than my share of the glittering prizes. Not until I was in my late twenties was I figuratively driven to my knees. It wasn't something bad in my own (rather charmed) life that drove me to my knees. It was my involvement, as a parish priest, with people who were dealt cruel blows—people (many of whom) I loved as much or even more than myself. Their suffering drove me to my knees. If your own lack of motivation, your own weaknesses, your own vulnerability, your own suffering don't force you to your knees, your anguish over those you love will do so.

God always answers prayer—sometimes in his infinite wisdom he gives us an answer we don't like or cannot understand. This week both Jews and Christians celebrate the central defining event of their religion—in which God responded favorably and with dramatic clarity. Jews celebrate the Passover: God's saving of the Israelites from the armies of Pharaoh as they escaped Egypt. And Christians celebrate Easter: the resurrection of Jesus Christ from the dead. In these events God answered human prayer in a decisive way. The Israelites were spared, the early Christians experienced Christ alive in their lives.

God does sometimes answer our prayers in a dramatic—what we might call miraculous—way. More often, however, God answers our prayers—gives us insight into things—in a quiet way. And you have to listen carefully to hear him. If you are listening for an answer to your prayers and yearnings (I say yearnings because our deepest prayers are often not articulated in words), if you are listening for God's response, you may well (to your surprise) hear it. God gives us occasional glimpses into the meaning of things in small, quiet ways.

When I was a student at Cambridge and studying philosophical theology, I became quite deeply troubled (as many before me had been) by the problem of evil. The Cold War tensions—including the Cuban Missile Crisis—were at their peak in my Cambridge years and there was much talk of the extinction of the human race. As I was in the midst of stewing about the problem of evil and the prospect of the triumph of evil in a nuclear holocaust, a friend of mine and I decided to bicycle to Ely—a distance of about fifteen miles from Cambridge. This is one of the flattest regions of England, but the road to Ely is a steady incline up all the way, a tough ride over, an easy coast back. Midway to Ely we paused to catch our breath by the side of the road and talked to a farmer—who was catching his breath at the side of his field. We could see the vestiges of an airfield on his land. The U.S. and Royal Air Forces built many airfields in this area in World War II because it's so flat and so near the continent. The farmer said, "Yes. The Americans came in here. They leveled everything. Poured poison all over the ground, then gravel, then concrete, finally asphalt. I remember the U.S. Army engineer saying, 'Nothing will grow here for a thousand years.' Look at it now." Everywhere the asphalt was disintegrating, the concrete below was cracked, and vegetation was reasserting itself through the cracks. It was 1961—a mere fifteen years after the war had ended.

It was as if God had answered my unspoken prayer and at least hinted that ultimately good triumphs over evil and life over death.

I'll give you one other—again seemingly trivial—example. When I got to London two weeks ago, I was at low ebb—exhausted, disillusioned by the terrible way a treasured colleague had been treated, worried about the sickness of one friend and the collapsing marriage of another. I had lost perspective. I was running on empty.

To add to my self-indulgent despondency, I was on a local train to Canterbury. On a fast train you can get from London to Canterbury in an hour and a half, but I had missed the fast train, so I was on a local that took two hours and stopped at every station in England. The train, like most British local trains, was made up of old equipment—railway carriages (as the British call them) from the 1950s. British railway doors of that era only opened from the outside, so to exit the train you have to pull down the window, lean out and turn the outer door handle. All manner of people got off the train at each little station—ladies in their eighties, mothers with babies, businessmen, and scruffy school kids talking and joking loudly. I'm sorry to have to admit that I found these people ugly and depressing. In fact I found everything about the journey ugly and depressing. Then suddenly I noticed that as each passenger got out, he or she pushed the window down, reached outside to open the door, and then—this is the significant thing—closed the window and closed the door. I watched this happen perhaps twenty times. Not a single person left the window down or the door open. Not a single one was so wrapped up in himself that he didn't take the time to close the window and close the door. This small act of responsibility, of thoughtfulness —repeated over and over—changed my mood, transformed my outlook. Maybe the human race wasn't so ugly and depressing after all.

If we are looking and listening, God sometimes gives us glimpses of the meaning of life, surprises us with joy, renews our hope.

Above me—on the frieze of this hall—is an eighteenth century paraphrase of the first line of the Founder's favorite psalm, Psalm 90: "O God our help in ages past, our hope for years to come." God was here long before the Founder, long before us, and God will be here long after we are gone. It is we who come and go—act our fleeting little role on the stage of life, and then exit. In ages past, God was there for our forbearers—and he is our hope now and in the years to come until our earthly life is over. That's why the psalmist of Israel says, "Lord, Thou hast been our refuge from one generation to another."

This Lord has inspired men and women with new hope in every generation. At the lowest point in the history of Israel, in 587 BCE, when Nebuchadnezzar's conquering Babylonian army laid siege to the City of Jerusalem, the prophet Jeremiah—the prophet who had made himself unpopular by warning his people that this disaster was coming—purchased a piece of property on the outskirts of the city. He invested in Israel's future at a time when its future looked absolutely hopeless.

"These are the words of the Lord of Hosts, the God of Israel," said Jeremiah. "The time will come when houses, fields, and vineyards will again be bought and sold in this land." God is our hope as he was Jeremiah's. When you are unmotivated—when you are living in the human hell of paralysis and ennui—God can give you new hope, new energy, new life.

In 1652, when England was bleeding to death in civil war, a man named Robert Shirley built a church. When he died, a plaque was erected in his memory in the church. This is what it says: "In the year 1652 when throughout England all things sacred were either profaned or neglected, this church was built by Sir Robert Shirley, Bart., Whose special praise it is to have done the best things in the worst of times and to have hoped [the best things] in the most calamitous [times]."

Hope is not optimism. Hope is realistic. It recognizes that life is hard, that it is unjust, that it is dangerous, that it ends for us in our death. But hope finds a reason to live, the motivation to live well in the midst of life's realities. Hope recognizes that we are weak and vulnerable and that we need help from a source beyond ourselves—from the God who has been "our help in ages past" and who is "our hope for years to come." All of you are going to die—some sooner, some later. What will they say about you? My prayer is that they will say about you what they said about Sir Robert Shirley: that in the worst of times you did the best things, and in the most calamitous of times you hoped the best things.

22

Charity

T. PAUL speaks of three abiding virtues—faith, hope, and love—and he concludes by saying "the greatest of these is love." This morning I want to speak about love. It's difficult to speak about this greatest of virtues because the word "love" is used in so many different ways in the English language.

"I love football," said a boy to me at Coach Guerra's football camp this summer. He clearly didn't mean sexual love, or brotherly love; he meant, I really enjoy football, I really like football.

Recently a young alumnus—speaking of his girlfriend—said to me, "Now I know what it means to be in love." Here the use of the word "love" clearly indicates erotic love, emotional infatuation. My friend Tony Campbell, in fact, says we shouldn't talk about "being in love"—but rather about "being in heat." When this young alumnus in heat told me about being in "love," he clearly meant something different from the boy who said, "I love football."

When your family, friends, or teachers tell you they love you, they do not mean what either the boy who loved football or the alumnus in love meant. They mean, "I care about you." I heard a father this summer say to his obnoxious son, "Right now I don't like you—in fact, I dislike you, but I still love you." This is the love that St. Paul calls the greatest of virtues. This is the love I want to talk about this morning.

This love has little or nothing to do with attraction, little or nothing to do with liking. You don't "fall" into this kind of love. It's not something that happens to you. This love is a willed concern that you have to initiate. It's not even something that necessarily "feels good." It's often difficult and inconvenient, unpleasant and costly.

Love Is Putting on an Act

Last December I took aside a member of the school community and told him that people often found him negative, snappish, short-fused, and self-absorbed, and I told him things had to change. Virtually overnight he changed. Virtually overnight he became what St. Paul meant by a loving person. In May, I told him how pleased I was by how he had changed. I said, "People now find you cheerful, upbeat, open, patient, and sympathetic." He responded by saying, "I'm glad you're happier with me, but I have to tell you it's all an act. I haven't changed on the inside at all."

The first thing I want to say about love is that it is an act. Love is acting patient on the outside with others when you are burning on the inside with some concern of your own. Love is acting patient when you're feeling frazzled, put-upon, and harassed. Last month I was celebrating Mass at 9:00 on a Saturday morning at my parish in Dorchester. After that I was going to drive to New Hampshire to have lunch with a couple who are longtime and dear friends of mine. Our time was limited, because both they and I had afternoon engagements. I was just about to leave the church for New Hampshire when an old man I'd never seen before—who was not a member of the parish—appeared. He wanted to tell me all his troubles. I wanted to scream, "Why me? Why now? Why today?" Forty-five minutes later I was still listening to an apparently endless list of problems. My patience was a complete act. Inside, my real self was shouting at the old man, "You self-centered old windbag, go off and bore someone else with your stupid problems." Instead, I acted the role of the loving priest: "Oh, I'm sorry to hear that," "Oh, how did that happen?" "Oh, what a terrible thing." To all appearances I was the very soul of sympathy, understanding, and patience, the quintessence of love. It was all an act. Love is often an act: it is the curbing of your own natural desires, it is willed caring for another person when you'd really like to be caring about your own needs.

Those of you who have been at this school for a while know that—

following ancient Jewish custom—we try to show particular concern for strangers and visitors who come to here. Last year I witnessed a Roxbury Latin boy struggle with himself. I was inside Rousmaniere Hall; I'd just turned out the lights. The door was propped open into the loggia. I stood inside the door, in the darkness under the balcony, watching this little drama. Bounding along the front loggia, the boy bumped right into some visitors entering the School's front door. First, he walked by them. His first instinct, like mine in Dorchester, was to escape: I don't have time today; I'm in a rush; I have something important I have to do; I'll do the right thing the next time. But this was a tough kid who wasn't able to rationalize running away from his obligation to love, and so—reluctantly—he stopped and turned around and said to the visitors, "Can I help you?" "We're looking for the admissions office," they replied. He started to give them directions. Then he said—rather sourly—"Never mind. I'll take you there." Then hearing the edge on his own voice, he added in a much sweeter tone: "I'm so-and-so, and I remember being lost when I first visited the School." And as he walked away with them, he conversed with the boy, asking him questions and making comments about the School.

It was an act. He had things he wanted to do. He was not feeling generous with his time. He was feeling put-upon, but he *acted* generous. He was busily occupied with his own life, but he acted patient. He was all wrapped up in himself, but he acted interested in them. That is what St. Paul means by love: willed concern for others when you don't feel like it.

A lot of people will advise you to "be your real self." It's terrible advice. Your real self is egocentric and self-seeking. If the boy I've just been talking about had done what his "real self" had urged him to do, he'd have trucked right on by those strangers and done exactly what he wanted without any interruption or inconvenience. So I'll give you the opposite advice: "Don't be your real self."

Love—the virtuous love St. Paul talks about—is not usually natural or instinctive. You don't usually feel it, it doesn't happen to you. You have to will it. And far from feeling good, it is often inconvenient and costly. It requires maturity, self-control, and toughness to overcome your natural instincts in order to love. Love is often a mask we put on that hides our real selves. Love is often putting on an act.

Love Is Intolerant

When you put on the act of love, the first thing you do is to put yourself in the other person's place. The Roxbury Latin boy did this when he said to the visitors in the hallway, "I remember what it was like when I first visited the School." Love first seeks to understand, to see where the other person is coming from.

Bobby Kennedy used to say that a quarter of the world is opposed to everything all the time. He was really talking about the "NBC" crowd—the naggers, bitchers, and complainers, the people who approach life with a chip on their shoulders, the people with an "attitude." Love not only seeks to understand, but love assumes good, looks for good, seeks, if possible, to affirm, seeks to see others in the best possible light.

During the Olympics I watched a local TV station interview the mother of a small child who had been rescued from her burning home by a teenage boy who lived nearby. In the interview, she said, "I feel terrible. I've always thought of him as a loser. Now he's done something that makes him deserve a medal more than anyone in the Olympics. He's a hero and I always thought he was a loser." We often do that with others. We see only what's wrong with them, not what's good. Love seeks to understand, love looks for good in others, love seeks to affirm.

And yet—and this seems to contradict what I've just said—"Love is intolerant." The 1990s have elevated toleration to top rank among the virtues, so to call love intolerant goes against the spirit of our time. But the fact remains that love is intolerant.

Each year a number of seniors ask me to read their college essays. And I'm happy to do so. Several years ago one of the class's strongest students gave me his essay to read. I expected great things, but what he gave me was an extremely pretentious and excruciatingly boring essay on his recipe for the reform of world government. It was pompous windbaggery of the highest magnitude. I tried to be as sensitive as I could, but I had to tell him that his essay was atrocious. He was furious: "No," he said. "It's an excellent essay. I'm sorry you can't understand how good it is." I explained to him why it was terrible, and his anger turned to hurt. Finally, in tears, he said, "You're always telling us how much you love us and yet you've just torn me to shreds." I said to him, "I haven't torn you to shreds, I've torn your essay to shreds. It's because I love you so much that I've told you that your essay is atrocious." (Love is intolerant. If you love a person, you are sometimes intolerant of things he does and says.) This was a smart kid and he ended up writing a brilliant essay in the end. In less than a week he was saying, "I can't believe what garbage that first essay was."

It's my experience that the people who "speak the truth in love" to you—even when they're wrong (and they sometimes are)—are the ones who really love you, the ones who really care about you.

When I was a boy at St. Mark's School, we had a track meet for the entire school at the end of each year. My best athletic talent was sprinting and I was sure I'd be first in the school in the 100 and 220 as a sophomore. But I finished second in the 220. When I crossed the finish line, I uttered a four-letter word—I didn't shout it, but it was audible to the master who was timing the race. He walked over to me, grabbed me by the front of my T-shirt, slapped me very hard on the face, and said, "Don't you ever say that again. You're too good."

That night I went to see him. After I finished apologizing I asked him, "Could I inquire what you meant when you said, 'You're too good.'?" He said, "I see you as a great kid who should have the inner strength to be a good loser, to handle disappointment with class. I struck you to get your attention because I care about you and have high hopes for you." *That* is love, willed caring, intolerant of what is second rate.

People who take the time to criticize you are often, in my experience, the ones who love you the most.

One of the saddest events of the summer was an accident in which a teenage boy who'd been drinking was driving a car, hit a tree, and killed two of his buddies. Several of his friends knew he'd been drinking and all of them knew they should have prevented him from driving. There they were—on TV, when it was too late—saying, "We should have stopped him." Love is intolerant. It risks unpopularity and unpleasantness to do the right thing.

Happiness Comes from Loving

Love, then, is hard. Love demands that you intervene with a friend, even if it will make you unpopular, even if it will involve unpleasantness. Love is also costly. It demands that you squelch your own needs, squelch your own impatience, squelch your own desires, in order to treat another person with compassion, patience, and understanding. Love is often inconvenient—as it was for the boy who stopped to help the visitors at the front door.

If love is often hard and costly, if it sometimes causes unpopularity and inconvenience and postponement of your own needs, why then should we love?

The answer, again paradoxically, is that real happiness in life only comes to those who are able to care about others at some cost to themselves.

For one thing, when you act in a loving way, you often become loving. You are able to take on the role and you become nearly as good as you act.

Some years ago we had a sophomore here who, despite our best efforts, remained arrogant, disdainful, unwilling to curb his own selfishness, unwilling to take the time or effort to be kind to or concerned for others. He was a brilliant kid—and he had all sorts of rationalizations for his behavior. Finally, we had a showdown with him and threatened to boot him if he didn't change. He was very angry. He told his advisor, "You can force me to change my outward behavior, but you'll never change the real me. I don't value being patient or generous or kind the way you do. I'll never change inside." His advisor, wisely, told him that all the School had any jurisdiction over was his outward behavior. And, in fact, the boy's outward behavior did improve dramatically, and we were satisfied.

Shortly after his graduation from college, he called me and asked if he could take me to lunch or dinner. A few nights later, at dinner, he reminded me (which I'd forgotten) about our ultimatum to him in Class III and his response. He then said, "That confrontation was the most important thing that ever happened to me. You forced me to break out of my lifelong pattern of behavior. You made me act kind and patient, and I found I actually liked being kind and patient. By forcing me to change my outward behavior, you actually changed who I was on the inside."

This boy was not the first—nor will he be the last—to discover that the outward practice of love leads to an inward disposition to love. He was not the first—nor will he be the last—to discover that the practice of love brings with it an inner happiness. He discovered what many had discovered before him, that after you have done something loving you are glad you paid the price to do it, that the cost and inconvenience are small in comparison to the reward of inner happiness.

I have been present at a number of deaths. I've never yet heard a dying man or woman brag about how much money he made or how successful he was. My experience is that a dying man looking back on his life is proudest of having helped people, of having used his time and talents to do something for others.

If you want to be happy, then, you must learn to love: to pay the price of caring for others, of putting them first, of inconveniencing yourself. That is the pathway to happiness. And the time to start is now. John Wesley, the great nineteenth-century founder of Methodism, put it best when he said, "I expect to pass through this world but once. Any good I can do, therefore, or any kindness I can show to any fellow creature, let me do it. Let me not defer or neglect it, for I shall not pass this way again."

You only get one life. Let it be said of you, "He had the courage and strength to love, the courage and strength to conquer his own selfishness in order to care about others."

23

Divine Irresponsibility

OST PEOPLE live in confined little worlds. You are no exception: up early, classes, sports, and activities all day, homework all evening. Many of you believe that this confined little world promises certain rewards: work hard, get good grades, get into a good college, get a good job, become happy.

You seniors think—ah, a few more weeks and I'm on to the nirvana of college. But of course, college is more of the same: work hard, get good grades, get a good job, become happy. Last summer I had lunch with a college senior a few days before he went to New York to his high-paying new job. "This is what I've been waiting for," he said. "Now finally I get to the payoff—a great job, a great salary, a great life." When I saw him a month ago, he looked exhausted. He told me he was working fifteen-hour days in order to get promoted. And when he gets promoted, he will undoubtedly work even harder to get promoted again to an even more demanding job.

Studies show that, increasingly, very successful Type A people—such as most of you are—are "waking up" in their late twenties or early thirties and asking, "Why am I doing this? All my hard work and success are not bringing the promised happiness."

Last week I was called by a young man in his late twenties who was diagnosed with what will be, in all likelihood, a quick and fatal cancer. He has always been a person of depth and substance, and when we met there was no beating around the bush about using the word "death." In the course of our conversation I used with him a phrase made famous by the great French existentialist, Albert Camus. Though Camus was an atheist, many of his insights are remarkably similar to the Judeo-Christian understanding of the meaning of life. Camus talks about—and this is the phrase I refer to—"the divine irresponsibility of the condemned man."

If you are condemned to death—if you discover you're going to die— you are strangely liberated. In March 1980, Billy McDonald, the captain of our football team, died after a long struggle with cancer. Minutes before he died, he smiled and said to me, "No more Latin homework!" In the face of life's only certainty—death—the world we live in (whether at school or in business or law or medicine) suddenly seems much smaller and less significant. The prospect of death brings perspective, conveys a divine irresponsibility: we suddenly see how small our world is, and we suddenly realize the unimportance of all the things we considered so important.

It is the perspective that death provides, and the divine irresponsibility that results from that perspective, that I want to focus on this morning.

Faith

We all have a faith—a belief—about the meaning of life. Many of you live by a tiny and confined faith: the one I've already talked about, the faith that if you work hard, get good grades, get into a good college, get a good job, then—here's where the faith comes in—you will be happy.

This is a pathetically tiny and confined faith—one that experience doesn't support and one that doesn't take the realities of life into account. As one very successful Roxbury Latin grad in his thirties put it to me, "Work hard, exhaust yourself, get rich, and die. I want more than that!"

There is more, lots more. There is the far broader and more realistic faith that comes to us—at least to us at Roxbury Latin—from both our classical heritage and our Judeo-Christian heritage. Socrates said to his fellow Athenians, "Gentlemen, I am your very grateful and devoted servant, but I owe a greater obedience to God than to you, and so long as I draw breath and have my faculties, I shall never stop . . . exhorting you. . . . I shall go on saying, in my usual way, my very good friend, you are an Athenian and belong to a city which is the greatest and most famous in the world for its wisdom and strength. Are you not ashamed that you give your attention to acquiring as much money as possible, and similarly with reputation and honor, and give no attention or thought to truth and understanding and the perfection of your soul? And if any of you disputes this and professes to care about these things, I shall not let him go or leave him; no I shall question him and examine him, test him and . . . reprove him for neglecting what is of supreme importance, and giving his attention to trivialities."

Jesus says, summarizing the whole tradition of Judaism: "For what will it profit a man if he gains the whole world and forfeits his own soul? For what does it profit a man to gain the whole world and lose himself?"

Both Socrates and Jesus urge us to go beyond conventional faith (the conventional faith of every age that happiness comes from success and money). Both Socrates and Jesus goad us to a much more daring faith. Only a few in every generation go beyond the conventional to the daring. When I was in London I heard P. D. James—Baroness James, as she now is, in her seventies—the popular novelist who has hit the TV and film jackpot and achieved all the successes promised by the conventional faith (work hard, get rich). She said, arrestingly to me, "There is much, much more to life than striving. Life is more than getting, more than accumulating." She then uttered the striking phrase (taken from English hymnody): "There is another country." There is a much, much larger world, a world vastly beyond the tiny and confined world of those who put their faith in the work-hard-get-rich philosophy.

Former Governor Mario Cuomo alluded to this in a recent speech: "Isn't America searching for something? Despite all the wealth and grandness that is so apparent, insinuating itself is a feeling that something is missing. There's no hero, no heroine, no great cause, no soaring ideology. We are riddled with . . . answers that seem too shallow, too short-sighted. . . . We need something real to believe in, to hold onto. Something deeper, stronger, grander that can help us deal with our problems by making us better than we are—instead of meaner. That can lift our aspirations instead of lowering them."

This school has always existed—in its best eras—to goad and persuade its students to that deeper faith, that wider perspective.

There are people who never experience a Beethoven piano concerto—who are never transported beyond the narrow confines of their lives to another country, to an experience of something beyond. I hope you won't be among them. Some of what we teach you here is practical, useful in the confined world of "get ahead—be happy." But the highest goal of our endeavors here is to take you beyond those narrow confines—to another country.

I believe that, when Camus talked about "the divine irresponsibility of the condemned man," he was urging us to see the shallowness of the conventional faith. He was urging us, to use P. D. James's words, to see that "life is more than striving, more than getting, more than accumulating." Camus was urging us to base our lives on a profounder faith, one that takes account of death, of life's shortness, of life's deepest and most ultimate questions, one that—to use the words of Socrates and Jesus—takes into account the well-being of our souls. A faith that takes into account life's shortness and life's deepest and most ultimate questions is the only faith that can bring us real happiness.

Most of your contemporaries believe that happiness comes from accumulation and success. Dare to be different. Dare to be among the few who believe that happiness comes from risking defeat in trying to do something great with your lives.

Hope

We all have our hopes. We all hope certain things are going to happen in the future for us. Hope, like faith, however, can be confined and conventional or it can be daring and soaring.

This past winter, a senior (a boy I really love and admire) said to me, "I've already learned that you should not build up hopes about people. I'm realistic. It's best not to open yourself up very much, it's best not to trust anyone very far. That way you're never disappointed, that way you never get hurt."

Well, he's right. If you never take any risks, you'll never lose. If you never make yourself vulnerable to another person, you'll never get hurt. If you never attempt anything great, if you have never set big goals or have high hopes, you'll never be disappointed. But what a narrow and, frankly, cowardly way to live. If you spend your whole life trying to avoid pain in human relationships, you'll never find any joy, because joy in human relationships comes when you risk letting people see who you really are—a risk that makes you extremely vulnerable. If you share your inner self with someone, he could betray you. If you invite another person to do something with you, he may say no and you will feel hurt and rejected. But he also may say yes and you will feel happy. No risk of pain, no chance of gain.

Hope is central to all deep human relationships. Hope gives you courage to be vulnerable, to risk the hurt of possible rejection.

Hope is also central to happiness in every other realm of human experience. Most people don't dream great dreams or hope great hopes. Their hopes are confined and limited: get a job, earn a living. I talked this vacation with a young Harvard graduate who is prepared to set aside all the conventional hopes—and lucrative opportunities already offered him elsewhere—to start a school in the inner city of Boston for disadvantaged children. You can just imagine how many people have told him to "be practical" and get on with his life. You can just imagine how tempting it is for him to set aside his dreams and hopes to do the conventional thing. But he's going to risk everything and leave himself wide open to the distinct possibility of failure.

I pray that, in your own lives, you will dare to have high hopes, not only in your relationships with others, but in what you do with your lives. Cast fear aside. Let your hope be divinely irresponsible. No risk of pain, no chance of gain.

Love

Finally (and you can see this coming), I urge you to love with divine irresponsibility.

Cynics will tell you that there is no such thing as selfless love, that there is no such thing as a good person. The press today regard it as their principal calling to go all out to try to find the feet of clay of everyone who appears to be good. It's almost the national sport now to debunk, to tear down, to point out imperfections.

By the narrowest definition, I suppose absolutely pure selfless love is rare. I have myself said, on numerous occasions, to a boy, "I love you, and I don't want or expect anything back from you in return for my love." In the narrowest sense I suppose that's not absolutely true. I sometimes get something back: a sense of satisfaction, I suppose, if I can see my love for someone helps him. I also get something back, I suppose, if he thanks me at some future point. Deep inside, we probably all want to think we've had some impact or made a difference, and we all want to be thanked. But often I don't get anything back—no sense of having an impact, no gratitude. If you love someone without expectation of getting anything back, that is selfless love. And there is, I submit, a lot of selfless love in the world.

One—I suppose, spectacular—example of selfless love happened to British soldiers in World War II. Ernest Gordon, a Scotsman, tells the story in his book, *Through the Valley of the Kwai.* These British soldiers, mostly troops of the Scottish Argyll regiment, were prisoners of the Japanese, and they were being worked and starved to death by their Japanese captors.

At the end of a terrible day of slave labor in the hot sun, the Japanese took a quick count and declared that one of the shovels was missing. The Japanese guard insisted that one of the prisoners had stolen it to sell to the Thais for food. He lined up the prisoners and demanded that the thief confess or else, he shouted, "All die! All die!" To show that he meant it, the guard "pulled back the bolt, put the rifle to his shoulder, and looked down the sights ready to fire at the first man he saw at the end of them. At that moment [a young Scottish soldier], stood stiffly to attention and said calmly, 'I did it.'" The soldier had not stolen the shovel, but he knew that unless someone died for all the others, everyone else would die. He was brutally beaten to death in view of all his fellow soldiers.

196

Later that night when the tools were counted again, no shovel was found missing.

There are many similar spectacular stories of selfless love. But, in a way, it's the less spectacular examples of selfless love that are—for us—more relevant.

I know there's such a thing as selfless love because I experienced it and have received it. When I look back on my life, I can see many instances in which I have been loved selflessly by another person. Sometimes I've thanked that person, sometimes I haven't.

Many of you have loved others selflessly—you have been patient with an elderly relative (when you could be doing something much more enjoyable), you have been kind to a younger child, you have helped a neighbor or a friend and expected nothing in return.

In my second year here, I—for the first time—asked students in assembly one morning to take the time to be kind to strangers and show them where the admissions office (or whatever they were looking for) was. I wandered into the faculty room later that morning and one faculty member—who didn't see me come in—was saying, "How naive can you get? Kids are never going to stop and greet strangers. Tony just doesn't understand boys."

He was wrong. I can't tell you how many times in my twenty-three years at Roxbury Latin, I have myself been picked up off the floor by the selfless love—the kindness and sweetness—shown to me by a Roxbury Latin boy or master.

Love—selfless love that expects nothing back—is the most powerful force in the universe. Its impact on both the giver and the receiver is incalculable.

Christian scripture says "God is love." And in the Hebrew tradition there is the wonderful story—which Rabbi Jacobvits, Britain's former chief rabbi, likes to tell—about Solomon's Temple. When Solomon first tried to build the Temple of the Lord in Jerusalem, everything went wrong. Finally, in frustration and despair, he decided to withdraw to his army—in a field on the outskirts of the city—and wait for some unmistakable sign that God wanted a temple to be built. No sign came. Then one night a man walked from his house in the center of Jerusalem to a field on the city outskirts adjoining the field where Solomon was encamped. The man moved a sheaf of drying harvest wheat from the right side of the field to the left. A bit later that same night, another man came from his house in central Jerusalem and moved a sheaf from the left side of the field to the right. This happened for several nights and it really puzzled Solomon. Finally, Solomon had the two men brought to him: "What are you doing?" he said to the first man. The man replied: "My brother has no children and I thought that if he had an abundant-looking harvest he would know that, even with no children, the Lord had blessed him." Then Solomon turned to the other man and said, "What are you doing?" And the man said, "My brother has many children and many mouths to feed, and it seemed to me that he would benefit from having a larger harvest."

Solomon then said, "Where there is such concern for another's well-being, where there is such concern for another's needs, and where there is such desire for God's blessings to be upon others, that is where God truly dwells and that is where I shall build the Lord's Temple." And he did.

God dwells among those who take the divinely irresponsible risk of loving one another selflessly.

Conclusion

When I was a student at Cambridge I did some debating. I was once sucked into a debate on one of those sophistical topics the Brits love so much: "Resolved, cynicism is better than idealism." I was the negative, defending idealism. My opponent concluded his rebuttal by saying, "My honorable opponent is grounded in unreality. He's a hopeless idealist, a naive believer of pie in the sky," and he sat down to great applause.

I responded by saying, "I plead guilty. Show no mercy. I don't regret a word of what I said. I accept the accusation of being an idealist as a crown upon my head, as the ultimate compliment. I rejoice in the accusation with my whole being." Then I turned to my opponent and said,

"You, my honorable opponent, are a gutless wonder, hiding in fear behind your cynicism, the last refuge of all sniveling little cowards such as yourself. And let me tell you, when you die, no one will ever accuse *you* of having tried to make a difference."

I hope I'd put it more charitably today—but I still hold the same view. I dare to hope that many of you will happily plead guilty to the accusation of idealism. I dare to hope that many of you will have the guts to choose the path of the few, that you will dare to live large lives—divinely irresponsible lives—characterized by great faith, high hope, and selfless love.

24

Committees of One

HIS SUMMER, as I traveled about the country, I had a chance to catch up with a number of alumni I hadn't seen in several years. I want to begin by telling you about one of them who graduated about a decade ago.

At School we all liked him; he was a great kid. You were glad to see him walking toward you in the hallway. But he was a very weak student academically. He struggled through Class VI and then through Class V. He was a frequent topic of discussion at faculty meetings and at the end of his Class IV year we concluded that—much as we liked him—Roxbury Latin was too hard for him and that we would hurt him if he stayed with us. I was delegated to "counsel him out."

So in all my persuasive wisdom, I said to him, "It's just not worth the high price you're paying in hard work to stay here and scrape by with low grades when you could go to another school and get much higher grades with much less effort." Each time I said it—and I put it to him brilliantly in about ten different variations—he replied, quietly but firmly, "I want to stay." I finally caved in. He stayed, worked hard for a barely C average, and graduated. His SATs and Achievements—his "stats"—were predictably low, and he went to a college that most of you would regard as a "safety" and where he again struggled to get by.

I visited him this summer in his spacious office at the international headquarters of one of the most powerful financial institutions on earth—of which he is already an important officer. By the world's usual standards of success, he would appear to be by far the most "successful" person in his class. His salary, I would estimate, is ten times that of his infinitely wise high school headmaster. But by standards far more significant than the world's he is equally successful. He has interests and involvements beyond his work in high finance; our talk ranged from art exhibits and new plays to baseball and politics. He also repeatedly expressed interest in involving his classmates in the financial support of the school, of which he is already an extremely generous supporter. He is obviously at peace with himself, happy with his life as a whole. By whatever measure of success you might use, it certainly appears that no one in his class has "done better" than this young man who ranked last in his class academically.

I tell you about this alumnus because I think there is a tendency for you—not to mention your parents—to see grades and test scores and college admission as the be-all and end-all of school. But to see things that way is to prostitute the Founder's clearly-stated goal which, I remind you, makes absolutely no mention either of grades or of college admission. John Eliot said that the purpose of his school was to "fit students for public service both in Church and Commonwealth." We say today in our catalogue that "we care most of all what kind of person a boy is" because we believe that personal qualities are far more important than academic success in fitting students for public service. And the principal reason for this school's existence is not to produce students who get high test scores or enter allegedly prestigious colleges; the principal reason for this school's existence is to advocate, advance, and inculcate in students certain great personal qualities.

I want to talk with you this morning about three of these qualities that are seen in the alumnus I just described and that we dare hope to see in every one of you.

Discernment

The first quality is discernment. I'd like to call it "discrimination"—the ability to distinguish between good and bad, morally and aesthetically. But the word "discrimination" has acquired so pejorative a popular use that I'll use the word discernment.

Discernment begins with ourselves, with self-awareness. As children, we naturally and instinctively lie and cheat and steal. As we mature we become aware of these tendencies and acquire the inner strength to control them. We become aware that we shall be tempted, and we learn to control ourselves and overcome that temptation. We expect to have to teach little children not to lie and steal and cheat. When a person becomes twelve years old, however, society expects that he will have become aware of himself, learned to control and master his natural desires to lie and steal and cheat. And society is less forgiving of childish behavior in people who are no longer children. Such behavior in adults is called criminal, in fact, and society does not condone it.

Discernment, though it begins with self-awareness, extends beyond ourselves (our awareness of our instincts and our weaknesses) to awareness of others. Children are almost completely centered on themselves. I stayed a few weeks ago with friends who have young children. One of them was cold in the night and, like all small children, he cried out at three in the morning—for everyone in the entire house to hear, "Mommy, I'm cold." I did not enjoy being roused from my peaceful slumbers, but I did not regard this crying out as a criminal act: the child is only three. However, if I spent the night at the house of one of you and you shouted out in the middle of the night, "Mommy, I'm cold," I would, I assure you, when awakened from my slumbers, harbor murderous thoughts toward you.

Discernment comes—or should come—as we grow older. We become aware of our own tendencies, and we become aware that there are other people in the world whose existence and needs must be taken into account. The mature person can get outside of himself into the lives of others. He can ask, for example, "And how was your summer?" and wait for an answer. At this more advanced level—and I dare to hope for this in each of you—discernment extends beyond ourselves so that we become aware of and sensitive to the pain, the loneliness, the hurt in the lives of those around us. We are not all wrapped up in ourselves.

I've been talking about growth in moral discernment. But the same growth can and should occur in aesthetic discernment. As much as you all may have enjoyed the Mother Goose stories, I doubt that any of you at bedtime tonight will ask your mommy to come and read you one of these tales (at least I hope that's the case). I doubt that any of you will fall asleep tonight clutching a teddy bear in your arms. You have gone beyond those things, outgrown them. If this school does its job well, you should be able ten years from now to look back and see—in a similar way—how childish and shallow and even silly some of your present perceptions are.

My freshman year at college we had a fireplace with a large area over the mantle. After some discussion, I prevailed upon my roommates to let me decide what should go there. I had been to a print shop in Cambridge and I knew just the thing: Salvador Dali's *Columbus Discovering America*. It was big, lavish, splashy, full of the parade and panoply of politics, the splendor and glory of religion, in all ways a stunning picture. I adored it. And at immodest expense I bought it, had it framed, and placed it over the mantelpiece to the figurative cheers of the art lovers around the globe. About two years later, as my knowledge of art increased and I still gazed each day at what I had come by then to regard as an embarrassingly inferior work of art, I finally took it down, put it in the back of my closet, and sold it the following fall for a tidy sum to a freshman who thought it was gorgeous.

I am glad I can look back now and be embarrassed about things I said or did ten years ago. As we grow in aesthetic awareness, we leave behind earlier, shallower perceptions. It is my hope and expectation that those of you who experience here in your course work the sufferings of Job or the humiliation of Oedipus or the madness of King Lear will not be satisfied by spending your time watching *General Hospital*, *As the World Turns*, or *The Bold and the Beautiful*.

I was in London a few weeks ago at the same time as Madonna and she was staying a block from where I was. Crowds lined up at all hours to catch a glimpse of her and forty thousand people a night saw her for three nights in Wembley Stadium. I was offered a ticket and chose instead to go to see Anthony Hopkins as King Lear at the National Theatre. Most of you would have chosen Madonna; so would I at your age. Only fifteen hundred of us saw *Lear* that night (though actually I guess more will see *Lear* than saw Madonna before the play ends its

London run). I say this not to denigrate either Madonna or you. Madonnas come and go and they provide an interesting diversion in life. But twenty-five years from now, Madonna will be a footnote in a dusty book on late twentieth-century popular music, someone else will bring out forty thousand to Wembley Stadium for three nights, and people will be lined up to see the latest production of *King Lear*. A few things endure; most things do not endure. We seek at this school to bring you into contact with the great scientific and mathematical perceptions of the universe, with great lives in history, with art, music, and literature, things so enduring that they deserve the name "immortal." And that—as enduring and immortal—give all of us a standard by which to measure and judge everything else.

Our efforts here will have failed if you do not know yourselves, if you are not strong enough to see and control your temptations, if you are insensitive to the feelings of those around you. Our efforts here will have failed if you do not grow in your awareness of the beauty and order of the universe and of the great achievements of your fellow men and women.

To me the epitome of such a failure of discernment was a Harvard classmate of mine who visited me while I was a student at Cambridge, regarded by many as the most beautiful university on earth. I took him after dinner for a walk through the lavish gardens and noble college courtyards. He talked to me incessantly (so he heard nothing). He looked at me as he talked (so he saw nothing), and he smoked cigarette after cigarette (so he smelled nothing). He had closed himself off from beauty, from enriching perceptions, from others, from growth and enrichment. And not surprisingly his life has been a tragedy.

Vision

Discernment, then, is the first quality I hope you will attain. The other two qualities, you'll be relieved to learn, take far less time to describe. The second of the three qualities I hope for is vision. Perhaps no quality is as alien to the spirit of our age as vision. We live in an age that craves instant gratification—pleasure now, profits now. Vision is the quality that enables us to look beyond the immediate, beyond the present, to see our lives in a larger context, to postpone gratification in order to achieve long-range goals. If you have a mental picture of what you hope to achieve, or if you have some idea what you might do with your lives five or ten or twenty years from now—if you have some idea of the work you might engage in, of the lifestyle you might choose for yourself, then you are, of course, better able to utilize the present to achieve your long-range goals. The vision of the future gives you something to strive for now in the present. I do not mean that you should have decided by now exactly what you want to do with your life, but I do mean you should have had some vision of possible careers, some vision of what you want to accomplish.

Important, though, as such a vision is (regarding career and lifestyle), it is nothing like as important as an overall vision for your whole life. We might call such a vision existential; it has to do with the discovery by you of some meaning and purpose to your whole existence. Inevitably such a vision must entail not only finding meaning in your life but meaning also in your inevitable death.

Most people never seek or achieve such a vision. Matthew Arnold wrote about such people:

> *What is the course of the life*
> *Of mortal men on the earth?—*
> *Most men eddy about*
> *Here and there—eat and drink,*
> *Chatter and love and hate,*
> *Gather and squander, are raised*
> *Aloft, are hurl'd in the dust,*
> *Striving blindly, achieving*
> *Nothing; and, then they die—*
> *Perish; and no one asks*
> *Who or what they have been. . . .*

For the founders of our school the existential vision of life was inextricably and inexorably bound up with God. So it was also in the concentration camps of Nazi Germany where the vision of life's ultimate meaningfulness enabled a few brave souls to cling to the hope of the meaning of things while all the evidence shouted that existence was hopeless and meaningless. Such a vision of the Divine Purpose enabled John Eliot to carry on his work among the Indians when all the world—his many friends, his many detractors, the terrible weather, the obvious dangers—all shouted for him to give it up.

Amid the trivialities of our lives together in this school, when we sometimes become petty and bickering and lose our vision or when the discussion becomes obsessed with where you'll go to college, I sometimes recall a TV program I once saw about a monastery. As I hazily remember, the monks were all squabbling, sniping at one another, complaining about their hard work, complaining about the food, complaining about the abbot's leadership. The abbot was driven almost to despair by all of this—and his vision was almost lost. Almost. But in the depths of his despair, he was able to hold on to the vision: "How utterly meaningless all this would be," he said, "if God weren't watching."

Without a vision for our life, we lose perspective, we lose the sense that there is meaning and purpose to our existence, and we become squalid little people who gather and love and hate, who strive blindly and achieve nothing.

Courage

The final quality we hope to encourage is that without which the others are useless: Courage.

A young man may come to the awareness that stealing is wrong—he may, in fact, be able to tell you quite clearly why, rationally, it is wrong to steal. Yet all his intellectual understanding, his awareness, and his discernment and even his vision are not enough: he must also have the courage to resist the inevitable temptation when it comes his way. Moral reasoning is not the same as acting morally. Almost every boy who lies or steals or cheats knows that lying and stealing and cheating are wrong. What he lacks is the courage to control those instincts within him. In the face of temptation he is a coward. That is why Winston Churchill, when asked what is the King of Virtues, instantly replied: "Courage—because it is the guarantor of all the others."

Without courage we also wallow in our natural mediocrity. We don't get beyond soap operas or Madonnas; we're too lazy. They're good enough. Why stretch? Without courage we remain wrapped up in ourselves. I've got enough problems of my own without worrying about world hunger, or without noticing or figuring out why the kid who sits next to me in math is so obnoxious or so unhappy. It takes courage to seek a great vision for our lives and much greater courage to make the sacrifices along the way to follow that vision. It is easy to sit around whining and complaining and blaming. It takes courage to lead, to aspire to greatness.

John F. Kennedy was fond of saying that the quality of our nation's life depended on committees of one: on individuals—we might say—of discernment, vision, and courage. In any given generation there are only a few men and women of discernment, vision, and courage. Only a few. Only a very few. Jesus said to his tiny band of apparently insignificant ragtag followers who went on to turn the world upside down: "You are the salt of the earth." A few tiny grains who could transform the taste of the whole meal. A few individuals of discernment, vision, and courage who could transform a whole society in their generation.

The reason for this school's existence in every generation is to produce just such individuals, just such committees of one, who will be in their generation the salt of the earth.

25

Thoughts on Vince Lombardi

F YOU'RE A SCHOOLMASTER you inevitably come into contact with parents. One of the most memorable parents of my career was the father of a student in my former school. This father was your classic macho male. I don't think he'd ever been an athlete himself: I think the most violent exercise he ever got was lifting the beer can to his mouth watching Monday night football on TV. But he was a fanatic spectator who could tell you at great length and in detail all the flaws of every player and every coach.

In virtually every conversation, this father would utter what he regarded as the two ultimate truths about the human experience. And he did not plagiarize. These two great truths were always heralded by the words, "You know what Vince Lombardi says?" And then, in case you didn't, he would quote the great philosopher: "Winning isn't everything, it's the only thing"; "Show me a loser and I'll show you a loser."

I am grateful to this father—not just for his reiteration of these profound insights, but for the absolute consistency with which he uttered them. I have no idea if this father was correct in attributing these quotations to Vince Lombardi. Many a stupid saying has been attributed to Vince Lombardi. But—whoever uttered these statements—I want to take them as a starting point this morning: "Winning isn't everything, it's the only thing"; "Show me a loser [i.e., a good loser or a bad loser] and I'll show you a loser."

The Inadequacy of These Truths

Even a seventh grader could point out the inadequacy of these alleged truths. By this definition of winner, Stalin was a winner: he stayed in office by killing millions and by threatening tens of millions. And the prophets of Israel and Socrates and Jesus were all losers who died at the hands of winners. But in the long-term judgment of history, Stalin is now seen as a loser, and the prophets and Socrates and Jesus are perceived universally as winners. Of Stalin we'd have to say, "Show me a winner and I'll show you a loser." And of the prophets of Israel and Socrates and Jesus, we'd have to say, "Show me a loser and I'll show you a winner." It is, I think, universally agreed that to win in a bad cause makes you a loser, while to lose in a good cause makes you a winner.

We know this from our own experience. We have all seen a winning athlete who is a jerk, a loser. And we've all admired an athlete who fought hard but lost with dignity; no one regards him as a loser. So who the real winners and losers are is not as simple a determination as it might at first appear.

Let me cast further fog on the issue by recounting something that happened to me in my parish in Dorchester about a decade ago. We had a teenager (I'll call him Loni) in the parish. This hapless youth was the sort of boy who is a day late, a dollar short, and a lap behind. "The other guys don't include me. They leave me out. They all think I'm a loser," he lamented to me. Well, to make a long story short, the phone rang in the middle of the night one Friday night (actually, Saturday morning), and it was a lieutenant at the Dorchester police station. "Father," he said, "I have a couple of your boys down here at the station." He told me what they'd done and I got out of bed and went down there. By Sunday morning, of course, the whole parish was abuzz about these two nimble-fingered nitwits. Loni, the boy who was always left out, came bounding up to me and said, "Father, you hear what happened to Luke and Kevin?" "Yes, Loni, I heard." "I was at home," he said. "They didn't let me go with 'em. Thank God I'm a loser!"

No intelligent person could possibly assert that winning is everything or the only thing or that a loser is always a loser. Also most of us have had the experience of Loni and been glad we've lost, and (equally paradoxically) most of us have regretted winning at some time or other.

I want briefly to explore with you this morning what it really is that makes and defines a winner and what it is that makes and defines a loser.

The Definition of a "Loser"

This is how I'd define a loser: a loser is someone who doesn't have significant long-range goals for his life, an overall sense of purpose that gives his life meaning.

A few weeks ago in Norfolk, England, I was having dinner with some friends of mine. Their son had just graduated from one of England's more prominent schools. He and a friend came in as we were ending the meal. Both boys—aged eighteen—sat down and had dessert with us. As is quite normal at even the best schools in England, neither boy was going on to college. One was going into commercial art and the other was going into accounting. Immediately following dessert both boys lighted up cigarettes. Without, I hope, coming across as judgmental, I asked them how much they smoked (they both said a pack a day) and how many of their schoolmates smoked (quite a few, they said). Then one of them said, "Don't the students in your school smoke?" I said—accurately, I think—"No, almost none of them smokes." "I suppose they're into weightlifting and jogging," said the other boy to me with a put-down smile on his face. "Most of them are pretty health-conscious," I replied. "Getting in shape and staying in shape is pretty much the in thing."

Then the first boy said, "I like my puny body!" This elicited a gleeful response from those sitting at the table. (Guess that takes care of the health-conscious American!) And I have to admit there was a certain charm about this boy. His comment was a nice antidote to the macho narcissism of some weightlifting American youths. But after his clever and charming remark the sad reality remained: he had a puny body and so did his friend.

As we talked, I more and more realized that neither of these boys had any important long-range goals, any overall plan for his life. They were sort of stumbling onward, without much sense of purpose, without important goals to strive for. If you have no long-range goals, you have no reason to give up any present pleasures. In their case, there was no reason not to smoke a pack a day, no reason to be fit. It is only when you have worthwhile long-range goals that you are able to resist destructive pleasures day by day.

I saw the ultimate example of this when I was working on the railroad during my college summers. We serviced a plant of the Industrial Rayon Company. We often arrived in the morning about the time of one of their breaks. As we came into the siding we'd find a large group of middle-aged men and women ferociously puffing away on cigarettes. You couldn't engage them in conversation; their minds were empty. My boss on the railroad crew often commented, "These people live from cigarette break to cigarette break. That's all there is in life for them: a succession of cigarette breaks." They had no important long-range goals for their lives, no overall sense of purpose, no reason not to indulge themselves in every possible present gratification (no matter how dangerous or destructive).

We could discuss all morning whether or not that's their fault or society's. But none of us would deny that these people define the word "loser." And, sadly, for all their charming excuse-making, the two English boys would also have to be called losers. They have no important long-range goals, no overall sense of purpose to their lives, no reason not to indulge themselves in destructive present gratifications. In all likelihood, they'll never amount to anything.

I think also of a schoolmate of mine. He was the picture of your successful schoolboy athlete, the idol of our school, the hero of our town. He had a valid long-range goal: to be a pro-football player. Most of us who knew him believed he would make it. He kept in superb physical condition, he went all out to achieve his worthwhile goal; he sacrificed many present pleasures to achieve his long-range goal. His life had a sense of purpose.

Sadly, as things worked out, he just missed making the pros. When his goal was denied him, he totally collapsed. There was nothing to live for, no long-range goal to strive and sacrifice for, and he let himself go, abandoning himself to gratify every present pleasure. Physically his once finely tuned, superbly conditioned body is now a grotesque ruin. He's never done anything with his life. This man—who as a young man was the epitome of a winner—is now the epitome of a loser.

You can set out in life with a worthy long-range goal—and being a pro-football player is a valid long-range goal—and you may sacrifice much for that goal; you may work hard and deny yourself pleasures in order to achieve that goal. But you must also remember that, despite your sacrifices, you may not reach your goal and you must be prepared to deal with the consequences. This man was a loser because he'd never asked himself: What is my real purpose? What is it I want when I seek to be a pro? Where will I be if I don't make it? What is my life's overall purpose and how can I achieve it by other means if I fail at this?

The Definition of a "Winner"

So much for life's losers. Who are life's winners? What distinguishes them? I think the winner has two qualities: He has well-thought-out goals and the courage to pursue those goals.

Every year I see certain boys return for the new school year in ardent pursuit of a worthy goal: "This year I'm going to get all B's," for instance. Then the first marking period comes and they have mostly C's. There are only two ways to respond to those C's. The loser, in the face of this setback, whines, "Oh the hell with it, no matter what I do I always get a C." And he gives up. The winner says, "OK, back to the books. I'm not going to give up." The winner has considered the possibility that he won't achieve his goal easily or quickly, and he finds the courage to pick himself up out of the dust and struggle onwards.

Or consider the boy who is burning for Brand A college and who fails to get in. The loser will regard his rejection as a world-class tragedy, because he has never set this goal in a larger context. The winner has anticipated the rejection and with a positive attitude he sets about constructively trying to figure out how he can make Brand B college serve the larger purposes and goals of his life.

Almost every one of you in this room meets the first qualification of being a winner: you have set high goals for yourself. You want to do something with your lives, you want to be somebody. You are able to deny yourselves passing pleasures in the present in order to achieve some worthwhile goal in the future.

Meeting Frustration and Defeat

Since most of you have this first qualification of a winner (high goals for yourselves), I want to focus on the second qualification of a winner, namely having the guts to continue pursuing worthwhile goals when you meet with obstacles and frustrations and defeat.

The other night I was reading the paper, paying no attention to the blaring TV in my kitchen. Just as I finished the paper, I glanced up and someone was interviewing a woman at her twenty-fifth high school reunion—I think at Brookline High School, but I'm not certain. She had a face of what I would call great beauty. She held up her left hand; on that hand she had no fingers. "High school was hard," she said. "Kids are only interested in the beautiful people; they hate imperfections." Then they asked her about her life. "Are you married?" "Yes, I am." It then transpired that her husband had gone to fight in Vietnam and that he had been emotionally crippled there and was unable to work. "He's never really recovered from the war," she said quietly. And then they showed her swimming. "And now you have multiple sclerosis," the reporter said. "Yes," she said. "I'm just trying to keep going." "What keeps you going?" asked the reporter. "You have to hold onto your sense of humor and you have to keep a positive attitude," she said.

Think of the goals she set out to reach and how each was undermined and taken from her: a deformed body, a husband destroyed by war, multiple sclerosis. Think of her courage in getting up and going on. How easy it would have been for her to squander her life in self-pity, to indulge in feeling sorry for herself, to give up, to take on the identity of a victim, to say, why bother, no matter what I do I always get knocked down. But she is not a loser. She saw one goal after another removed as a possibility and she has set for herself one great final goal that no one can remove: to face pain and inevitable defeat—which m.s. will bring her—with poise and dignity and courage.

Nine Septembers ago, the captain of our football team returned to school with his classmates: Billy McDonald, Class of 1980. The previous May he had been diagnosed as having an inoperable malignant tumor on his heart. Through the early months of the summer they had tortured him—almost to death—with a new killer chemotherapy and radiation treatments. This blond-haired 6'2" Adonis went from over 200 pounds down to 108 pounds, and all his hair fell out. After enduring a month of excruciating pain, he was told, "We think we've arrested the cancer temporarily." Weak as he was he returned to school wearing a wig. "I know we all have to die," he said to me acknowledging the ultimate reality of all our lives, "and if I have to die of cancer I can accept that. But—in the meantime—I'm going to fight it with everything I have." Through the ensuing months, the frequent returns to the hospital, he never said, "Why me?"

After he battled cancer week after week for several more months he wrote: "The last seven months have for the most part been Hell. Therefore I have tried to take things one at a time. In order to do this, I have set six rules for myself which I consider mandatory:

> 1. Agree to all treatment
> 2. Look my best at all times
> 3. Lead as normal a life as possible
> 4. Don't get emotional
> 5. Don't feel sorry for myself
> 6. Don't quit."

I was with him when he died in March of his senior year. His sense of humor, his concern for others remained with him right to his last agonizing breath. The *Globe* headline the day after his death read, "Death beats Billy McDonald to graduation." As it happened, that was literally untrue. The trustees presented him with his diploma that spring before he died. But, that headline was untrue in a far more significant way than literally. Death didn't beat Billy at all, not in any way at all. Much as he wanted to live, he did not cower in the face of death. Disease and suffering did their utmost to reduce him, to bring him down, to destroy him. But Billy faced those forces of destruction and used them as an opportunity for greatness and for heroism. And he died with dignity and courage. He may have lost, but he won.

The Qualities of Life's Winners

Life's winners, I submit, have three great qualities:

First, they each remember to count their blessings. We were not born without fingers, we do not have multiple sclerosis, we are not dying of cancer. Let's remember, when we start to fall into complaining about all of life's very stupid, very petty annoyances, not to feel sorry for ourselves for the small crosses we are given to bear. We could have been born in another country, we could have been born in hopelessness and poverty along with most of our fellow human beings. But we were born in the best of times, and no one has been given more opportunities than we. Let us not waste time in the obscenity of complaining and self-pity. Let us recall our good fortune, count our blessings, and let us remember that "from those to whom much has been given much will be expected."

Second, life's winners do not see life in terms of its obstacles, but in terms of its possibilities. In Volume 8 of Martin Gilbert's life of Winston Churchill, Gilbert recounts a story that Queen Elizabeth II told about Churchill when he was seventy-nine: "She and her Prime Minister were travelling up the Thames [River] together on the bridge of the [Royal Yacht] Britannia. '[We] saw this dirty commercial river as [we] came up,' the Queen recalled, 'and he was describing it as the silver thread which runs through the history of Britain. . . . Churchill saw things in a very romantic and glittering way [said Her Majesty]; [and the rest of us realized that perhaps we were] looking at [the river] in a rather mundane way.'" You cannot set great goals for your lives, my dear children, unless you see life in terms of its romantic, yes glittering, possibilities. Dream great dreams, strive to accomplish great things.

And finally, life's winners are courageous. Pray for courage. You will need it in order to hold onto your dreams, in order to cling to the great goals you've set for your lives. This same Winston Churchill, when asked what was the greatest of all virtues replied at once, "Courage— because it is the guarantor of all the others." Without courage all the other virtues are useless. Courage is what gave Billy McDonald strength—in the face of terrible pain and certain death—not to feel sorry for himself, not to quit. Pray for courage.

26

The Life of the Mind

 WANT TO ADDRESS the subject "The Life of the Mind" because the nurturing of the Life of the Mind is, at least on the surface, the reason we are all here.

Being Led Out of Ourselves

Let me first remind you what you already know: the word "education" comes from the Latin words *e-/ex* and *duco*. Education has to do with being led out of ourselves.

Let me confess right at the outset that there exists a school of thought that holds that we do not need to be led out of ourselves. This theory of education flourishes in the sort of elementary school that some of you attended. Underlying the philosophy of this kind of elementary school (and of some secondary schools) is the belief that children are inherently inquisitive and that if you just encourage them a little they will happily run off and learn things and engage in creative enterprise.

A couple of years ago in the admissions season I talked with two parents—both liberal academics—whose son was applying from such an elementary school. They were initially ardent believers in the every-student-is-eager-to-learn-and-to-create theory of education. But they had become doubters. They described how the school had let their son go off on his own and pursue his interests: the first year, for example, he was interested in dinosaurs and for a year spent almost all his time in school focussed on dinosaurs. He may have found out a great deal about dinosaurs, but he paid a price: he learned precious little about math or history. Now, after several years in the school, testing revealed that he was a poor math student and that he was, all things considered, a modest writer. When I chatted with the boy, I found him remarkably self-absorbed, wanting to talk about his own rather confined interests, unable to say much about the range of subjects I asked him about. He even complained that his parents "won't let me alone" and that they wanted him to broaden his horizons. Not surprisingly, his essays were flaccid and badly written, full of spelling mistakes. When I gently pointed out these recurring errors, he responded, "I don't think it's important to spell. It's only your ideas that matter." Unfortunately, his shallow ideas showed clearly that no one had ever criticized or challenged him or told him he could think more deeply.

As I talked with this boy, I recalled a poster I once saw in an elementary school similar to the one this boy was attending: the poster read "I am perfect just the way I am." My visit occurred at the height of the "positive reinforcement" craze, and the two teachers whose classrooms I observed both spent the entire period telling each student how wonderful he was and how wonderful the work he'd done was. I asked both teachers about grades. Both said grades were A Very Bad Thing. I asked about written comments. Both said, "Never say anything critical. Never be negative." Now I believe that all good teachers engage in positive reinforcement, but what a wildly unrealistic picture of the universe these teachers were giving their students! I bet most of the students were tired of the incessant praise and, at some level, realized that their teachers were debasing the coinage of teaching. After these teachers had heaped praise on mediocrity, what was left to say when a student actually did something first rate? You may have guessed by now that I believe such a philosophy of education is rubbish. At the end of my discussion with these teachers, I found myself wanting to shout, "If these kids are perfect, then why the hell do they need to go to school?"

I submit that we need to be led out of ourselves because, by nature, we are confined. By nature we wallow in ourselves, by nature we are wrapped up in ourselves, by nature we don't challenge and push ourselves.

Early this summer I attended the meeting of the Country Day School Headmasters' Association at Reed College in Portland, Oregon. I decided last February that I would set aside the three days it takes to go by train. And I did so in mid-June, taking first the Great Lakes Limited to Chicago and then the Empire Builder to Portland. (I was the only person in the country that day to go from Boston to Portland on the train.) In the afternoon and early evening before the third night on the train, we wound our way through the Rockies and the southern part of Glacier Park—and by merely looking out the window we were privileged to see what must be the most spectacular vistas on this continent.

Before I went into the dining car for dinner I decided to have a glass of wine in the lounge car. I knew its huge windows would afford the best possible view of south Glacier Park. I sat down, as most of you would, enraptured by the amazing sights. I soon realized, however, that more than half of the people in the lounge car were glued to the huge screens at both ends of the car watching some blood and guts adventure film. Here we were in the midst of the most stupendous wonders of nature, and these people—and I don't mean children or teenagers because most were adults—were glued to these screens watching a movie they could have seen in their hometowns or could have rented from a video store. What they could probably never see again was the beauty passing by them right outside the window.

By nature, we like what is familiar. We do not see and hear most of what surrounds us. That is why the essence of education is to lead people out of themselves. Had I been headmaster of Amtrak I'd have turned off the damned TV and required people to look out the window to see the magnificent and ennobling sights of Glacier Park.

In July I was in northwest Spain in Santiago de Compostela, the shrine of the Apostle St. James which was once, with Jerusalem and Rome, one of the three great ancient shrines to which pilgrims came from all over the world. This summer, being a holy year, it was crammed with pilgrims.

I went to Santiago by bus with a group of Spanish-speaking tourists.

Because I have not spoken Spanish since my senior year in high school, I was happy to discover that two grandmothers in the group had brought their eighteen- and nineteen-year-old granddaughters on the trip. These girls lived in Miami, and though they spoke Spanish with their grandmothers and the rest of the group, they could speak English, so I frequently chatted with them over the course of our trip through Spain. When we got to Santiago, I took a city bus the short distance into the old city. Santiago thronged with tens of thousands of teenagers and twenty-somethings. The lines to the shrine of the Apostle stretched hundreds of yards; the vast cathedral was crammed to the rafters at all times of the day and night.

When I returned to our hotel on the city's outskirts after dinner (it was shortly before midnight because the Spanish don't eat until 9 or 10 P.M.), there, in the hotel's lobby, were my two girlfriends drinking Cokes. I sat down and began to enthuse about the day. "Did you like it?" I asked them, only to discover that they hadn't been into the city at all. They'd gone to the nearby huge shopping center, El Corte Inglés—in English, "The English Cut"—and shopped all day until they got tired and went to a movie in the cineplex adjoining El Corte Inglés. I told them then that if I were their principal, I'd make them spend all the following day seeing the great historical and cultural sites in Santiago. They laughed, but they asked me if I'd take them into the city the next morning.

Somewhat to my surprise, they showed up at the time I set. When we got off the municipal bus in the old city, they were amazed to discover that it was filled with people their age who were obviously really interested in the sites. Since they were fluent in Spanish (not to mention attractive looking), they quickly fell in with other teenagers. The next day at breakfast they regaled me with all they'd done. Then they told me—with, I'd have to say with some amusement—that their grandmothers had spent the day watching Spanish television in their hotel rooms and shopping. So while the girls were exploring the city, their grandmothers were watching soap operas or buying cheap souvenirs. It turned out, in fact, that the girls had told their grandmothers that they were "reporting" them to me. So I then had the pleasure of two roiled grandmothers telling me passionately in florid Spanish that they were not about to stand in line to visit the Apostle's tomb or any other cultural sites for that matter, that it was none of my business what they did with their time, etc., etc.

By nature, left to ourselves, we instinctively close ourselves off from new experiences. We wallow in the familiar, confined to our narrow selves.

By nature, we do not, most of us, lust to learn. You all, for example, instinctively enjoy summer, when, to a large degree, you can wallow in your own interests, do what you like, lie around, sleep late, watch TV, whatever you want. School—education—is unnatural. Teachers pull us away from our instinctive narrowness; they lead us away from ourselves—out of ourselves, to something beyond. We do not instinctively enjoy the process. We're not just dying to read the next novel in English, or to learn the subjunctive in Latin, or to master the glories of Algebra 2. These things are unnatural. But most of us—at least most of you here—know that it is "good for you" and so you come along cheerfully and with some semblance of enthusiasm.

Opening Ourselves

Now the hope is that, once we reach a certain age, we will not need the external force of school in order to be led out of ourselves. The hope is that we will have acquired the habit and discipline of—on our own—opening ourselves to what is beyond us. All people of substance, all people who aspire to do something great with their lives, somehow acquire the habit of resisting their natural inclination to wallow in their own confined interests and succeed in opening themselves up to experiences beyond themselves. And many of these substantial people acquired these habits when they were your age.

Now, in all honesty, when I was your age and a student at St. Mark's, I cannot say that I got to this stage. I really pretty much saw education as something they did to me. I cannot remember consciously ever thinking to myself: "I must now, on my own, begin to open myself up to fresh perspectives, to new experiences." I pretty much "did" school because "they" told me to.

I can think of only three occasions in those years when I led myself out of myself. The first was in the eighth grade in public school in Ohio. We all had to take a course called Industrial Arts, popularly known as "shop." It was a course in metalworking and woodworking. We all hated it: four months making a wood shoe box, then four months making a metal trowel. But it happened that our teacher had about twenty years of back issues of *Popular Mechanics* magazine in the shop. He was always urging us to borrow them to get ideas for projects we could make in the future if we continued—which he urged us to do—to take shop in the ninth grade. Now I had no intention of taking one more minute of shop than was absolutely required, but one day, to kill time, I languidly flipped through an issue of *Popular Mechanics*. It was about ten years old—from the year 1942. I was thirteen years old, and 1942 seemed to me then about the time of the Pharaohs of Egypt. But within seconds I was mesmerized by the magazine—not by anything mechanical, but by the articles about the war, about military aircraft, guns, ships, and descriptions of what to do if an incendiary bomb landed in your attic. This magazine hurled me right into the midst of the Second World War in an intensely gripping way. On my own I went on to search Mr. Sanderson's magazine dump for every issue from the war. I devoured them. My point is this: I had, admittedly by accident, just had my first experience of leading myself out of myself.

A couple of years later I was a student at St. Mark's. Now I loved St. Mark's, but I found it wearing in one regard: it was a boarding school and there was hardly any privacy, hardly any place you could be alone. Each day there was a small gap of time between sports and chapel (which was at six each night on the way to dinner). I discovered that there was a place in the library, hidden from view amid the stacks, where nobody went at that time and where I could sit by myself. It was all mine, and it remained all mine through all my time at school. I soon discovered that the adjoining shelves were entirely taken up by bound copies of the *Illustrated London News*, the British weekly magazine. I opened the most recent bound volume. Its date was 1945 and it naturally focused on World War II. I was immediately entranced and devoured it until the bell rang for chapel.

In the ensuing days and weeks I read nearly every word of all fifty-two issues of the *Illustrated London News* for the year 1945. I then went to the previous volume, 1944. By my senior year I had read ninety-four years of the *Illustrated London News*, from 1945 to 1851 (I believe the first year it was published) backwards. It was a gold mine of information and I learned more by reading those issues—all on my own, nobody knew— than I learned in all my history courses put together at St. Mark's and Harvard. That magazine opened the whole world to me.

These two experiences occurred outside the classroom. Regrettably, through my school years, I fear it never really occurred to me that anything I was taught inside the classroom might be interesting, or might lead me to new delights. I never experienced the thrill that I could sense in some of my classmates about some discovery in science or some perspective in math. I never grasped the mystic overall structure of language that I know some of you have discovered here in your study of Latin and French. The sole exception for me was a sophomore music history—or music listening—class. Now I have described how, when I was a boy, my elementary school dragged all of us to Severance Hall in Cleveland once a year to hear the Cleveland Orchestra, then, by universal admission, the finest orchestra in the world. I liked Elvis Presley and rock and roll, and I hated the idea that "they" were trying to ram classical music down my throat. I knew what I liked. Don't disturb me with this classical music. Don't try to change my confined, narrow taste, don't try to enlarge my vision.

Anyway, here I was at St. Mark's in this music listening course with Doc Sheppard. We were given certain pieces of classical music to listen to and become familiar with. Then we were tested on them and required to identify the composer and the work. At first, most of us rebelled. "This stuff all sounds the same. There's no way to tell the difference." Some of us were indignant, claiming we were required to hear things that weren't there to be heard. Our indignation grew as some of our classmates began to "hear" things. Now we were mad not just at the course but at our classmates. Well, to make a long story short, eventually we all "heard" the music and a whole new world of enjoyment was opened to us, a world that made our previous narrow tastes seem embarrassing.

Having had my ears opened, I pursued further delights in this area and enrolled in Advanced Music when I was a senior. It wasn't a popular course. Out of the forty-six boys in my class, only two of us took it. As we had hoped, our teacher—Doc Sheppard—again opened up whole new vistas of beauty to us. I not only heard things I'd never heard before, but I also experienced the rapture of composing music, of creating something.

These are the only three experiences from my school years that I can recall actually, in part at least, leading myself out of myself. That may seem pathetic to you, but at least I had discovered a taste of the joy of—on my own—being led out of my own narrowness into a broader perspective, into the "broad sunlit uplands" of the Life of the Mind.

Suspending Disbelief

The goal of what we, the faculty, are trying to do here is to give you a taste of the things that have intrigued and delighted us, in the hope that some of those things will intrigue and delight you so that you will—on your own—pursue them and be led out of yourself, out of the narrow confines of your present interests.

I see a few boys every year—boys who reach their senior year—to whom the thought has never occurred that any of this stuff they learn could be interesting or valuable or delightful in and of itself. School—education—remains for them something "they" (the faculty) inflict on "us" (the students). There is no suspension of disbelief on their part, no sense that this material could possibly interest or excite them or make them happy. In a way, I greatly admire some of these boys because day after day they joylessly grind their way through the required work to do what "they" tell them to do.

I had such a senior a couple of years ago in English. I said to him—pleadingly—"Could you for just one second imagine that this book could bring you delight and pleasure?" He looked at me as if I were crazy. And when I repeated my plea he said, "Are you kidding?" I loved this boy and I admired him tremendously for joylessly grinding out his work day in and day out. But I was also intensely sad for him.

I was sad because he was missing so much happiness, the delight that can spring from being gripped by a new and delightful idea, a new and delightful insight, a new and delightful sound, a new and delightful way of seeing something.

The Life of the Mind is mostly counter-instinctive. It begins with the willingness to suspend disbelief, to open yourself to the possibility that there is something interesting, beneficial, and even delightful beyond us.

The Life of the Mind is uncomfortable. It requires an openness to new and different things when we'd rather wallow in our narrowness and watch TV or do the same old things we're familiar with.

The Life of the Mind requires guts, the courage to be vulnerable, to risk new and different experiences rather than to hide behind what we're already familiar with.

My prayer for you, then, is that you will risk suspending disbelief, that you will risk opening yourselves to new insights—which will lead you out of your confined outlook on life to delight in the new and broader and richer perspectives that are as yet beyond you.

27

Unless You Become
Like a Child…

ET ME BEGIN by sharing with you one of the most
beloved and also one of the most misunderstood stories in
the Bible. It is found in all three Synoptic Gospels—
Matthew, Mark, and Luke.

Here is Mark's version:

> *People were bringing children to Jesus, that he might touch them.*
> *But the disciples rebuked them. When Jesus saw what the disciples*
> *were doing he was indignant, and said to them, 'Let the children*
> *come to me; do not hinder them. For to such belongs the Kingdom*
> *of God. Truly I say to you, whoever does not receive the Kingdom of*
> *God like a child shall not enter it.' And he took the children in his*
> *arms and, laying his hands on them, blessed them. (10:13–16)*

Dramatis Personæ

Though this story is really only a vignette, it has a quite well-developed cast of characters.

First, there are the parents who bring the children. Biblical commentators usually point out that it was common for Jewish parents to bring their children—on their first birthdays—to a rabbi (such as Jesus) for a blessing. But St. Mark does not use the word "blessing." The parents, he says, brought their children to Jesus "that he might touch them."

There was something utterly compelling about Jesus. People were drawn to him everywhere he went. He was a charismatic teacher, a rabbi whose teachings moved his hearers, a rabbi whose whole life reflected and radiated the insights and vision he taught with his lips. Those who longed to discover meaning in their lives were drawn to him. But, as is always the case with charismatic figures, some were drawn to him because he was a celebrity. All of us are thrilled by contact with famous people. It is fair to say, I think, that I am not an ardent admirer of Governor Dukakis. But last summer, when I was ushered into his office, to shake his hand, and share maybe forty-five whole seconds of conversation with him, I was (I have to tell you) thrilled. That's why—even today—people thrust their babies into the arms of presidential candidates.

So here were these parents—drawn to Jesus by the radiant goodness of his life and teachings, drawn to Jesus by his celebrity, and St. Mark tells us "they brought their children to Jesus that he might touch them."

Next on the dramatis personae list are the disciples. St. Mark tells us simply, "They rebuked the people." The disciples are sometimes portrayed as ogres, as child-haters. But their behavior is much more plausibly explained if we understand that they were trying to protect Jesus: "Quit bothering him! Can't you see that you're harassing the poor man! Give him a break! You're interrupting something important, you and your children. Can't you see the man is trying to speak?" The disciples were trying to shield Jesus from the crush of the unruly crowd that was disrupting his teaching.

But the central figure of the story is Jesus, the itinerant rabbi of Nazareth. St. Mark says, "When Jesus saw the disciples rebuking the parents, he became indignant." This is one of the few times when the New Testament describes Jesus as angry or vexed.

Why was he indignant? Because to Jesus, no one was unimportant. Jesus did not divide people into categories—most important to least important. There were no little people to him. No one was contemptible to Jesus. No one was unworthy of his time. No one was unimportant. This was the rabbi who taught that "he who would be greatest among you must be the servant of all."

That's why Jesus with some impatience overruled his protective disciples: "Let the children come, do not hinder them. For to such belongs the Kingdom of God. Truly I say to you, whoever does not receive the Kingdom of God like a child shall not enter it."

Then Jesus did a striking thing. The parents had brought these children to Jesus "that he might touch them." But, as so often, Jesus did more than they asked, Jesus gave them more than they sought. St. Mark tells us, "And Jesus took the children in his arms and, laying his hands on them, blessed them."

That's the vignette. The phrase I want to focus on with you this morning is Jesus' statement: "Whoever does not receive the Kingdom of God like a child shall not enter it." The essence of what I want to say to you this morning is that you need to become a child again if you want to experience life in its fullness.

That may strike you as odd. After all, haven't we been telling you over and over again for the past few years to "grow up," to "quit acting like children"?

What Jesus Did Not Mean

Let me try to clarify by saying first what I think Jesus did not mean when he talked about the desirability of our becoming children.

For starters, Jesus was not being sentimental. Perhaps no story in the New Testament has so often been used as the subject of stained glass windows. In these pretty windows, Jesus is seated in the middle with his arms outstretched and dozens of little children are gathered around him. They all have the faces of angels, they are all beautifully dressed, and they are all enraptured and entranced by what Jesus is saying to them. These pretty windows are, of course, a highly sentimentalized version of reality. Had we been there, we'd have witnessed a disorderly mob of parents with their noisy, smelly, sniveling children crowding around Jesus, interrupting him as he was trying to teach. It was anything but a pretty scene.

Jesus was not being sentimental. He knew—just as any parent of a two-year-old knows—that children are not little angels. Children can be—and often are—a pain.

Secondly, in telling us to become children, Jesus was not suggesting that somehow we could become innocent again.

It is a sure sign of mental illness in an adult when an adult reverts to behaving like an innocent child. Years ago I saw a middle-aged man in an asylum sucking his thumb, wetting his pants, talking baby talk. But sane people cannot revert to childhood. We can't lay aside all we have learned and pretend we don't know that certain things are wrong or dangerous. Jesus is not asking us to turn back the clock of our minds, to throw away all we know, to give up rational thought processes, to feign innocence.

Jesus did not say, "You cannot enter the Kingdom unless you become childish." He was not urging us to cast aside our adult sense of responsibility. He was not suggesting that we should childishly indulge every whim or childishly assume no responsibility for our actions.

What Jesus Did Mean

What, then, did Jesus mean when he enjoined us "to receive the Kingdom of God like a child"?

1. TO BE OPEN AND RECEPTIVE. The most striking thing about children is their receptivity, their openness to life. Things we adults have long since taken for granted, children are thrilled by. Children have a sense of wonder at the unfolding world around them. One thing after another catches their fancy, excites their interest.

Many adults—and teenagers—are no longer receptive or open. They have become weary, worldly-wise; they have lost their sense of wonder.

In *The Tempest* when Miranda (whose name means wonderful, full of wonder) first sees the men of the ship, she exclaims:

> *O, wonder!*
> *How many goodly creatures are there here!*
> *How beauteous mankind is! O brave new world*
> *That has such people in't!*

But her worldly-wise, pedantic father, who has "seen it all," wearily responds: "'Tis new to thee."

Robert Sam Anson's book on the controversial death of Edmund Perry, contains this comment by one of Perry's fellow students at Phillips Exeter Academy: "We were sitting around having the usual Exeter conversation, telling each other how terrible it was and how we couldn't wait to get out." Some people think it's cool to affect an attitude of smug superiority, of rather bored wisdom. This arrogant, cynical, closed attitude is the very antithesis of the openness and receptivity Jesus enjoined when he urged us to become children.

A great scientist once said to me that the key to great achievement in science is the retention of this sense of wonder at the mystery of things, this sense of excitement and possibility. Children dream great dreams, they let themselves go in fantasies. I followed a little boy up St. Theresa's Avenue during vacation. He lurched from one side of the sidewalk to the other, steering a space ship on a rescue mission. He talked—even shouted a couple of times—and he gesticulated wildly. He was oblivious to his surroundings; he was caught up in his fantasy; he was dreaming a great dream.

The truly seminal minds in every generation have this quality. They retain (or they recapture) this sense of wonder. They fantasize and dream; they see life in terms of exciting possibilities.

Without that sense of wonder we might as well be dead, said Wordsworth:

> *My heart leaps up when I behold*
> *A rainbow in the sky:*
> *So was it when life began*
> *So is it now I am a man;*
> *So be it when I shall grow old,*
> *Or let me die!*

I might as well be dead if I can't see the wonder of life.

Children are open not just to their natural surroundings but to the people around them as well. Children are not self-reliant, and they know they're not self-reliant. They are by instinct open and receptive. They live by receiving from others. They learn to trust their parents; they know they will be fed and clothed. They are not only receptive but hopeful, expectant. Watch a toddler run towards his father, his arms outstretched as he calls out, "Daddy!" Dependent, receptive, trusting, hopeful, expectant.

Most of you have spent the last few years trying to become independent, to carve out your own separate life, to become self-reliant. You'd rather not need anyone. That establishment of independence is a necessary and desirable phase to go through. But it is tragic if you never get beyond that phase. And some people never do. Their development becomes arrested in this I'm-a-tough-guy-I-don't-need-anybody phase. As adults they are therefore incomplete, emotionally retarded.

Jesus tells us that we need to go beyond this adolescent phase. We need to recover the child in ourselves that we lost for a while when we were trying to establish our self-sufficiency in adolescence. The really fulfilled adult rediscovers the child in himself—the sense of wonder, the openness to others, the enthusiasm, the readiness to trust.

2. To Be Honest About Our Feelings. In addition to being open to their surroundings, children are also honest about their feelings. If they are unhappy, they cry. If they are happy, they smile.

As you have moved into adolescence, you have all learned to mask your feelings. If you don't get a good grade, or if you don't get much playing time, or if you don't get invited to a party, you pretend that you don't care, that it doesn't matter. You pretend even to yourself a lot of the time. Adolescents and adults rarely admit: I'm really disappointed, I'm really hurt. We protect ourselves, we cover up our feelings, hold up our shields. We're also afraid to show excitement and enthusiasm, lest someone laugh at us. So, we hide our enthusiasm by putting on a mask of blasé, cool indifference.

But Jesus tells us that we must go beyond this phase of cautious, wary self-protection. Again, we have to recover the child we have lost.

In this second childhood, we need to show and tell to others our real selves. That is a terrible risk. They might not like the real us underneath the mask. They might not respond to us. We could be hurt. Some adults are so fearful of hurt, they never get up the courage to reveal what's behind the mask

But Jesus tells us that real happiness comes when we become children again, when we show and share our honest feelings, when we acknowledge how fragile and vulnerable we are, how much we need others.

3. To Let Things Go. Finally, when Jesus urges us to become children again, I believe he is thinking of how quickly children let things go. A child will be bereft at one moment, sobbing with utter abandon, the picture of desolation. Then you pick him up or make a funny face at him and suddenly, instantaneously, he is smiling radiantly. In seconds he has gone from fathomless despair to rapturous joy. Tears still on his cheeks, he is laughing with abandon. In a flash, all is forgiven and, in a flash, all is forgotten.

How different that is with most adults. I know adults who remember in detail every wrong ever done them, adults who bitterly nourish and endlessly replay every hurt ever inflicted on them. They forgive not, they forget not.

Jesus tells us we need to be children again. To let the past be past. That's what Jesus meant when he said—with characteristic oriental hyperbole—"Let the dead bury the dead." Let the past be past. It's over. Become a child again, quick to forgive, quick to move on in trust. There will be hurts, there will be tears, but while the tears are still on our faces, let's smile and go on.

"In my beginning is my end," writes T. S. Eliot regarding this tremendous mystery. In my beginning is my end. Only in going back to my beginning, by becoming a child again, can I discover life in all its fullness and joy. For life's fullness and joy come to those who lay aside their cynicism and who, with hope, open themselves up again to the wonder of their surroundings, who see life in terms of its possibilities, who dream, who risk being hurt by opening themselves honestly to others, who are quick to forgive and start afresh.

I have focused with you on what is to me the operative sentence in St. Mark's little story, Jesus' words: "Whoever does not receive the Kingdom of God like a child shall not enter it."

But those words are not the final words of the story. St. Mark adds, you will recall, one further sentence: "Then Jesus took them into his arms and, laying his hands on them, blessed them." And so, sophisticated, worldly-wise adults-in-the-making—I submit that if you seek to be blessed, that is, if you are looking for a life of happiness and fulfillment, you will find it only if you rediscover and reaffirm the child within you.

28

Beyond Self-Absorption

AST WEEK I was returning from London on the plane. Scarcely a minute after I sat down in my assigned seat, a very attractive teenage girl claimed the seat directly in front of me. We were both in the center section, in aisle seats, and across from this girl sat her mother and younger brother in the two seats on the side.

Eavesdropping over the next several hours, I discovered that this girl was a sixteen-year-old American enrolled at a prestigious New England boarding school. She had just spent three weeks in England with her family, and it was not, I gathered, her first trip. It was easy to eavesdrop; in fact, it was impossible not to eavesdrop. Everyone within ten rows in each direction had to listen to her because everything she said was either very loud or extremely loud.

At first I was absorbed in my newspaper and only vaguely aware that she was constantly leaping out of her seat, wandering around, and then bouncing back down again. Just as I finished the paper, the stewardess brought drinks and I sat contemplating the pleasant prospect of the cool, refreshing Coke resting temptingly on my tray table. Suddenly, however, the Coke literally bounced off the tray table and into my lap. This girl had literally jumped into her seat (the one to which my tray table was attached) and slammed the back of it, sending my Coke flying—spilling onto a fairly embarrassing spot.

She had now arrested my attention, and I realized that I was just the last of many others whose attention she had by now attracted. I will not bore you with all the details about what she did and said, but a sample would include permanently parking her legs and feet in the center of the aisle, despite repeated requests from the stewardesses, so that everyone had to step over them: "But I feel so crowded, I have long legs; I need more room," said this 5'7" girl. She picked a fight with her mother for not buying her a leather jacket she wanted in London. Her mother finally said, "You've already got a leather jacket and anyway I let you buy several thousand dollars worth of clothes for yourself in London." But the girl was obviously determined to get her mother, so she said, "This whole trip's been so boring. I've hated every minute of it." Everything she said was punctuated by repeatedly jumping up from her seat, and then crashing back into it. I was carefully clutching a second rapidly warming Coke, when suddenly onto my tray table flew one of her socks. She had decided to go barefooted and just tossed her socks into the air. All the while she continued to contort herself into every known position, ceaselessly banging against her seat back, as if trying to break it down.

The elderly English couple next to me—on their first trans-Atlantic trip—were by now enraged, and I had to keep reassuring them that this princess was not a "typical American teenager." I was enraged, too, but I have to admit I was even more fascinated. This girl was a virtually perfect study in self-absorption. She was utterly self-absorbed, apparently unaware of anything but her own needs and desires. It was as if the rest of us were an inanimate backdrop to her life, a stage set for her act. I'm sure there's another side to this girl, though there was not the slightest evidence of it for the seven hours and ten minutes the flight lasted. I'm sure that, if I should ever converse with her on some other occasion, she would reveal that she's involved at her boarding school in some politically correct activity, such as Save the Whales. But even involvement in so noble a cause would not, I think, alter the judgment of everyone who observed her on that flight that she was basically a self-absorbed little brat, imprisoned in her own life.

We might expect that someone who can remain so totally focused on herself—to the exclusion of concern for anyone else—would be happy. But, of course, such self-absorption does not bring happiness. This girl was not happy. She never opened her mouth except to complain.

Our Own Self-Absorption

I tell you about this spoiled American preppie not only because I was fascinated by her, but because I think we see in extreme form in her the same self-centeredness and self-absorption that all of us instictively share. In her we see nature untamed; in her we see raw, unmasked self-centeredness (which most of us by adolescence have learned to temper and control).

As babies we are locked into our own lives. When as babies we cry out for attention, we are not aware of disturbing our parents or making problems for others. It only gradually dawns on us as children that there are other people on earth who have to be taken into account. As we mature we become more consciously aware of the needs of others who share the world with us.

But life also involves a continual temptation to return to self-absorption. At a weeklong music festival in England this summer I observed a group of ten Texans who ate every meal together in a tight circle, sat together at the concerts, and talked exclusively to each other. In effect, they pulled the wagons into a circle and kept out all non-Texans. By doing so, they missed ninety percent of the festival experience. When I was a student at Cambridge in the early sixties, there were only about fifty Americans in the whole university. But half of them huddled together—talking condescendingly and suspiciously about "them," that is, the English. The self-absorption of these huddled Americans made them miss many an enriching experience in their time at Cambridge.

There is a great tendency in all of us to withdraw into ourselves, or into safe little cliques of like-minded people—to live sheltered, claustrophobic, risk-free, boring little lives.

Our first inclination is to step back safely into ourselves, into our little group. When we see a homeless man begging for money on the street, we try to look the other way and walk by him. We instinctively recoil from contact with him. A boy said to me last year, "You know, you're always telling us to offer help to strangers when they come into the school. Well I've watched visitors come in before, but I've never gone up to them; someone else always does it before I do. But today I was the only one in the whole hallway. I almost turned around and went the other way. It was really hard to stop and say hello and take them to the admissions office." All encounters—even minor ones such as this boy's—are demanding. It is easier to remain wrapped up in the cocoon of our own little lives.

We all nod gravely and approvingly when we hear the parable of the Good Samaritan, but in real life we find it very hard to stop and help someone; we're constantly warned of all the possible risks. "Don't get involved" is the motto by which many people live.

Risking Involvement

I was standing in line at the post office in Hereford, England, this summer to mail some books back to the United States. Shortly after I got to the window I felt something at my feet and looked down and it was the head of the old man who had been standing in the queue behind me with his wife. He had just crumpled, slumped to the ground. I stepped aside quickly and looked down at him. I was almost as stunned as he was. His wife was wringing her hands and whimpering. As I dithered, a teenage boy towards the back of the line quietly stepped forward, bent down, and said, "You're all right, old dad. We'll get you up and going." And he turned to me and said, "Come on, get his other arm." I obeyed and we soon had the old man on his feet, shaken but mobile.

After this boy had gone to the window, I stopped him and said how impressed I was by his presence of mind. I discovered in chatting with him briefly that he was seventeen and that he had quit school at sixteen (which you can do in England) to become a farmer. He was depositing part of his farmhand earnings in the National Savings program which is run in Britain through the post office. So here was a mere seventeen-year-old who, in American terms, wasn't even going to finish high school—who showed more presence of mind, more willingness to take a risk, more readiness to get involved, more leadership, than the high and mighty headmaster of The Roxbury Latin School. He didn't withdraw, he didn't avert his eyes, he didn't wait for his elders to take charge, he didn't say, "What's this old guy doing on the streets anyway?" He quietly, simply, unofficiously, and immediately got involved.

The course of western history was not changed by his leadership and involvement, but the lives of an old man and his wife were certainly greatly benefited.

This small act of involvement—this capacity and willingness to triumph over our natural tendency to be self-absorbed, our natural tendency to focus on our own needs—has in it the same ingredients as those great acts of involvement that occasionally do alter the course of western history. We saw a veritable raft of Soviet leaders this summer who waited to see which way the wind would blow in the coup. Boris Yeltsin—whatever you may think of his ideas—stepped up and said, "No, this is wrong." And most observers in the West at the time felt he would not survive. He could have evaded and avoided. He didn't need to get involved. He had plenty of excuses not to risk his neck. He could have said, "I'm a Russian official, not a Soviet official." He could have equivocated. But, like the Hereford farm boy, he stepped in, involved himself, took charge, took a risk. And the course of western history was altered.

We hear a great deal today about toleration—about the need to be tolerant of those who are different from us, or who hold opposing viewpoints. Now I'm certainly for toleration. Toleration is right up there with Mom, apple pie, and the American flag. Everybody I know is for toleration. But I'm awfully tired of people stopping at toleration. Toleration is the absolutely minimal good relationship we can have with others, it's the first baby step away from self-absorption. But it is only a baby step away. In a funny way, people practicing toleration are still self-absorbed. They see everything from their viewpoint and condescendingly allow the existence and free expression of others. Toleration involves very little if any risk, and very little if any involvement. One can be tolerant and still be distant, uninvolved, apart. That Hereford farm boy could have been very tolerant of old people (people different from himself), but he also could have remained absolutely aloof from involvement in their lives. Boris Yeltsin could have used toleration as an excuse to equivocate: "Well, after all, everybody is entitled to his opinion. We need to study the matter. These are difficult times; we need to pull together. I'm prepared to give these men a chance to prove themselves," he could have said tolerantly.

The Quality of Our Involvement

The Judeo-Christian revelation on which this school and all it stands for is built, calls us to something greater than toleration. It calls us to involve ourselves in the lives of other people. It calls us to go against our natural, innate tendencies to self-absorption. It furthermore calls us not just to go beyond toleration to involvement, but it calls us to a certain quality of involvement: it calls us to care. It calls us not just to tolerate, not just to involve ourselves, but to love one another.

I was walking towards the cathedral down a narrow pedestrian way in Hereford. At the end of this pedestrian way, two other streets (with car traffic) come together at the edge of the cathedral precincts. As I'd noticed each day, there were two teenage boys at this junction who had obviously been hired for the festival week. They were checking each car in order to make sure that only those cars with special authorization got into the cathedral close. I passed by these boys every day but I hadn't really looked at them. There was nothing unusual about their appearance. They were just ordinary kids, about sixteen years old (I would guess), dressed in T-shirts and jeans.

As I arrived at where they were, pretty much self-absorbed, I paused at the crossing. It was maybe five seconds before I noticed a blind woman who was standing nearby, tapping with her white stick, searching for the curb—which had ended right there at the perimeter of the cathedral grounds. Before I said or did anything, one of the boys noticed her plight and said, "I bet you're trying to get to the cathedral and you've come to the end of the curb." He put himself right in her place. Self-absorbed people—often tolerant people—simply cannot or will not do that. He then went right to her and said, "Here, put your hand on my arm and I'll walk you over to the cathedral—special escort service. And I want you to know that everyone is looking at us because I'm extremely handsome." This boy didn't just involve himself—a risk, an inconvenience, in itself, who could ask for more? But he involved himself with humor and charm and grace. The blind woman not only got to the cathedral, but she enjoyed the trip. That is love.

This kid was hired to park cars, not walk blind women to the cathedral. He had several cast iron excuses to avoid getting involved, to let someone else do it. He could have waited for me or some other adult to help her. He could have been worried about how it would look to others, about whether his buddy or some other kid might laugh at him. But he overcame all the internal and external pressures not to involve himself with this woman. And when he did involve himself he did so with a charm and humor and grace that are the very ingredients of love. My mother used to say, "It's not just what you say, it's the way you say it that's important." It's not just what he did, but the loving way in which he did it that was so stunning.

This boy—and the farm boy in the post office—broke out of the prison of self-absorption. Neither of them changed the course of history, but I submit to you that it is by just such small acts—in which we burst the prison of self and risk involvement—that the whole tenor of a school's life—or a nation's life and even occasionally the world's life— is changed.

The supreme irony, of course, is that while self-absorption brings unhappiness, happiness results from self-risk, inconvenient involvement, self-sacrifice, and costly love.

Am I asking you to be heroes, to risk yourselves—maybe even to risk your lives—for what is right and good? Yes, in all honesty I hope some of you may someday have the opportunity to be Boris Yeltsins. But I also hope you will remember these two—unlikely—Hereford boys who, in their far smaller worlds, heroically burst the prison of their own self-absorption and reached out with love.

I used to be quite despondent about the human race, quite cynical about human nature. And, God knows, there is a great deal to be despondent and cynical about. As I have experienced more of life, however, I have come to think that there are a lot of good people in the world—people who have broken out of themselves, people who risk loving others—not enough such people, but a lot. I dare to hope and pray that each of you will be such a person—that you will have the courage to burst out of the prison of self and to involve yourselves with grace and charm and humor in the lives of others. I hope, in short, that people will say of you when you're gone, "Here was a man of courage who made a difference."

29

Manners Makyth Man

ANNERS MAKYTH MAN is the ancient motto of Winchester College—one of the great schools of England. When I first heard this motto more than twenty-five years ago, it struck me as shallow in its total focus on form and outward appearance. Is it true: manners makyth man? Do manners make us who we are?

If we picked a motto for our time, I think it would probably be "Do your own thing" or "If it feels good, do it; it must be good if it feels good."

When I first came to this school in the early 1970s, an English teacher couldn't correct a set of papers without some student telling him that he was not allowed to object to anything he wrote because he (the student) was "expressing himself." "If that's how I feel then it's valid; you can't criticize how I feel." Never mind if his precious self-expressing thought was a non sequitur or illogical or incompletely reasoned out or just plain wrong. "Self-expression" carried the day. After "self-expression" came self-satisfaction, self-contentment, self-fulfillment, self-realization, and self-everything-else.

These "self" words still remain the fashionable buzz words of our time.

Manners Are Unnatural

Concern with manners is not fashionable. Manners have fallen into disfavor mostly because they are regarded as "unnatural" and "artificial." And, above all, it is fashionable in our time to be "natural" and "real" in our self-expression. Manners are unfashionable because they are curbings or denials of self-expression. As such, manners, in our time, are often considered as "fake" or "hypocritical" or "dishonest."

Any discussion of manners must begin with the admission that manners are unnatural. When we use underarm deodorant we are being, I suppose you could say, dishonest. We are "covering up" our real honest-to-God self-expressing smell. The same goes for brushing our teeth in the morning or combing our hair or taking a shower each day. All are unnatural, artificial denials or curbings of our natural selves.

Manners are unnatural; that's why little children have to be taught manners. Little children defecate in their pants. Little children interrupt. Little children eat with their fingers and don't use a napkin. Little children wake up their parents in the middle of the night if they're hungry or thirsty. They are expressing themselves; they are being their natural selves. They have to be taught manners—forms of behavior that deny or curb their natural self-expression. In that sense, of course, you can call manners dishonest or artificial or fake or whatever pejorative word you want to use. Manners are unnatural.

When I say to a boy, as I will say dozens of times in the next few days, "How was your summer?" I am not always, at the moment when I ask, dying to hear his response. Sometimes I've got a lot of other things on my mind and sometimes it's a struggle to listen to the response and to appear interested. My expression of interest—"How was your summer?"—is not always, in the purest sense, genuine. You could therefore make a case that manners are, in that limited sense, dishonest.

Alexander Solzhenitsyn, the Russian philosopher now living here in New England, writes:

> *When Western Society was established, it was based on the idea that each individual limited his own behavior. Everyone understood what he could do and what he could not do. Since then the only thing we have been developing is rights, rights, rights, rights, at the expense of duty.*

As he often does, Solzhenitsyn oversimplifies, tends to make out that the present is terrible and the past a golden age. But his distinction between rights (such as self-expression) and duties (which usually involve curbing our self-expression) is a useful one, I think. There's no getting around it: manners are an unnatural duty. They involve an unnatural limiting of our natural selves, an unnatural curbing of our rights.

Manners As the Minimum

Let me pause here briefly to define what manners are not. This summer I visited Ireland's most prestigious university, Trinity College in Dublin. I decided to take the tour of its buildings and arrived at the appointed place at 10 A.M. with several others. We were greeted by a twenty-five-year-old graduate student who was spiffily dressed in a bow tie and vest, who was carrying a rolled-up umbrella, and who spoke (what I would call) decorated English (never use a one-syllable word if you can use a four-syllable word). With elegant superficial manners he proceeded to say snotty things about the English (which, as you can imagine, endeared him to me), then about the church, and then about how terrible American education and television and everything else in the United States was. When an American woman in the group asked him a question about the college, he replied, "Madam, I doubt you would understand my answer to your question, so I won't bother to give it to you." He was, in short, an obnoxious little twit (and I deserve the Nobel Peace Prize for not strangling him!). He's the sort of person who gives manners a bad name. Under the veil of superficial good manners, he both did and said ugly things. He was using manners not (as they are designed) to curb his self-centeredness, but to enhance his self-centeredness.

Manners are the most rudimentary way in which we acknowledge the existence of others in the world, in which we curb our natural selfish instincts. They are small, simple acts. Instead of plunging headlong through a door, we pause (we curb our desire to get where we're going) so our elders can go before us. When we're seated in the subway and an older lady comes in, we give up the comfort of our seat out of respect for her existence (and out of recognition that we shall someday perhaps need it as she does now). Such acts are inconvenient; they go against our natural selfish inclinations. At this school, we greet one another in the halls and we acknowledge each other's existence by calling one another by name. We say not just "Hi" or "Hello," but "Hello, Mr. Jarvis" or "Hi, Jim." Since ancient Israel the use of people's names has been the most rudimentary sign of respect. We bother to stop to ask, "How was your summer?" "What did you do?" "How are you?" when we might well rather be on our merry selfish way. We also stop, inconveniently, to ask a visitor to our school if we can help her find what she's looking for.

That is what manners are: the mundane basic recognition that others exist and have as much right to their place on earth as we do. Manners are the fundamental curbings and limitings of our own self-expression.

Beyond Manners

Manners are the first step away from self-centeredness. But only the first step. If we continue on the journey away from self-preoccupation we go beyond manners to kindness, to concern for others. Kindness could be defined as manners with feeling and imagination, manners with grace and charm, manners with extra effort.

Kindness goes beyond manners. Manners greets someone at the door and says, "Can I help you?" Kindness goes beyond—it doesn't just give directions. Kindness impels us to say, "I'll take you there." I'll give you an example: This summer, without calling ahead, I walked into the ancient and renowned Royal School in Armagh, Ireland. A tall floppy teenage boy working intently at some sort of project across the room jumped up from his chair and came over to greet me. "Good morning," he said. "Can I help you?" I told him I was from the United States and wondered if I could see the school. His face broke into a radiant smile (what dramatic effect a smile can have!) and he said, "Welcome to Ireland! I go to the school and I'd be happy to take you around myself." Off we went, he showing me every part of the school with enthusiasm and humor. Here was manners with grace and feeling and charm. Here, in fact, was something more than manners. Here was kindness.

One of the rages of the 1950s—when I was your age—was a card game called Canasta. I never hear of anyone playing it today and you've probably never heard of it—but it was the fad of the fifties. My grandmother loved Canasta, and she was sharp as a tack at it. Since most of her friends seemed to be dead or dying, or unable to remember their cards, she couldn't play as often as she wished, and my mother was always saying to me or my sister: "Go play Canasta with your grandmother!" We were always responding, in the Midwesternese of the era, "I don't wanna." And my mother would repeat, "Go and play Canasta with your grandmother, and act as if you enjoy it!" The "act as if you enjoy it" was, of course, the kindness part. I not only had to play Canasta, I had to go beyond that and act as if I enjoyed it. Now when I was about fourteen, I became extremely wise and I said to my mother one day when we were going through the whole Canasta routine, "I'm not going to act as if I enjoy it. You're asking me to be dishonest. I'm not going to pretend. That's insincere. I can't lie. I won't do it." My mother didn't buy my response and she replied, "Then be dishonest in this one area." Now I had her: "But you're always yelling at me [my mother rarely yelled at me, but at this stage I referred to every motherly admonition as "yelling"] You're always yelling at me to be honest. Now you tell me to be dishonest? What are you asking me to be: honest or dishonest?"

"I'm asking you to be kind," said my mother, "and you're making up excuses to be selfish."

And so I went off to be dishonestly kind to my grandmother, and, as usual, in pretending dishonestly to enjoy playing Canasta with her, I ended up, in fact, actually enjoying doing it.

That happens regularly, I think, when you put on an act. Yesterday at the end of the afternoon when I was extremely busy, a boy came into my office and started in on his summer. With considerable effort I feigned interest, and, then, remarkably, I didn't have to pretend anymore. I suddenly was interested. If you try to show an interest, if you try to whip up enthusiasm in order to be kind, you sometimes are swept up in your enthusiasm and suddenly it's not such an effort anymore.

If manners are the first step and kindness is the second, the third and final step away from self-centeredness is self-sacrifice. It is possible to go beyond even kindness, so that you are willing to make enormous sacrifices of time and energy for no self-gain whatsoever. I was struck this summer by the inscription on the World War I memorial in St. Patrick's Cathedral in Dublin. This is what it said: "When you go home, tell them of us and say that for their tomorrow, we gave our today." Those soldiers didn't want to die, but they were willing to die for something and someone they loved more than their own lives. "Greater love," said Jesus, "hath no man than this, that a man lay down his life for his friend."

We can now see the complete sweep of human possibility. We began with the entirely self-centered baby. We moved first to manners—then to kindness—and finally to costly self-sacrifice.

A Manners Miracle

I want to conclude by telling you something that happened to me on my third day in Dublin this summer. Back when I was a student in England in the sixties, an elderly priest said to me as we walked along the street one day, "Always give something to any beggar who asks you. It might be God himself you're giving to." For years I have done that, as I know many of you do, though the innumerable beggars on the streets of Boston (as of the past couple of years) now provide a huge challenge. My third morning in Dublin was one of those rapturously perfect days you get once or twice a summer: sunny, warm but not hot, a light breeze, no humidity, deep blue sky. As I stepped out of the building where I was staying in St. Stephen's Green, I inhaled the fresh morning air and almost floated down the steps lost in the beauty of the day. As I reached the sidewalk, however, I became unpleasantly aware that sitting on the sidewalk was a mother and baby, both filthy. The mother held up her dish begging for money. I was jarred. I said to myself, "I'm on vacation; I don't need poverty. How dare this woman ruin my perfect morning?" With considerable lack of grace I reached into my pocket, and threw a few coins in her dish. In doing so I wasn't being kind or sacrificing myself; I was acting out of the very lowest form of manners.

As I tried to dash off, she called to me: "Wait! Stop!" Damn, I said to myself, this woman not only wants my money, she wants my time. And I turned around and without an ounce of kindness snapped, "What?" She said, "Thank you! God bless you!" I—barely—said a curt "Thank you" and fled.

I walked a couple of blocks to one of Dublin's "institutions," Bewley's Oriental Cafe. I think I even may have avoided walking where I'd seen a beggar the previous day. I bought the *Irish Times* and arrived at Bewley's at the same time as I'd arrived the previous two days, only today there wasn't a line. I zipped through to get a roll and coffee and sat down to read my paper. After a couple of minutes I looked up and there was a line of about thirty people. I said to myself, "Boy, I lucked out today—there was no line a minute ago when I came through."

The Number One item on my Dublin agenda was to see a play at the Abbey Theatre—probably the most famous theatre in the English-speaking world. Boucicault's *The Shaughraun* was playing, but the notices all said the theatre was sold out the whole time I was to be in Dublin.

On a whim, I said, well, what the heck, I'll walk over to the Abbey and see if by any chance I can get a ticket. The sign there said, "Tonight's Performance Sold Out." There was just one man standing in front of the box office window so I waited. When he left, I stepped up and said, "You don't by any chance have a single ticket for tonight, do you?" "You're in luck," the box office man said. "The man in front of you just turned in his ticket. I'll sell it to you!" "Fantastic," I said, and gave him twelve Irish pounds. "Is it a good seat?" I then asked. "Fourth row center," said the man and handed me the ticket. "Wow," I said.

All my adult life I've heard of the Turner watercolors at the National Gallery of Art in Dublin. By terms of the donor's will more than a hundred years ago, they can be exhibited only during January, the month with the least sunlight. That way they won't fade—something watercolors easily do. I knew all about the will but I wanted to see the rest of the gallery anyway, so I decided I might as well ask about the Turners. "By any chance could I see the Turner watercolors?" I asked the lady at the desk. She replied, "They're on display during January and at a few other special times," but when I told her how long I'd be in Dublin, she said she was sorry but I wouldn't be able to see them. I said, "OK, thanks a lot" or some such, but I must have looked disappointed. And as I started to turn away she said, "You look so downhearted." I said, "Oh no, that's the breaks. I just thought I'd ask." "Well, wait a minute," she said. "Let me see if I can do anything." And she picked up the phone and embarked on what was obviously a fairly insistent conversation with an unenthusiastic person on the other end. And in a minute or two we were scrambling up several flights of stairs, going through doors with combination punches, until suddenly we were face to face with a man in a darkened room. "You want to see the Turners, I understand," he said. "Yes," I said. "Stand there," he said. And he drew the long black curtain, the overhead lights went on, and there magically spread before my eyes were the fifty Turner watercolors. I just gasped.

Two hours later—after I'd toured the rest of the gallery—I was back on the street walking toward Dublin Castle. As I approached the first street corner the "Walk" light went on and I went straight across without a hitch. As I reached the next corner, the "Walk" light again clicked on as I arrived at the curb. When the same thing happened as I approached the third intersection, it suddenly hit me: no line at Bewley's Cafe, the single ticket at the Abbey Theatre, the special viewing of the Turner watercolors, the lights turning to "Walk" at each street corner. I remembered the woman saying, "God bless you."

That morning I had thought that I was the generous giver and she the probably undeserving recipient. After all, I gave her my money; she had no claim on it. Now I realized that, in the great mystery of things, she had been the giver and I the graceless, grudging, ungrateful recipient.

That's the moral of this story: even if you are—like this woman—reduced to the dregs of life, to the lowest circumstances in which a human being can find himself, no one can take away from you your fundamental civility (the basic manners that are the foundation of civilization) and no one can take away from you that even higher virtue: the option, the right, to be kind. The woman not only said "Thank you" but "God bless you." We know from many accounts that even those who were imprisoned in the Nazi concentration camps, stripped of every possession (even their hair shaven off), degraded by every form of abuse and indignity, still had the option to be kind, still had the capacity to reach out to others.

And never doubt the amazing power of kindness. The kindness of this poor, filthy woman in Dublin—whom I had so resented for disturbing my perfect day—and who could so easily have focused on her own problems, who could so easily have reserved her kindness (as we so often do) for someone who deserved it (rather than asking a blessing on someone who already had far more than she had), the kindness of this woman brought a blessing on my whole day.

I reached the curb at that third intersection and stopped. The people behind me bumped into me as they hurried to cross the street. With some difficulty I turned around against the tide and started walking back to St. Stephen's Green where my day had started. I wanted to see her again, really, this time, to look at her and—a belated thought—I wanted to thank her. With each step I walked faster and faster. By the last block before St. Stephen's Green, I was nearly running. Panting, I burst round the last corner into the Green . . . but, of course, she had vanished.

30

Three Phrases to Live By

'D LIKE TO TALK BRIEFLY about three words, three simple phrases. They are phrases we need to use often, phrases we need courage to utter.

First, the words "I'm wrong." How we hate to say them: to people in authority, to our friends, perhaps especially to our parents. We feel humiliated, ashamed, vulnerable when we say them. And the temptation is strong to try to evade saying them.

I suppose the classic public example of this effort to evade is Watergate.

President Nixon's secretary Rosemary Woods maintained that she "accidentally" erased twenty critical minutes of a tape by reaching for her phone. When she demonstrated how she did this, she had to contort and twist her whole body out of shape and nearly everybody felt she was really twisting and contorting the truth.

President Nixon himself obfuscated and in the guise of compassion deftly sought to place on others the responsibility for being wrong. Listen carefully to this segment of Nixon's interview with David Frost:

> *I'm convinced that if it hadn't been for Martha (Mitchell) and God rest her soul, because she, in her heart, was a good person. She just had a mental and emotional problem that nobody knew about. If it hadn't been for Martha, there'd have been no Watergate, because John wasn't minding the store. He was letting Magruder and all these kids, these nuts, run this thing. Now, am I saying here, at this juncture, that Watergate should be blamed on Martha Mitchell? Of course not. I'm trying to explain my feeling of compassion for my friend, John Mitchell.*

When the president's assistant Alexander Haig was asked how he thought the tape was erased, he passed the buck to the ultimate recipient attributing the erasure to "some sinister force," something like the fate or destiny that the gods decree on hapless humans in classical literature.

Those of you who have studied Western Civilization will be familiar with the greatest buck-passer of them all, Moses' right-hand man, Aaron. While Moses was away on Mount Sinai, the people—as the people are wont to do—reverted to crass materialism. They said to Aaron, "Up, make us gods, as for this Moses . . . we know not what has become of him." And Aaron, eager to be popular and to accommodate the people, collected their jewelry and made them a golden calf to worship, just like the one the Egyptians had. When Moses returned and saw the people, now debauched in materialism, dancing before the golden calf, he was enraged and demanded of Aaron an explanation. Though he (Aaron) had been left in charge, he passes the buck, blaming the people. "And Aaron said, Let not your anger wax hot. Thou knowest the people, that they are set on mischief. For they said to me, make us gods . . . And I said to them: Whosoever hath any gold, let them break it off. So they gave me it. I cast it into the fire. And: out came this calf!" Who? Me? Responsible?

How hard it is to say, "I was wrong." How tempting it is to make artful excuses, to pass the buck to someone else or to some force beyond our control. How tempting it is to lie, and obfuscate, and evade. How terribly hard it is to face up and to say, "I'm wrong."

One of the greatest attributes of the ancient Hebrews was their willingness to record all the worst as well as the best aspects of the character of their nation's great leaders. An example is the Prophet Nathan's confrontation of King David. Again you remember, David conspired to have Uriah the Hittite killed by having him placed in the center of the battle so that he (David) could then marry Uriah's wife, Bathsheba. When Nathan realized what David had done, he came to the king and told him this story.

There were two men in a certain city, the one rich and the other poor. The rich man had very many flocks and herds; but the poor man had nothing but one little ewe lamb, which he had bought. And he brought it up, and it grew up with him and with his children; it used to eat of his morsel, and drink from his cup, and lie in his bosom, and it was like a daughter to him. Now there came a traveller to the rich man, and he was unwilling to take one of his own flock or herd to prepare for the wayfarer who had come to him, but he took the poor man's lamb, and prepared it for the man who had come to him. Then David's anger was greatly kindled against the man; and he said to Nathan, "As the Lord lives, the man who has done this deserves to die; and he shall restore the lamb fourfold, because he did this thing, and because he had no pity." Nathan said to David, "You are the man. Thus says the Lord, the God of Israel, 'I anointed you king over Israel, and I delivered you out of the hand of Saul, and gave you the house of Israel and of Judah; and if this were too little, I would add to you as much more. Why have you despised the word of the Lord, to do what is evil in his sight? You have smitten Uriah the Hittite with the sword, and have taken his wife to be your wife, and have slain him with the sword of the Ammonites.'"

What did David say? "Who do you think you are, making such outrageous and unprovable (and they were unprovable) accusations?" What did David say? "This man Nathan poses a threat. Take him out and silence him." David could have said and done these things. He had the power to do so. But, instead, the king said, right there, in the open, for all to hear, "I have sinned against the Lord." He said, in short, "I was wrong." And he repented.

It is a sad fact of my own experience, and I think of most people's experience, that if we set about to do anything, to accomplish anything, we will, at times, be wrong. The only way to avoid being wrong is never to do anything. There is a class of people, of course, who attempt little of significance in life, whose life's work is mainly to stand on the sidelines and criticize the players. They attempt nothing great and so make few mistakes, and they delight in the mistakes of others. But, since most of you are attempting great things—now and in the future—you will make mistakes and need from time to time to come to grips with being wrong.

People who are afraid to admit they're wrong cannot, of course, learn from their mistakes. Courageous people face up to their mistakes. They're truthful to themselves and to others. They don't succumb to the temptation to evade, to lie, to obfuscate, to pass the buck. They are able to admit that they are wrong. And they learn from their mistakes.

"I'm Sorry"

If it is hard to say "I'm wrong" it is even harder to say the second of the phrases I want to talk about: "I'm sorry." When we say "I'm wrong" we take responsibility for our own mistake. When we say "I'm sorry" we recognize that our mistake affects not only ourselves but others.

A few years ago here at Roxbury Latin I had just harangued the School in Hall about eating—reminding students that eating was not allowed in a number of areas (and I named them) including the Reception Room. The very next day I walked into the Reception Room and sitting right there on the couch, just returned from an open campus outing, was a junior reaching into his brown paper bag. With considerable anger I said, "You heard what I said, Andy. You know perfectly well you're not supposed to eat in the Reception Room!" And I stormed on, concluding, "Your open campus privileges are revoked for the rest of the term." After a brief silence, Andy said quietly, "I'm on the stage crew and I've just been out on my free period to get this bag of nails for the set." And he reached into the bag and brought out a handful of nails.

A fireworks of emotions exploded in my mind. I felt cornered and I wanted to wriggle out. It occurred to me to say, "Well, it may be nails this time, but it was food before." I felt angry at myself for being so stupid as to be trapped, and I sought in vain for an escape—someone to pass the buck to, some way of evading responsibility. Somehow, amid all this mental explosion, I said, "I'm sorry, Andy. I was wrong. I thought you had food in the bag. I'm sorry. I owe you one." The room was full of boys, and I hated to have to admit I was wrong and to say I was sorry. At such moments we feel, perhaps, an exaggerated sense of shame and embarrassment. It was almost as if I could hear Dan Rather saying on the evening news: "And this afternoon in Boston, at the oldest school in continuous existence in North America, the headmaster, heretofore regarded as an honorable and decent man, falsely accused a junior of eating food in the School's ancient reception room. A humiliating public apology ensued, and the School was reported quiet by day's end." (Or perhaps waking up to the *Herald*'s headline the next morning: "JR. NAILS HUB HEAD.")

Now when I said to Andy, "I'm sorry. I owe you one," the "owe-you-one" was a token of my repentance in deed as well as word. And scarcely an hour went by before another junior came to my office and said politely that Andy respectfully requested my presence in the Reception Room. Repairing there, I discovered him with most of the Second Class, eating about a ten-foot long submarine sandwich. It was hard, it was very hard, but I owed him one and I said nothing, biting my tongue. Andy also said nothing; he just smiled, biting into his submarine.

Saying you're sorry is sometimes very galling. You feel ashamed, disgraced, disadvantaged. A coward cannot bear to admit he's wrong or to say he's sorry. A coward cannot bear to be vulnerable in that way.

There is a lie making the rounds on television and in popular magazines. The lie is this:

"Love means never having to say you're sorry." Nothing could be further from the truth. Nothing is more destructive of a real relationship than the unwillingness to be vulnerable, than the unwillingness to realize and admit that you can do and say things that hurt others and for which you should be sorry. Love means having to say you're sorry often.

"Thank You"

The third and final phrase is "thank you." Europeans frequently comment on how Americans expect life to be good to them. Despite the fact that many people of the world are hungry and homeless, despite the fact that most of the world's population do not live in a democracy or enjoy material advantages and opportunities for education and advancement, we Americans tend to take all these things for granted. A European teacher, now transplanted to this country, said to me: "Americans nourish and indulge their children to such a degree that they leave them ill-prepared for the harsh realities of life." Americans do expect much from life. They do take things for granted.

What he says of Americans may be true, but taking things for granted—ingratitude, if you like—is a human, not just an American, characteristic.

St. Luke records this healing by Jesus in his Gospel: "There met him ten men that were lepers, which stood afar off. And they lifted up their voices and said, Jesus, Master, have mercy on us. And when he saw them he said to them, Go show yourselves to the priests. And it came to pass, that as they went, they were cleansed. And one of them, when he saw that he was healed, turned back, and with a loud voice glorified God and knelt at Jesus' feet and gave him thanks (and he was a Samaritan). And Jesus said, Were there not ten cleansed? Where are the nine? None returned to give glory to God except this foreigner."

Where are the nine? They got what they wanted. They're off to the next thing in life. All of you have experienced what Jesus experienced here. You have all performed some (perhaps costly) act of kindness only to watch the recipient walk off without showing the least hint of gratitude or offering even a murmur of thanks.

That is why you can understand how critical the words "thank you" are in human relationships. When we say "thank you" we affirm the existence and even the importance of others. We recognize that we are not the central sun around whom all other planets revolve. We stop to acknowledge that others give us shelter, help, support, and affection without which our lives would be very different.

Life is not—as some want it to be—a rose garden. Those who expect life to be fair, those who expect life to be for them easy and accommodating and filled with exclusively happy experiences doom themselves to a life of bitter disillusionment. And we all know people whose lives are one long complaint about being treated unfairly, about not getting their just deserts, about not being recognized, about not achieving their heart's desire. We all know people who spend their lives focusing on all that's wrong.

The opposite of that kind of life is what we might call living thankfully.

And it seems to me that those who have grown up, who have "put away childish things," realize that life is hard. They do not expect everything that happens to them to be favorable, they do not assume that only good things happen to good people, they do not take the blessings they presently enjoy for granted. They assume nothing; they take nothing for granted. And they live day by day finding each day something to be thankful for.

I remember the change that Billy McDonald, Class of 1980, underwent when he met some of the other children at the Floating Hospital. Billy knew he was dying of cancer and that he had only a few months to live, and yet he was able to say, "Boy, compared to them, I'm lucky. They're really young. They never got to do anything. I have a lot to be thankful for."

It is my experience that the happy people are those who assume nothing and who live each day aware of their good fortune—giving thanks for all they do enjoy, however little that may be. Happy are those who "count their blessings."

I will close with part of a poem that says this far better than I can— a poem written by Dietrich Bonhoeffer, the German Protestant pastor who opposed Hitler and who was imprisoned throughout the war. These are the words he wrote to his parents at New Year's 1945, a few weeks before he was executed. They express for me—and I hope they will for you what it means to live each day thankfully:

> *With every power for good to stay and guide me,*
> *Comforted and inspired beyond all fear,*
> *I'll live these days with you in thought beside me,*
> *And pass, with you, into the coming year.*
> *The old year still torments our hearts, unhastening;*
> *The long days of our sorrow still endure;*

Father, grant to the souls Thou hast been chastening
What Thou hast promised, the healing and the cure.
Should it be ours to drain the cup of grieving
Even to the dregs of pain, at Thy command,
We will not falter, thankfully receiving
All that is given by Thy loving hand.
Today, let candles shed their radiant greeting;
Lo, on our darkness are they not Thy light
Leading us, haply, to our longed-for meeting?
Thou canst illumine even our darkest night.

31

Getting Away
with Murder

OST PARENTS have certain expressions they use over
and over. The expression my mother most frequently
used with me was: "You think you can get away with murder!" I can hear her now at the dinner table: "You didn't
mow the lawn today, did you?" "No," I would reply—offering some
excuse. And my mother would respond: "You think you can get away
with murder." During the school year she'd say something like: "I
suppose you 'forgot' to do those extra arithmetic problems for Mrs.
Englebret?" "She didn't ask me for them," I'd respond. "Did you do
them?" "No, I forgot." And my mother would respond: "You think you
can get away with murder!"

She was right. I often *did* wear down adults and get away without
mowing the lawn or doing the arithmetic problems.

My Life in Crime

My most memorable moment in getting away with things came in
the summer before fourth grade. I was playing with Rusty Stewart—in
his house across the street. It was time for lunch, and I was going out
the Stewarts' backdoor. There on the kitchen table was a fifty cent
piece—money, I knew, left out for the egg man who came in once a
week through all our backdoors to deliver eggs. Without missing a
beat, I glanced deftly over my shoulder to make sure I was alone, and
then with a single brilliant stroke, swept the fifty cent piece into my

hand and glided out the door. When Mrs. Stewart questioned me that afternoon, I put on my injured-innocence act ("Me? Mrs. Stewart, do you really think I would steal something of yours?") and she was the one who was left feeling guilty.

I had no sense of guilt whatsoever. Rarely, in fact, have I felt such exhilaration, such sheer rapture, at the discovery that there were a lot of stupid adults in the world and that I was smarter than they were. Bathed in self-congratulation, I instant-replayed my dazzling execution of this theft over and over in my mind. What a feat of brilliance and of daring on my part! How great to have been born smart in a world of stupid people!

There was certainly an element of rebellion in what I did. As little kids we are told, "Don't steal things," "Don't lie," etc. This often creates—it did in me, anyway—a rebellious reaction.

I was allowed as a boy—before the days of television—to have a radio next to my bed on condition that I never listen to anything after 9:30. But every night I rebelliously kept the radio on later than that. My father would sometimes sneak up to my bedroom door and quickly open it to catch me. But I could see his shadow break the crack of light under the door and I always had the radio off before he caught me. Since I won this game every time, I came even more to realize how naive, how stupid, adults were—and how brilliant and daring I was.

In *King Lear*, which the seniors read last term, Edmund plays on the naivete, on the stupidity, if you like, of his unsuspecting father and brother—both of whom foolishly trust him and both of whom end up being duped. Edmund speaks of his "credulous father"—a father who foolishly believes him—and his "noble" brother "Whose nature is so far from doing harms/That he suspects none; on whose foolish honesty/My practices ride easy."

That's the way I felt. You could lie to people and they would stupidly believe you. Since most adults were stupid and I was smart, I didn't have to play by the rules. I could get away with murder. And I did—playing easily on the "foolish honesty" of my noble parents and my kindhearted neighbors. The New York multimillionaire hotel magnate, Leona

Helmsley, put it best when she bragged, "Paying taxes is for the little people." Smart people—big people—don't have to play by the rules.

Such an attitude is bolstered by all sorts of rationalizations: Even at age nine, I could say to myself, "If Mrs. Stewart is so stupid as to leave money on the table, and others are so stupid as to pass it by and not take it, that's not my problem. I have the guts and I have the smarts to grab it. She'll never miss the money, anyway. And besides I get one of the smallest allowances on the street—a quarter a week, outrageously little." By the end of this process of rationalization, I had become in my own mind not just brilliant and deserving of this stupid woman's money, but I had transformed myself into Robin Hood stealing from the rich to help the poor; I had become Karl Marx inventing a just economic system and redistributing the world's wealth.

I was never caught for this theft; I got away with it (and with a lot of other things). Mrs. Stewart has gone to her grave without her fifty cents and without knowing I was the thief.

Most of you—in childhood—had to come to grips with the issue of honesty, and most of you had to develop a moral code by the time you got here. You know you will be tempted to lie and steal and you are pretty well armed to resist temptation when it inevitably comes your way. Incidents of lying and stealing here are extremely rare.

You are—by now—basically and generally honest. Some years ago, a psychologist friend of mine and I decided to conduct an experiment. I placed a five dollar bill on the windowsill by the stone goddess on the stairway outside my office. The psychologist and I had placed a bet with each other about how long it would take for some boy walking by to pocket the five dollars. Within five minutes, however, a freshman boy coming down from homeroom, picked it up, took it into the office and said, "Someone left this on the windowsill. He'll be looking for it." We repeated this experiment for the next few days—each time with the same result. Within forty minutes back came the five dollars to the office. The results of this experience leave little room for cynicism about your honesty.

Lying and stealing are rare, but pressures to cheat are far greater in a place like this where almost every student is striving to achieve excellence. From all I hear, we have less cheating than most schools, but every year there are boys who are "caught" cheating.

There are also, I am sure, boys who cheat here and who do not get caught. Such students apparently "get away with murder." Watching a kid cheat when I was your age—or catching one when I became a teacher—used to upset me. My perspective is different now: I now believe that the lucky ones are not those who get away with murder; the lucky ones are the ones who get caught. They learn something relatively early in life about reality; they are forced at a relatively early age to do some painful and hard thinking. I've repeatedly had the experience of men in their twenties and thirties and forties telling me years later that the best thing that happened to them in school was getting caught. One said to me in New York a few weeks ago: "I watch these guys cheat on their taxes and get caught at age thirty-five, or cheat on their wife and get caught at age forty-five. They thought they'd go through life getting away with murder. I learned at school when I was fourteen that you don't get away with murder."

Rationalizing Our Crimes

What we always hope for, when we catch a boy cheating, is that he will say, simply, "Yes, I'm sorry. I did it. I make no excuses. I'm prepared to pay the consequences." And that often happens—with the toughest kids, the ones with the guts to face up to themselves.

Sometimes, however, a boy doesn't face up. The most striking example (that I know) of this inability to face up is an incident I dealt with as a teenager, when I was a lifeguard one summer. We had a nine-year-old boy who each day was observed by his friends and by us lifeguards peeing in the pool. I took him aside privately and told him he'd have to stop. He said, "I don't pee in the pool—it's unsanitary and it's wrong because there are others in the pool." He then went on to elaborate a list of reasons not to pee in the pool that was far longer and better thought out than the list I was giving him. I was puzzled, but I thought, well, I guess he won't do it anymore. But the very next day, one of the kids suddenly shouted, "Jon's peeing in the pool!" I was nearby and could see him and I said to him, "Jon, stop it." "I'm not peeing in the pool," he stated emphatically. "I would never do such a thing." "Look down," I shouted, "You are!" Despite repeated requests, however, he would not look down. It was simply too painful for him to see the evidence. He wanted to believe he didn't pee in the pool at the very same time he was doing so.

Occasionally boys caught cheating here can't face up to the reality. Their first line of defense is usually, "I know it's wrong to cheat. It might look like I'm cheating, but I would never do that." They know it's wrong, so they don't want to think of themselves as cheaters. A smarter, more verbally facile boy will try to talk his way out of things, will try the redefining-terms routine: "Do you really think that's cheating? What exactly is cheating?" etc. And a debater may even try intimidation: "Are you accusing me of cheating? Is that what you're saying? If so, you'd better have very solid evidence."

After such a person has been well and duly cornered, he usually marshals a raft of excuses. The first is always: "Everyone else cheats. Why are you picking on me?" (This is rather like getting caught for speeding and saying, "About fifty cars have gone by me. Why are you picking on me for exceeding the speed limit?") The answer in both cases is: "Even if everybody else was cheating or speeding (and they weren't), you are the one who was caught and you know it's wrong."

A second excuse often arises at this point, "I was under a lot of pressure and I was only going to cheat this once. I really intended to go back and learn it all correctly." But, of course, it is exactly when you are under pressure that you find out who you are. If there is no need for you to cheat (if you're not under pressure), then there's no virtue in not cheating. It's only when you feel the need to cheat, it's only when you are under pressure, that you discover whether or not you have the guts to be honest.

A third excuse can run something like this: "If he's stupid enough not to cover up his answers (or if the teacher's stupid enough not to watch what's going on right under his nose), then it's not my fault." This excuse contains the hidden admission that the cheating was not hard to accomplish because another person made it so easy. In this school and in the offices you will someday work in (and school and the real world are remarkably alike!), it will be easy to cheat. It will require no brilliance, no cleverness, no guts. Any fool can do it. You may—like I did when I was nine stealing the fifty cents—tell yourself you are brilliant, but such an act really requires no brilliance, no guts.

My all-time favorite excuse, however, was that offered by a boy here several years ago. "Why did you cheat?" I asked him, and received this solemn reply: "I did it for my parents. Grades aren't important to me, but to my parents they're everything. I did it for them." Very adroitly, of course, he had neatly turned his vice into a virtue. He had convinced himself that cheating was an act of love.

Smart boys think up smart excuses. Brilliant boys think up brilliant excuses. The smarter you are the better you can rationalize, the better you can lie to yourself.

Deluding Ourselves

So far I've tried to make two points: First, that it is possible—even easy—to "get away with murder." I did so as a child. Perhaps you did. You all know people who have done so. Second, that the lucky ones are those who get caught at an early age and who then take stock of themselves and become strong adults able to overcome temptation and rationalization. (The unlucky ones don't get caught till they're older when their careers and personal lives can be endangered or destroyed.)

What I've said so far is pretty conventional stuff, things most of you have thought about in some depth. My final point is one that I have never spoken about before, nor have I seen it expressed elsewhere. But it is something that, in talking with people in the "outside world," I have observed more and more frequently. My final point is this: more and more I see people getting caught who don't know they've *been* caught, people who *think* they're getting away with murder who are not.

Let me give you one example from school life. Years ago at my former school—where I was teaching psychology—I conducted an experiment of the sort I just described, using the three ninth grade history sections I taught. (Since the experiment involved entrapment, I discussed it with an administrator, and we agreed that no one except me would know what happened and that no disciplinary action would result.) To each of my three history sections I said, "I didn't record the results of the test I handed back four days ago in my grade book." My disingenuous statement led them to believe that I had forgotten to record the grades; in actuality, while I technically didn't record the grades, I had xeroxed every boy's test. "Could you tell me the grade I gave you?" Most did, but a few said, "Can I tell you tomorrow? I'm not sure what I got." I waited. When I had all the grades, I checked them against my xerox copies. Everyone in the first section had told the truth. Everyone in the second section had told the truth. Everyone in the third section had told the truth, except one boy, who had raised his grade by seven points (we marked by numbers, not letters). The next day I asked all three sections, "Could you bring in all your tests? I want to make sure there are no mistakes." For two of the three sections, obviously, I was just going through the motions. Inevitably, there were three or four in each class who had not saved their tests as they were supposed to, and, for the sake of consistency, I asked each of them, "You're sure about the grade?" "Yes, I am," said each. Finally I got to the third section, where I wasn't going through the motions. The boy who was lying was, of course, one of the three who'd "lost" his test. I looked each of the three in the eye and asked, "Are you sure this was your grade?" Each of the three, including the boy who was lying, said, "Yes." I'm not sure how I would handle it today, but I recorded the grade the lying boy told me he'd received in my grade book, and never said anything to him. I let him get away with murder, in other words. Two years later I went back to speak at his graduation and told him (privately) what I had done. He admitted it and then said, "You mean you knew all along?"

I recount this incident that happened long ago, because I am more and more struck by similar tales I hear from friends of mine in the outside world—from bosses in business offices who are in a position to promote or block someone's promotion. I'm struck by how often I hear about people who think they're getting away with something when, in fact, they are not.

Let me give you a few examples, in somewhat altered form, that I've heard about.

A young man repeatedly comes to work a little late. His boss speaks to him about it several times, but soon again he's often a little late. To him it's not important; he thinks it's something he's getting away with. To his boss, however, it's important, but his boss gets tired of confronting him. The young man is surprised when the other new guy in the office gets a promotion and he doesn't. Sadly, the young man never finds out the reason, never knows that he didn't get away with what he thought he was getting away with.

Another young man picks up the check (which will go on an expense account) at the restaurant where he, his boss, and two clients have just had dinner. After paying the bill, they walk out together, and the young man says, "Did you enjoy your free drinks? The idiots forgot to put the drinks and the wine on the check." The young man thinks he's gotten away without paying the full bill, and he has. What he doesn't realize is the bad impression he's made on at least one of the three people with him. His boss doesn't say anything to him, but he gives the next promotion to someone else. The tragedy is the young man will never know why he didn't get the job. The young man's bragging ended up costing him dearly, but he will never know that.

An office manager said to me recently, "I require long reports from my younger employees about every two weeks. I tell all of them they're important. When they're first here I send their reports back if they're not good enough. After a while, however, I get tired of that. If they go on writing sloppy reports, I eventually give up on them and stop sending their reports back. They think they're getting away with sloppy work, they think their coworkers who are devoting hours of meticulous care to their reports are fools. They're always so surprised when the others get promoted and they're left behind. They are the fools: they thought they were getting away with murder."

Even when you don't think people are looking, they often are. People form impressions of you in seemingly insignificant situations. They probably won't tell you they think you're irresponsible; you just won't get the promotion. They probably won't tell you when they think you're not completely trustworthy, you just won't get the promotion.

It is also true that you sometimes won't know why you got a promotion. A few years ago, a Roxbury Latin boy was working at an ice cream shop. His parents told me that the manager had promoted him over the head of the other teenagers working there, even though he was one of the youngest. I stopped by the shop one night, after going to the movies nearby, to say hello. I asked the manager if the boy was there. He said, "Why, are you his father?" "No," I said. "I'm one of his teachers." And he said to me, "He's not here, but let me tell you, he's one hell of a kid, about the best I've ever had here." "Really?" I said. He said, "Yeah, he's absolutely honest. If I leave money around, he always brings it to me. He came to me once to show me he'd accidentally undercharged a customer and offered to make it up out of his pay. He broke up a fight the other night by getting between two kids who were about a foot taller than he is." I said to the manager, "Did you tell Matt all this?" "No," he said. This boy had done the right thing over and over just because it was the right thing. He expected no reward and he was not aware that the whole time the manager was noticing everything he did.

My point is this: people who think they're getting away with things in life often are not—but they'll never know it. And people who think they're doing the right thing and nobody notices or cares often are noticed and people do care.

The older I get the more I believe that people rarely—in any important or long-range sense—get away with murder. Other people are much smarter and much more observant than they are given credit for by those who think you can get away with things in life. The real fools are not those who are trustworthy and trusting; the real fools are those who try to get away with murder and who never realize that others come to see them for who they are.

In the long haul of life, honor and honesty are best. St. Paul said all of this better than I can when he wrote this advice to his little band of followers at Philippi, and so I'll conclude with his words to live by: "Whatsoever things are true, whatsoever things are honorable, whatsoever things are just, whatsoever things are pure, whatsoever things are lovely, whatsoever things are of good report; if there be any virtue, if there by any praise, think on these things." Truth, honor, justice, purity, loveliness, reputation. These are the virtues that characterize a life worth living.

32

The Fine Art of Rationalization

VER SINCE the School's 350th birthday party, I have heard over and over how wonderful the boys of Roxbury Latin were: helpful, courteous, friendly, hardworking, responsible.

To all of us, however, there is a darker side: a me-first, others-be-damned, I'm-number-one, why-should-I-care side. And it is this side of ourselves that I'd like to examine this morning. In particular, I'd like to focus on the capacity within all of us to rationalize our discourteous, self-centered, irresponsible, and selfish attitude and behavior.

Elementary Level Rationalization

Let me begin some time ago on a Monday morning after a Friday night school dance. As usual, one of the classes had sponsored the dance, and the members of the class had agreed to be there to help out. The dance started at eight, I think. At about nine a small group of boys from the sponsoring class took off—they thought stealthily—for a party elsewhere. How clever they were: no one would miss them at school, and their parents would think they were at a well-supervised school dance.

I myself talked individually with two of the boys on Monday morning. Each responded in his own way.

The first took what I'd call the "sweet innocence" approach: his eyes clouded over with a mystified look and he said, "Gee, I didn't look at it

269

as evading responsibility. I see what you mean. I just never thought of it that way." I said to myself: either this kid defines for all eternity the word "clueless" or else he is an Olympian liar. He soon tipped his hand by going too far: "I just don't think of myself as a person who matters that much, and there were plenty of others there who were enjoying themselves," etc., etc. There is nothing quite as sad as listening to someone who believes the lie he is telling. This kid had convinced himself of his basic innocence.

What he was doing, of course, was rationalizing: if I can convince Mr. Jarvis (or if I can convince myself) that I just didn't realize that what I was doing was wrong, then I will absolve myself of any guilt. The oh-gosh-I-never-really-thought-about-it rationalization is one that almost all teenagers have in their repertoire.

The other boy was a refreshing contrast, because he offered no rationalization. "Yeah," he said to me, "as I skipped out I said to myself, I shouldn't be doing this. I said I'd stay. Probably someone will notice. And I did tell my parents I'd be at School till the dance was over." No glazed-over eyes, no mystified look, no verbal rationalization. His honesty did not make up for his failure of responsibility, but it did leave me with a fundamental respect for his courage in facing reality. And I'd have to say that ever since then I've never been able to bring myself to trust the first kid, while I have felt great trust for the second, even though they did the same thing.

Closely related to the "sweet innocence" rationalization is the "I forgot" rationalization. Little boys do this all the time: "Did you clean your room today, like I told you?" "I forgot." "Did you wash your hands before supper?" "I forgot." "Did you give your teacher the note I gave you?" "I forgot."

We forget what we do not want to remember—we forget responsibilities that interfere with our doing what we want to do. Every teacher has dealt with the student who gives him a mystified look and exclaims, "I thought we had another week before that paper was due." This excuse is even more convincing if you can get one or two others to "remember" the same thing. I heard a Roxbury Latin boy saying last winter to a mother who had waited and waited for him and finally found him shooting baskets in the gym at six, "I forgot you were picking us up at five."

This rationalization is not limited to teenagers. In my first year here, there was a teacher who "forgot" to do his advisor letters. "Oh, I forgot they were due today," he said to me jovially. "I'll get them out this week." "By tomorrow," I said. "OK," he replied. Two days later he still hadn't handed in a single advisor letter. "Advisor letters?" I said to him. "Oh gosh, that's right," he said with that cheerful look of surprise I'm sure he'd used in similar situations for years. "Don't worry. I'll get them done." "Tomorrow," I said. "OK," he said. This went on for almost three weeks. I really think he believed his own lie—that he'd forgotten—each time he uttered it. He thought I'd forget. I didn't, and at year's end he departed to labor in another corner of the vineyard.

But sometimes you can wear people down and they will—apparently—forget. With considerable trepidation, I helped a Roxbury Latin grad get a job with someone I know in business. After he hired him, this friend of mine said to the Roxbury Latin grad, "Your reports are due every Monday morning at nine. No exceptions. No excuses. Every Monday at nine." In his first six weeks, this Roxbury Latin graduate finished not a single report by Monday at nine. The first few times he offered excuses. After that, when the boss stopped telling him how important the deadline was, he just assumed he'd worn the boss down. But the boss had not been worn down; the boss was simply devoting his energies to finding a replacement. When the Roxbury Latin grad was let go, I asked him, "What happened?" (even though my friend, his boss, had already told me). "I really don't know," he said to me. In the course of our conversation, I asked him, "Did you get all the required work handed in on time?" "No," he said, "but after the first few weeks it didn't seem to bother him. His Monday deadline was ridiculous." This young man thought he was getting away with something. But he deceived only himself: he was not getting away with anything. The boss had simply given up on him and was getting ready to dump him. Sadly, when this kid was fired, the boss felt no obligation to sit him down and explain things to him. I don't think the kid realizes to this day why he was let go.

I have observed this pattern over and over in my life—people convinced they are getting away with something, people convinced they have worn someone down, who are too stupid to realize that people are on to them and that eventually they will pay.

Intermediate Level Rationalization

But the "sweetly innocent" and "forgetful" tactics are not the only ones you can use to rationalize your behavior.

One popular tactic—especially among juniors and seniors—is to adopt an attitude of condescending superiority. In addressing your parent or other adult authority you adopt a sophisticated pose and you condescend: "When are you going to acknowledge that I've grown up? You're the only ones who treat me like a ten-year-old. It's embarrassing when you call and check if a kid's parents are going to be home. You're always asking me where I'm going. Don't you trust me?" I lighted my father up once by saying, "OK, if it's really important to you, I'll go to church."

This past spring I heard a conversation between a Roxbury Latin boy and his parents. When his parents said, "Be home by midnight," the boy responded, "You've got to be kidding!" When they reminded him that Sunday was set aside to do something as a family, he replied, "You can't be serious."

This tactic can be used with teachers as well. My first year as an English teacher, a student assailed me when I passed back his paper, "You count off for spelling—you must be joking!" "Yes," I replied, "I have a very, very tiny mind and I care about the most trivial things—such as spelling." Last year a senior—after having all summer to do his autobiography—said he couldn't get it in at the start of school. I said, "Stay up all night, but get it in." He replied, "You're joking. I know you're joking." "Moi?" I said: "I have no sense of humor whatsoever. I never joke."

Now if this "sophisticated" approach fails—and it sometimes does—there is an interesting variation you can try. It is the "You-are-hopelessly-out-of-date-and-I'm-with-it" approach. Certain adults are especially easy targets. They immediately fall for a smart teenager's flattery: The mother of one of my friends when I was your age was so pathetically afraid of growing old that we could always flatter her into anything: "Oh, Mrs. P., you're so cool. You really understand us. You're like one of us." She went for it every time. But even normal adults don't like to think of themselves as getting old, so it's always worth a shot with your parents: "Come on! We're not living in the last century. This is a new century. You're the only parents who don't get it. This is not the dark ages! Have you forgotten what it's like to be young?"

As a teenager I was an accomplished artist at this approach. I was gently condescending—affecting an I-live-in-the-modern-world attitude and an I'm-sorry-you're-so-behind-the-times air of superiority. Thank God I lived in a time when parents were not afraid of their children.

Last spring I talked with a twenty-year-old boy who, three years after taking some bad drugs, has still not recovered: "I thought I was so damned sophisticated," he said.

This summer I talked with a sixteen-year-old girl who had had an abortion. I was astounded when she said, "I wish my parents had been like [she mentioned a girl's name] parents. My parents always backed down every time I pushed them. Before I went out on the night I got pregnant, my parents and I had a fight and I said, 'You're so old-fashioned.' They backed down, just like they always did."

Advanced Level Rationalization

If all else fails, there's still another rationalizing approach that a teenager can take. This is the "I'm special" approach. It is a great favorite at this school.

This rationalization goes something like this: Life's rules are for the rest of the human race, not for special people like me.

Applied by you, this rationalization goes something like this: "We work much harder than kids do in other schools so we ought to be allowed to [fill in the blank]." We should not have to mow the lawn or devote any time to our elderly aunt. And we should (since we're specially hardworking) be allowed to take a spring vacation trip to Cancun with our buddies.

A slight variation on this theme goes something like this: "I don't hang out on street corners; I slave away at my homework night after night, therefore I should be allowed to [fill in the blank]." This is the teenager as martyr variation: you turn what is—in fact—a privilege into a burden. You never compare yourself to the bright and ambitious kids in your local public school who are working just as hard as you are or to the bright and ambitious kids in other independent schools who are home each night doing their homework. You always compare down: to the unambitious kid drifting through high school or to the teenage criminal. Then you can convince your parents—and if you're gullible enough, even yourself—that you are a martyr and that you deserve special privileges.

This rationalization is not, of course, confined to adolescents. Leona Helmsley—the hotel magnate who did time for cheating on her taxes—always used to say, "Taxes are for the little people." That was also the attitude of a highly successful lawyer whom President Clinton tried to appoint to the Cabinet. She said her life was so busy and pressured that she "overlooked"—or "forgot"—to pay the required taxes for her domestic help. A whole lot of people who have for years paid such taxes were very angry when she implied that she was too busy and important to remember such a small matter.

When I was a young parish priest I knew a teacher my age who free-lanced in the summer doing carpentry and other small repairs. He asked to be paid in cash and never reported the income he earned. When he mentioned to a mutual friend that he made a bundle in the summer "under the table," the friend said to him, "Aren't you, really, cheating on your taxes?" "Give me a break," said the young teacher. "I earn practically nothing as a teacher. You must be very naive—everybody does it. Nobody reports income like this." Note his thesis: I'm a special person; the law doesn't apply to me. Note his twisting of reality: everybody does it; nobody reports income like this. He got away with it for years. Long after I'd moved to Boston, the mutual friend told me that this guy had finally been arrested. He had become chairman of a department at his school and was a pretty good teacher. But his career was finished the minute somebody finally dropped a dime.

Essential to this "I'm special" rationalization is the favorable comparison. The student I was just talking about compared himself down in order to achieve a favorable comparison: "I don't hang out on street corners. I don't steal. I don't skip school." This young teacher compared himself up for the favorable comparison. This teacher was probably above the eighty-fifth percentile of people in his age group in his earnings. But he adroitly compared himself not to the eighty-five percent earning less than he, but to the fifteen percent earning more: he looked at what a doctor or a lawyer or a highly successful businessman was earning and then he was able to say, "I earn practically nothing as a teacher."

I've talked before about a boy on my street when I was a child—named Dickie Shaeffer—who was perfect in every way. My mother made frequent comparisons: "Why can't you be more like Dickie Shaeffer?" It infuriated me. When I was about ten or eleven, however, I saw, with precocious insight, that my mother's argument could be turned on its head. There was a notorious kid in my class who got into one scrape after another. And so every time I got in a scrape I would say to my mother, "Well, I'm not like Joe Schmoe (not his real name!). I've never been arrested for shoplifting. I've never stolen hubcaps. . . ." It was a favorable comparison down: it always moved *me*, even if it did not always move my mother.

When I was sixteen—a few days after I got my driver's license—I scraped the right-hand side of the family car from one end to the other pulling up too close to one of those rural mailboxes. It was rather like the Titanic hitting the iceberg—a nice clean rip from end to end. Even if the car didn't sink, I knew my fortunes were about to plunge into the depths. For six glorious days I had ruled the world with my new driver's license, until this accident. Even though I was humiliated, by the time my father got home from work that night, I pulled myself together and lined up my rationalizations. When he confronted me, I responded: "So I made a mistake. Big deal. You never made a mistake, right? It's not as if I was endangering lives by speeding. I've never gotten a ticket [I'd been driving all of six days]. It's not as if I stole a car or as if I got some girl pregnant," I contended, with brilliant use of the downward comparison, vehemently absolving myself of all but the tiniest of trivial infractions. I concluded with a great flight of rhetoric: "It's not as if I'd murdered someone. It's not as if I'd raped someone." After I subsided, my father looked at me icily and said, "Are you finished?" I pouted "Yes," and he said, "Go to Frank Stanton (he was the Ford dealer), get an estimate first, agree to what they tell you, get it repaired, and you pay for it with your money. When children make mistakes, somebody cleans up after them. You want the responsibility of being a man, then you clean up your own mess." It took every penny I had saved that summer and then some. My father did not relent. I was financially ruined.

One of my father's favorite sayings—which he repeated ad nauseam—was "You don't get away with anything in life." By the time I was your age I realized he was wrong. I did get away with some things, "pulled some things off," as we used to say. When I got to college I watched a kid cheat and never get caught. When I was a young clergyman, I watched a man lie and steal his way up the ladder in business, leaving his honest coworkers wondering if they were stupid to be honest. And I said to myself rather cynically: "My father was wrong. You can get away with things in life. Bad people do get to the top stepping on the backs of good people." There were plenty of times when I said to myself at your age—and there have been plenty of times I've said it since—that there is no justice in life, that bad guys get away with a lot and good guys get shafted.

Today I still do not believe that life is always fair—that goodness and honesty are always rewarded and evil punished in this life. But the older I get, the more inclined I am to think that my father was basically right.

The kid who cheated his way through college was never caught in college. But the one or two people who knew that this kid cheated told others (as people inevitably do) and at key times in his career he has been passed over because his contemporaries don't trust him. The young businessman I spoke of seemed Teflon-covered. He slithered up the greasy pole to a high position in a bank. Then when he was in his thirties, with a wife and several children, he was caught red-handed, exposed. He went to prison and lost his wife and family.

A few years ago a senior in the winter term began nickel and diming us on the shaving and dress code. (I discovered the following summer that he'd said, "Well, I'm into college, what can they do?"—though I didn't suspect that at the time since such an attitude is rare among Roxbury Latin boys.) Other faculty members and I said the usual things, "You can either shave every day or grow a beard." But he persisted. Eventually, after many, many such efforts we pretty much gave up. I'm sure he congratulated himself on wearing us down. But when you wear people down, you always do it at a price. You leave a residue of anger and resentment. But this kid hadn't a clue that a lot of people had simply written him off as a jerk. Fast forward: when he was a senior in college, he applied for a job. The person doing the hiring saw Roxbury Latin on his application and called me. The first question he asked me was "Is this young man cooperative? Will he follow instructions?"

So, as I said, at this point in my own personal journey, I've come to think that basically, "You don't get away with anything in life." By this point in my life I've seen people who are lazy, who don't pull their weight, who leave without finishing the job, people who cut corners, shade the truth, rationalize their own faults—who stupidly think no one notices. I have come to believe that those who rationalize their selfishness—those who play the sweet innocent role, who "forget," those who are too sophisticated and "with it" to bother with the rules, those who convince themselves that they are special and that the rules don't apply to them, those who rationalize their selfishness, almost always pay in the end.

That is why I have come to believe that honesty really is the best policy—even though it is often costly at the time. When you base your personal life or your career on honesty, you build on a rock that will anchor you through every storm. When you make a mistake in life—and you will—being honest about it is the best and safest way to clean up the mess.

And so I pray that you will be strong enough, tough enough, to be honest in all things and at all times. And I give you a great truth to live by: "You don't get away with anything in life."

33

The Road to Hell Is Paved with Good Intentions

 HERE WERE two ninth grade English teachers in the public school I attended in Ohio: Mr. Hutton and Mr. Jones. Mr. Hutton—C. Osborne Hutton in all his glory— was notoriously demanding, precise, and fussy. Everything had to be "just so," done thoroughly, turned in on time with no excuses. The previous summer we'd all been hoping we'd get the other teacher, Mr. Jones. He was younger; he directed the plays and his real interest was drama. We'd all heard that he could be easily distracted from the day-to-day grind of English. He described his grading system to his students as "impressionistic," and he rarely had a bad impression of anyone.

I therefore considered myself unlucky when I received my schedule on Day One of ninth grade and learned that Mr. Hutton was my English teacher.

Yet, callow as I was, deep inside I quickly realized that Mr. Hutton was good for me—rather like some terrible-tasting medicine you swallow knowing it will make you better.

As we went along, it turned out that the medicine was not that terrible tasting. I got swept up in Mr. Hutton's enthusiasm for literature. I actually enjoyed what we were reading. He also cared about how I wrote and how I spoke, and what's more, he made me start to care. In short, though I hardly realized it, Mr. Hutton "raised my consciousness" to great literature and to graceful writing and speaking.

He had an array of special projects—précis, book reports, short speeches, after-school discussions—for those who were turned on by his teaching. When he'd describe these special projects they all sounded great, and I signed up for one after another—as did a number of my equally captivated friends. The first one was a book report. I thought a lot about what book I'd do, how I'd do it, and I imagined how Mr. Hutton—and my friends—would be impressed by my efforts. But when the actual due-date came, I hadn't gotten around to doing it (it wasn't required, after all). He looked at me expectantly, and I replied, "I was going to do it, but I was real busy. I'll do the next one." To which he replied, "Mr. Jarvis"—he called us all by our last names—"Mr. Jarvis, the road to hell is paved with good intentions."

It was the first time I'd heard that aphorism. Unfortunately it was not the last. It became something of a theme in ninth grade English—as time after time I failed to translate my good intentions into good actions. I'd resolve to concentrate on my schoolwork at night, and then I'd end up listening to the radio. I'd set my alarm clock for 5 A.M., and then turn it off, roll over, and go back to sleep. Each time I had the best intentions. I really did want to do it. But time after time the due date would arrive and I would come to school empty-handed—once again to hear Mr. Hutton's refrain, "Mr. Jarvis, the road to hell is paved with good intentions."

Evidently, St. Paul had this same experience. In the Letter to the Romans he writes—plaintively—"For I do not do the good I want to do, but the evil I don't want to do is what I do." It is hard to translate good intentions into good actions. We set out with exalted goals—with great visions and dreams of glory—only to discover that we are too weak, too lazy, too self-indulged to make these visions and dreams a reality. The road to hell is paved with good intentions.

In early January this past winter I fell off my daily exercise routine. At first, I stopped for a day here and there, soon it was two days, and—perhaps you recognize the pattern—I finally stopped exercising altogether. I kept telling myself: I'll start up again as soon as I get this report done, as soon as I finish my work for the Headmasters Association, as soon as Lent comes, as soon as I finish my advisor letters, as soon as vacation starts. By the end of winter I had traveled far down the road to hell, and with every broken resolve the task of turning my life around became more difficult.

The bad news, then, is that the battle to translate good intentions into good actions is part of a war you'll have to fight all your life long. The good news is that there are things you can do to recover the vision, to translate intention into action. This morning I'd like to share with you some thoughts about how to avoid taking this trip to hell in the first place, and how to get off this bad trip once you're on it. I share these tips as a battle-scarred veteran.

Don't Deny the Evidence

If you want to get off the road to hell, the first thing you have to do is to hear and see the evidence that indicates you are on the road to hell. The first thing you have to do is to hear and to see—and to digest—the feedback that comes from your eyes and ears.

If you try to accomplish anything in life you will receive criticism: if you are a coach, you will be second-guessed; if you are a businessman, a lawyer, a doctor, whatever, there will be people who criticize you. Some of these people will be malicious and mean-spirited, some will be yappy little Monday morning quarterbacks who do nothing themselves but wait around to pounce on people who are trying to accomplish something. If you are trying to accomplish things in life, you are going to make mistakes, and you will find a corps of critics always waiting to point them out to you—and to everybody else.

Twenty years ago when people criticized me, I would immediately focus on the unjust part of their criticism, the part they got wrong, and then reject their criticism as a whole. If they were wrong in part, then I could reject their criticism in toto. Today I am more inclined to overlook the unjust part and to open my mind to the part that might just be true. I am more willing to listen for and to hear whatever grain of truth might be contained in their criticism.

I was talking with an older boy shortly before vacation about his advisor letter—which contained a number of criticisms. He had all sorts of reasons to reject those criticisms: his teachers, in his view, were mean-spirited, they weren't sympathetic enough to the special circumstances of his life, they didn't appreciate his good qualities enough. I felt for this kid, because I often think of myself as unjustly treated. I finally said to him, "Let's suppose your teachers' motives are mean and their criticisms invalid, is there anything in what you say and do that could give them an opening to criticize you?" To his credit, he returned the next day and said, "Yes. I do do things which enable them to criticize me." I say "to his credit," because he actually for the first time heard the feedback. There are mean-spirited critics in the world waiting like vultures to swoop down on your imperfections, but I think they are outnumbered by people who criticize you because they care about you, who want to give you critical feedback in order to help you. The people I have come to treasure most in my job are those who love me enough to take me aside and say: "That's not right," or "That's not good enough," or "I don't think you should say or do that." I don't enjoy such criticism—and they don't enjoy giving it (it's hard for such people to criticize someone)—but I benefit from it.

I have Jon Lawson this year in senior English and I have—with justification—been on his case about some things. A few weeks ago I summoned him to my office and expressed my displeasure that he never contributed to class discussion. Now this was in the middle of wrestling season and I was twice a week watching Jon destroy his hapless opponents on the mat, en route to his unprecedented third consecutive tournament championship. Anyway, Killer Lawson is sitting in my office, and I'm telling him in a forceful—yet gentle and persuasive—way that he has to speak in my class. And when I finally finish, Jon says, "I'm afraid to say anything, because you're so intimidating."

Now when I paint my own self-portrait, "intimidating" is the last word I'd use to describe myself. I picture myself as gentle, kindly, caring, compassionate, concerned, eager to help. There's nothing intimidating about me whatsoever, and I told Jon so, finishing with a great rhetorical flourish by saying: "Who do you think *you* are to call anyone else intimidating?"

But when I quieted down again, Jon repeated, in what the Bible calls a "still small voice": "You are. You are intimidating."

Even if Jon's accusation doesn't fit in with my own picture of myself and even if it's motivated (in some part, at least) by self-interest and excuse-making on his part, even if I don't desire or intend to be intimidating, I still have to stop and say to myself: "Could there by some truth in what Jon says?" And, painful as it was, I had to look for things I'd said and done that could be perceived as intimidating. Reluctant as I was to find such evidence, it was there.

The entrance to the shrine at Delphi contained the famous words people are always quoting: "Know thyself." But when people look in the mirror to see themselves, they frequently see not what's there but rather what they want to see. I would say that the first step in turning your good intentions into good actions is to know yourself—to know your limitations, your temptations, etc. And, if you want to know yourself, don't shut yourself off from outside criticism. Even if you doubt the motive behind that criticism, even if you can fault its accuracy, you can train yourself to respond by looking for what might be true about the criticism rather than what is obviously untrue about it.

And I would remind you again that many of those who take the risk of criticizing you (especially friends, who do so in private) are doing so because they care about you and want to help you.

Anticipate the Temptations

If you want to stay off the road to hell, then, the first thing you need to do is to listen for the voices of criticism from outside.

But you also need to have an internal alarm system that warns you when you get near trouble. Hemingway once said that every good writer needs a "built-in shock-proof [junk] detector," an alarm system that goes off inside his mind when he is writing rubbish. Every person who wants to stay off the road to hell needs a built-in temptation detector. I have often referred to the old Roman Catholic *Baltimore Catechism* (on which some of your parents and grandparents were brought up). It made an extremely useful point when it warned that a moral person's duty is not just to avoid sin, but also to avoid the occasions of sin.

Most of you have been—or will be—taught in driver's ed to anticipate: to anticipate that the driver in front of you or behind you will do something stupid, so that, as the Boy Scout motto puts it, you can "Be Prepared." A moral person has to anticipate the occasions of sin, the places he'll be tempted in life.

Each of us has his own specially tempting occasions—or places. Last year at this time I was trying to help a boy learn how to get his schoolwork done, and I said to him, "When I grade papers on Sunday, I give myself little bribes in order to get through the stack: I'll grade four papers and then take a short break to read a section of the Sunday *Times*. Then I'll do another four, and take another short break to read another section of the *Times*." It's a trick I've used for years. I suggested that the boy try something like this, and he did. But after a few days, he returned to me and said, "It doesn't work. If I take a break I never go back. It's fatal to take a break." He sounded rather like an alcoholic who knows he cannot take even a sip. What tempts one person greatly does not tempt another person, and vice versa. Another boy said to me, "It's fatal for me to study near a TV. I just can't resist turning it on." Both these boys have learned to avoid what are for them "the occasions of sin": one never takes a break, the other studies where there is no TV.

A few years ago a Roxbury Latin boy came into my office to talk. He lived in an apartment with his mother and she worked nights. He became close friends with a girl and the girl would come over to the apartment each night "to study." It wasn't very long before the two of them were spending the evening engaged in something other than study, and his schoolwork declined noticeably. "Believe it or not," he said, "we both keep trying to study, but the minute we're together, we just can't help ourselves." By the time he came to see me, they both had figured out that the only solution—unless they were going to throw away all they'd accomplished—was to avoid being together on school nights.

You have to depend not only on outside voices, but you have to depend on your own inner voice to anticipate and avoid situations where temptation will overcome you. There are people who put themselves again and again in situations where they will be tempted, and then they blame the situations.

If you know a short break from your homework will lead to a long break, then you need to be tough enough to avoid taking a short break. If you can't turn on the TV without addictively watching it, then don't go near the TV.

The morally mature person knows his weaknesses, he anticipates where he'll be tempted, and he avoids such situations.

Don't Let Yourself Off the Hook

Smart people, however, are expert rationalizers—experts at letting themselves off the hook. In February a boy said to me, "I tried to study last night, but I couldn't. The phone just kept ringing and ringing. It was one interruption after another, and I never had a chance to get my homework done." I suggested that he tell his parents to answer the phone and to tell his friends that he was not available to talk. He was disappointed in my response, because he wanted to think of himself as a helpless victim of the telephone. He wanted to blame the temptation rather than to avoid the temptation.

Early in the year a senior asked me for an extension on a paper. Even though I was dubious about his request, I gave him the extension. Still, the paper did not come in. When I pointed out that he was now losing ten points a day, he responded, "You never should have given me that extension in the first place. If you'd just made me hand in the paper the day it was due—instead of giving me an extension—I would never have gotten in this mess." Rather than deal with his own procrastination, this boy neatly took the burden of guilt off himself and put it on me.

At a recent parent conference in my office, a boy said to his parents, "You should have stopped me from watching TV at night." He'd worked it all out. It was not his obligation to avoid the occasion of sin, to anticipate being tempted, it was his parents' obligation.

I know adults my age who are still blaming their parents for something, who are still blaming some teacher or boss for something. These adults take full credit for everything that went right in their lives. But for everything that went wrong—that didn't turn out right—they have some scapegoat.

My final point, then, is this: Don't scapegoat. Don't blame others for not taking responsibility for your life. Take responsibility for your own life.

Listen when others point out things they think are less than perfect about you. Anticipate when you're going to be tempted. Anticipate temptation and avoid it. And when you mess up, take the blame for it yourself and try to learn and grow from your mistake.

Life is a struggle against our own weaknesses. Don't give up. Don't despair. The same St. Paul who talked about his own weaknesses also said, "We are never tempted more than we can bear." You are strong enough not to take the road to hell—paved with all the good intentions you never put into action.

Try to see yourself as God sees you: as called to live the best and noblest of lives. With His help you can hear those who point out your imperfections, with His help you can determine to avoid the occasions of sin, and with His help you can take responsibility for your own life.

A century or so ago, a ship in a storm was dashed against the rocks off the southern coast of England in Cornwall. A fifteen-year-old sailor swam to an off-shore rock and clung to it all night until he was rescued the next day. A reporter interviewed him and commented, "You must have been shaking all night as you clung to that rock." "Yes," the sailor boy said. "I trembled all night with fear and cold." Then he added, "But the rock never trembled once."

The psalmist of Israel wrote, "God alone is my rock and my salvation." Over and over the Hebrew and Christian Scriptures refer to God as the rock on which (and in whom) alone we can find safety and strength.

If you try to live up to your own good intentions, you will tremble and shake many a time as you try to find the guts to put your good intentions into action. Always remember that God is your rock and defense—nearer to you by a single word of prayer than any human being can ever be. And also remember that there are a lot of good people in this world who can help you—if you will let them—as you grapple with taking responsibility for your own life.

34

Three Pieces of Bad Advice

HAVE BEEN THINKING—as I do at this time of year—about the soon-to-depart seniors. This is my last shot at them, and there's a great temptation to try to give them one final inoculation of good advice with which to face the disease of modern life. But like them—like all of you—I have been on the receiving end of good advice. And this morning, instead of giving you more good advice, I want to share with you some of the bad advice I've been given by well-intentioned people over the years.

All Things in Moderation

One piece of advice I was frequently given as I trudged through school and college is advice you have also been given right within this room. It is the advice implicit in the often-quoted inscription on the Shrine gate at Delphi: "Nothing in excess," that is, "All things in moderation." This, I submit to you, is terrible advice; it is, in fact, a recipe for mediocrity.

Most of you seniors have pushed yourselves to the limit in academics and extracurriculars. Your lives have not been characterized by "moderation in all things." What you have achieved—often while trying to fulfill huge conflicting demands—what you have achieved (through excessive commitment on your part) has, in fact, won our profound admiration. We have watched you bound from a music rehearsal to a public speaking contest to a Model U.N. to a yearbook meeting and to a varsity sport—somehow also keeping on top of your academic work.

Occasionally you may blame the school for putting so much pressure on you, but underneath you realize that it is you who has chosen to do these things and that you'd probably do them anywhere else you went. Most of you have led lives of excess here. You have experienced the thrill that comes only from making an all-out commitment.

A few weeks ago, the parents of one of our Latin declaimers—a kid who was under immense pressure in other areas—told his advisor that their son would have to withdraw from the competition: "He just can't do this on top of everything else." And if "all things in moderation" had been his guiding principle he would have backed out. In the event, the boy did not back out. He pushed himself—excessively—to the limit and won.

Many of you have experienced the thrill of immoderate commitment in athletics. Over and over at the wrestling tournament I watched Roxbury Latin boys come from behind to win in the last few seconds. There was no moderation in the commitment of these guys—they made an all-out, excessive effort, calling forth the last one percent of their energy. I think of this year's J.V. basketball game against Belmont Hill—the meeting of two undefeated teams. It was a Friday night. Our kids—exhausted from a week of tests and extracurricular commitments—got behind ten by the end of the first half. When they came back after the halftime break I could tell they were going to make an all-out, no-holds-barred effort to retrieve the game. Exhausted as they were, they dug down to bedrock—to the last one percent of their reserves, and they won the game. There was nothing moderate about their effort; it was pure excess.

The same thing goes for the job you will have some day. And, let me tell you, I have never met a man or woman who loved his or her job who worked at it in moderation. Any job worth having is one in which you will have huge challenges, in which you will work to excess. Any job worth having is one that will drain you, make huge demands on your time and energy.

I bet twenty people have repeated to me in the last few years a currently fashionable saying by one of the modern "all things in moderation" philosophers, namely: "No man on his deathbed ever wished he'd spent more time at the office." The first time I heard it I was quite impressed. I have been less and less impressed ever since. Now I think it's a huge lie. As it happens, as a priest, I have been present at a good many deathbeds and heard a good many last words and final confessions. Never once have I heard any dying person express the least regret that he worked hard to accomplish something. Most of the regrets I've heard at deathbeds are exactly the opposite. A young man in his twenties—with AIDS—said to me last summer as he lay dying: "I wish I could have done something with my life." That reflection— sad in a young man dying—is, I submit, far sadder in an old man dying. One of the greatest consolations on your deathbed can be the knowledge that you worked really hard to accomplish something worthwhile.

People say if you like sixty percent of what you're doing in life you're lucky. I love ninety-nine percent of what I do. I work sixteen-hour days seven days a week—and, in all honesty, I do manage to let everybody know how hard I work and even to complain about the many demands I have to meet. But, in actuality, I work long hours not because I am a martyr, but because I love what I am doing and think it's worth doing. All the happiest people that I know, all of them, work too hard. Their commitment is not moderate.

And so, I submit to you that the famous inscription at Delphi is bad advice. If you want a life of comfortable mediocrity, by all means live by the motto at Delphi. If you want a boring life at the end of which you can look back at nothing more than having existed safely and comfortably, then by all means be excessive in nothing and moderate in all things.

If, on the other hand, you want a fulfilling life, you will choose a life that is costly, a life filled with challenge. You will persevere—because you are immoderate—while others fall by the wayside. On your deathbed, you may well have to reflect (I certainly will have to) that you were not successful at everything you attempted, that you were not able to climb every mountain you set out to climb. But you will have the consolation of knowing that—whether you were entirely successful or not—you set huge and challenging goals for your life and pursued them with excess and without moderation.

Play It Safe

The second piece of bad advice I was frequently given at your age is this: "Be Cautious"— or to state it both positively and negatively— "Play it Safe. Take no risks."

There are, of course, stupid risks. I mentioned one recently when I talked about the young man who blew his brains out playing Russian roulette. Experimentation with drugs is also a stupid risk. People who take risks of this sort are not brave or creative or interesting; they are simply stupid. I won't belabor that point because I believe everyone of you agrees with it.

In general, however, I submit that "Safety First" is bad advice and that you should take many risks in life. I was in Italy over this past vacation. At my hotel in Rome I met a couple who perfectly exemplify the "Play it safe; take no risks" philosophy. At breakfast the husband—two tables away—shouted at me, "Where'd you get that paper?" I had a British paper and I told him I'd bought it at the newsstand right outside the hotel, on my way into breakfast. He darted out, saying, "Maybe I can find an American newspaper." But he soon returned: "They won't take my money," he bellowed, so everyone in the dining room could hear. "These idiots refused to take American money!" I quietly pointed out that I know of no American newsstand that would accept Italian money. He replied, "That's different." He had arrived early the day before and had spent his entire first day in Rome in his room with his wife watching the only English language channel—CNN. He still had no Italian money. He had as yet seen absolutely nothing of the Eternal City. His wife said, "Well, he's gotta have his basketball, you know." I replied by inquiring why they'd come all the way to Rome if they wanted to spend all day watching American basketball on TV. "You could do that," I added peevishly, "in a motel room in Gary, Indiana." He replied, "We're going on a damn bus tour the wife arranged this morning. But let me tell you something, Sonny Boy, if I want to watch some damn basketball game on my damn TV, I will." His response thrilled me. I don't think I've been addressed as "Sonny Boy" since I was eighteen—it was a favorite expression my dad (and other adults) used when they wanted to dress down a teenager who was being rebellious or obnoxious or full of himself. This guy—with his "Let me tell you something, Sonny Boy"—made me feel like a teenager.

This man's basic problem is he's afraid. Plunk him down in Rome and he'll curl up in his hotel room, watch American TV, and try to do everything else he does at home. He's a coward: fearful of any change in his routine, any reordering of his interests, any new experiences or new way of seeing things. He incarnates the motto "Play it safe, take no risks."

I spent nearly a whole day in the Brancacci Chapel at Santa Maria del Carmine in Florence while I was in Italy. I was studying—with the help of two new books—the restored Masaccio frescoes—two of which (the *Tribute Money* and the *Expulsion of Adam and Eve*) feature prominently in the Western Civ slide lectures. I watched young people come and go, your age, the age I was (nineteen) when I first saw these frescoes. And I watched retired people as they came and went. There was little discernible difference between the young and the old. They all tried politely to look interested in the frescoes. But most were glassy-eyed, waiting impatiently to be whisked off by their tour guide to the next wonderful work of art. That's the way I was when I was nineteen— I'm glad it's not the way I am today. The goal of every life should be to grow in awareness.

I have grown in awareness—over the years—of some aspects of the human experience (certainly art and music), but there are experiences in other fields that are not open to me because I live in too limited a world. We all do. For that reason we must be constantly, consciously seeking new experiences, risking changes in our routine.

There is no better place to start than right where you are. Some of you have formed close friendships with like-minded and like-interested classmates. If you want to be a richer, deeper, more interesting person, open yourself up to a classmate who, right now, you barely more than nod at. Start with just one. Start this week. It will be a risk; he will more often than not rebuff your outreach, and you do risk humiliation and embarrassment. What a loss to you, however, if you live in this most diverse of all schools in a narrow and confined circle of friends who are just like you.

The weak and cowardly cannot bear the discomfort of risk. Like the basketball-obsessed man in Rome, they want to live in a closed-off little world where the lines are drawn and where everybody who is not just like them can be kept out. The motto of these people is: "Play it safe; take no risks."

If you want a truly fulfilling life—enriched by constant new insights and growth—then take all such risks. Do not play it safe.

Be Tolerant

The final piece of bad advice is the currently most politically correct piece of advice: namely, be tolerant. Implicit in this toleration is often a moral relativism: an outlook that asserts that we need to tolerate every viewpoint and that every viewpoint is the equal of every other viewpoint.

I had my seminary training for the priesthood in the heyday of what was called other-directed counseling. The basic principle was: the counselor (that is, the priest) should never express judgment. He should listen and ask questions, and somehow by this process—hocus-pocus— the person being counseled would find the right solution. This made a lot of sense to me at twenty-four. And when I was unloosed upon a large and unsuspecting parish I carefully followed what I'd been taught.

The first piece of marriage counseling I did was with a guy who was cheating on his wife. And I laboriously asked him week after week: why are you doing this? (Basic answer, reclothed somewhat each week: lust.) Much talk about his relationship with his parents, his wife's inadequacies, his own inadequacies. And after a number of weeks of my being ever so nondirective, he deserted his wife and got a divorce. Then several years later he deserted his new wife, and got another divorce.

However, I was not deterred and had many a session of a similar nature (and often similar result) over the next three or so years. My fourth summer a young married couple came to see me (we'll call them Steve and Jennifer). They seemed to me to have just about everything you could want in life. I saw them (I guess) for several weeks and it was always: She says this. He does that. She does this. He says that. Yap. Yap. Yap. The day of the fourth session with them was a bad day for me. It was 110 in the shade. I had had a long and very trying and utterly draining day and as they started in on the usual yap, yap, yap, I finally just exploded—all over the walls and ceiling. I said, "You two are the two most spoiled brats I've ever met. You deserve each other. You've got everything in life—good jobs, good health, good prospects and all you do is complain, complain, complain. I'm sick and tired of your self-indulgent bitching—go bother someone else with your stupid problems. Get out of my office."

They were, of course, shocked. Almost as shocked as I was. And I went home filled with guilt and remorse and regret and with Excedrin headache #97. I woke up the next day feeling hung over (without having had any alcohol). The next morning in my office I was sitting with my head in my hands contemplating the wreckage of my priesthood (I've always been given to melodrama) when the phone rang. It was Jennifer. Before I could say I was sorry, she said, "Steve and I have been up all night. You know, you really got through to us. I think you saved our marriage."

I'm as happy as the next guy not to say I'm sorry if it's not really necessary. So I gasped, "Oh, ah, well, good, yes, ah, that's what I hoped. Glad it's all worked out."

When I put the phone down I sat there astounded. It was a real light bulb moment: What I thought I'd been doing right was wrong and it rarely worked. And what I thought I'd done wrong—landing all over this young couple with a scathing judgment—was right and it worked. It changed my whole approach to counseling. I still get a card from Steve and Jennifer every Christmas.

The most moving address in my time here was given almost fifteen years ago by a boy named Bobby Oldenburg. He was then a twenty-year-old sophomore at Boston College who had managed to stay off alcohol for over a year. He was a Cleveland boy and a student at my old school—University School. He was a great kid, nice-looking, popular, personable. He started serious daily drinking when he was fourteen. By great stealth he mostly concealed this at home and at school, though by his sophomore year he was consuming nearly a bottle of vodka a day from a thermos in his locker. As things progressed, his problem became less and less hidden. After several crises, he was finally hospitalized. He told his story this way: "All the psychiatrists and counselors for the next three or four years asked the same questions: How do you feel about your mother and father? Tell me about what happened when you were three. What makes you feel you need to take a drink? It was question after question. I went through (I think it was) three hospitals and two detox centers and nobody—nobody— once said the words I needed to hear: Stop drinking. Everyone of them was so eager to be nonjudgmental, they couldn't bear to stick it to me: Stop drinking!"

He was asking for less tolerance and more judgment. That, he said, could have saved him a lot of pain. The couple I referred to were helped by my inadvertent enraged intolerance. But there remains, in society at large, a kind of bland tolerance—an unwillingness to judge.

Let me give you one example. Some years ago the City of Boston decided to make new curbs, plant new trees, and lay new brick and concrete sidewalks on Centre Street in West Roxbury. The City left piles of bricks and crushed stone along the side of the street. An alumnus who was a senior in college had picked me up in his car; we were going out to dinner. As we turned onto Centre Street, we saw a very respectable looking couple—I suppose in their late fifties or sixties—who were piling bricks into the trunk of their car. I saw what they were doing and (I regret to tell you) my gut response was not to "get involved." I rationalized my avoidance of responsibility by saying to myself that, after all, I'm not headmaster of the world. My former student—the driver—however, swerved to the side, jumped out of the car and said to this couple, "What are you doing?" "It's none of your business!" replied the woman. The man said, "We're just taking some bricks for our back patio." The alumnus said to them, "Isn't that stealing?" The woman responded, "Why don't you mind your own business?" The boy said (brilliantly, I thought), "This is my business. I and the other taxpayers own these bricks. These are my bricks! Now either you put them all back or I'll report you right now to the police." And he waited until they took every brick out of the back of their car and drove away.

This young man was not going to tolerate theft. And he was not afraid of being called "judgmental." He was not cowed by being told to "mind his own business."

I am not urging you to run around being self-righteous all the time (which hardly seems a danger), but I am pointing out to you that if you have high standards and values, you will at times have to be intolerant and judgmental in normal day-to-day life.

If you have seen great works of art you will find it difficult to tolerate cheap, tawdry, and shallow art. If you have read the works of great authors, you will have a hard time tolerating junk. If you are men of integrity, you will have a hard time tolerating fellow workers who lie and cheat. I have often been amazed in Discipline Committee meetings to hear how disgusted boys are by fellow students who cheat or steal. They don't want to be in a school community that tolerates such things, that is reluctant to pass judgment on those who are not willing to live by these standards.

Jesus said to his little band of disciples, "You are the salt of the earth." The ancient Jews used salt as a preservative. Salted meat did not rot. A few tiny grains of salt could preserve a large piece of meat. They also used salt, as we do, for seasoning. A few tiny grains of salt can change the whole flavor of a meal.

I say to you, especially you seniors, "You are the salt of the earth." Society needs your standards and values. Do not be intimidated into tolerating what is ugly, bad, and untrue. Eschew bad advice: Live life to the full—excessively, immoderately, with abandon. Take risks that will open you up to new experiences and thoughts; don't play it safe. And stand intolerantly for what is good and true and beautiful.

35

Friendship

SOME YEARS AGO *The New Yorker* magazine published (in several installments) the poetic autobiography of England's poet laureate, Sir John Betjeman.

Betjeman hauntingly evokes his grim and barren experience as a schoolboy (your age) at Marlborough: the sense of not belonging even though he was a member of a class, a house, a team; the sense of loneliness even though he could never be alone:

> *Luxuriating backwards in the bath,*
> *I swish the warmer water round my legs*
> *Toward my shoulders, and the waves of heat*
> *Bring those five years at Marlborough through to me,*
> *In comfortable retrospect: 'Thank God*
> *I'll never have to go through them again.'*
> . . .
>
> *Here, 'twixt the church tower and chapel spire*
> *Rang sad and deep the bells of my desire.*
>
> *Desire for what? I think I can explain.*
> *The boys I worshipped did not worship me:*
> *The boys who worshipped me I did not like. . . .*

What was agonizingly missing in the world of school (which Betjeman had to live in) was a deep relationship with anyone. What was missing was friendship.

I want to talk about friendship. I don't have to give you a learned definition of friendship because you already know what friendship is.

Everyone of you has at one time or another experienced the absence of friendship, right here at school: the longing to find another person with whom you have something in common, with whom you can relax, with whom you can share your feelings without fear of ridicule or betrayal.

Friendship is not, of course, a physical or sexual relationship, but friendship is nonetheless a critical ingredient in the most important relationship that most of you will someday enter, namely marriage. Sexual attraction may bring a man and woman together—and a sexual relationship is an ongoing expression of their togetherness—but it is friendship that keeps them together over the years. The marriage that fails to develop mutuality of interest, an openness and trust in which deep feelings can be shared, the marriage in which friendship is not developed, is doomed to failure. At the heart of every successful and enduring marriage is friendship.

The art of friendship—the ability to make and to keep friends—is perhaps the critical art, then, for all of life: not just for happiness now in school, but for happiness in the future at work, at leisure, and in marriage.

Risking Vulnerability

The first observation that needs to be made about friendship is that you can't have it without risking vulnerability. If you are unwilling to risk being hurt or being rejected, if you are unwilling to risk being ridiculed or humiliated, you can never enter into deep relationships with others.

You cannot become friends with someone without being willing to risk rejection and hurt. Most of you have experienced the terrible hurt that results when you make yourself vulnerable to another person only to be ignored or rejected or laughed at by that person. There is no more painful experience in life.

It takes two people to make a friendship, and the sad reality is that sometimes we will take risks—make ourselves vulnerable—and no friendship will result. As Betjeman put it, "The boys I worshipped did not worship me. The boys who worshipped me I did not like."

When somebody we want to be friends with rebuffs us, or when somebody we thought was a friend betrays us, our instinctive reaction is to crawl into our shell and resolve never again to take such a risk. If we never allow ourselves to be vulnerable again, we will not (it is true) be hurt. But if we never allow ourselves to be vulnerable again, we cannot enter into friendship with others; we foreclose the possibility of experiencing the rich rewards that come from friendship.

How we hate, how we fear, being vulnerable! But vulnerability is the indispensable foundation and basis, the sine qua non, of friendship. No vulnerability, no friendship.

If you can find the courage to risk vulnerability, then (I'd like to suggest) there are three qualities you can bring to a relationship that will help you to make and to keep a friend.

Hopeful Commitment

The first quality is hopeful commitment. Or, perhaps better, committed hope.

If you want to be friends with another person you have to maximize his best qualities and minimize his worst. There will be times when his good qualities seem few and his bad qualities glaring. That's when hopeful commitment comes in. I had a roommate in college who came back to our room at least once a week wildly enthusiastic about some new "friend" he'd made. Then—invariably—within two weeks, having discovered some imperfection in him, he'd discard his new friend: he's too interested in academics; she bites her fingernails; he talks too much; she always wants to study.

Friends are never perfect, certainly not as perfect as we like to think we ourselves are. If you want to become someone's friend, you cannot expect that person to be perfect.

When two people enter into the lifelong friendship that underlies marriage, they make a commitment to one another: "for better, for worse, for richer, for poorer, in sickness and in health." If they know anything about life, they realize when they say "for worse" that they are not talking about a remote possibility: they are talking about a reality that is certain to occur. There is no marriage, there is no friendship, in which there are not bad times. "For worse" is for real.

What does it mean to be a friend? I think St. Paul defined the role and function of a friend when he wrote (in quite another context): "To rejoice with those who rejoice, and to weep with those who weep." That is the calling of a friend: to be there, amidst the joys and sorrows of life, for richer for poorer, in sickness and in health, for better for worse.

St. Paul also speaks of "preferring one another in love." When we minimize (and forgive) the faults of another person we seek to go more than halfway. We have made a hopeful commitment to care about another person at some cost to ourselves. If you approach friendship primarily as a way of getting something for yourself, you will be disappointed. If you make a hopeful commitment to another person (to minimize the bad and to affirm the good and to be there to give affectionate support in the valleys as well as on the peaks), you will have taken a giant first step in friendship, because the first step in friendship is commitment to another person—a commitment that is motivated by the hope that you have something worthwhile to give that other person.

Openness

The second quality you can bring to a relationship in order to make it a friendship is openness: openness to differences in the first instance. Some people want their friends to look like them, dress like them, act like them, and share the very same interests. Such people are essentially narcissistic; they are so busy figuratively looking in the mirror that they can't relate to anyone else. We're always a bit frightened by people who appear to be "different" from us. But one of the greatest joys of real friendship is to come to appreciate differences in others. When I was nineteen I spent the summer in Europe with five college buddies. We had motorbikes and we covered over ten thousand miles together. One kid was very interested in cars and we all went together to several grand prix auto races. Another was very interested in Hemingway and we visited all of Hemingway's Paris haunts and traveled together to Pamplona in Spain for the running of the bulls described in *The Sun Also Rises*. Another was interested in architecture (guess who that was!) and we all visited Roman ruins and Gothic cathedrals. Another was interested in music and we all got tickets for the Salzburg Festival. All of our lives were enormously enriched by our friendships with people very different from us. When you decide to risk friendship, don't look for a xerox copy of yourself.

Be open to differences. Be open also to change. All real friendships change and grow. One summer day I was eating breakfast with my grandfather, to whom I was very close, and he suddenly said to me, "You know, your grandmother and I have been married sixty-two years and she still says and does things that surprise me, even shock me." Theirs was a marriage made in heaven because both of them continued to change and to grow every day. They didn't look backward to remind one another of the way they had been—or to rehash or regret past hurts, or to bring up past mistakes or embarrassments. They didn't resent or regret change and growth in each other; they expected it and enjoyed it. You kill a friendship if you try to put a glass case over someone and prevent him from continuing to emerge as a person.

I had a college classmate who was a great athlete and therefore something of a campus hero during our college days. When college was over, however, his heroic age ended. I had another classmate who was a virtual unknown in college but who has since emerged as a nationally prominent figure. When I was talking recently with the once-heroic athlete, he turned to me bitterly and said, "I saw you talking to X [our now nationally prominent classmate]. He was a jerk in college and he's still a jerk." He couldn't bear the emergence of his classmate. He couldn't bear the fact that our classmates had changed and grown. If he was the big man on campus then, he should be the big man twenty-five years later. But, of course, people do change. And real friendship allows room for people to change and to grow.

If you enter a relationship in order to dominate another person (or to feel superior to another person), that relationship will not be a true friendship. Friendship cannot exist where one person has control, where one person dominates. Friendship must be based not on controlling but on caring.

One of history's classic friendships is that between David and Jonathan. While Jonathan's father, King Saul, was insanely jealous of the popular young hero David (who slew Goliath), what is remarkable about the king's son Jonathan is his total lack of jealousy. Jonathan rejoiced in David's triumphs. One of the lamentable by-products of our competitive society is the feeling ingrained in many of us that: if so-and-so is up, I must be down. We are secretly (and sometimes not so secretly) resentful if someone does better than we do on a test, or plays ahead of us on a team, or wins some recognition or prize.

Openness to differences, openness to change, however, should enable us to rejoice in the successes of our friends without feeling jealous or put down.

Jealousy can also destroy a friendship if it tries totally to possess another human being. Beware of the person who seeks to prevent you from being friends with others, who plants the seeds of distrust between you and others, who is jealous of your relationship with others. Real friends are never jealous of your relationships with others. To be the friend of one person does not mean that you (or he) cease being friends with others.

Real friendship, then, is characterized by openness. You allow a friend to be different. You allow a friend to grow and to change. You rejoice in a friend's successes, you share in a friend's sorrows. Real friendship does not seek to close off, it does not seek to control or possess a friend. Real friendship is open: a commitment freely given that seeks a response freely given.

Loyalty

The final quality that you can bring to a relationship in order to make it a friendship is loyalty: genuine and abiding concern for a person "through thick and thin."

We have all experienced disloyalty: the discovery that someone has stabbed us in the back, the discovery that we cannot trust someone. Disloyalty can take many forms, some of them very sophisticated. I once had a friend who, I eventually realized, was always having one-on-one tête-à-têtes eliciting people's opinions about other people. Protesting loyalty (and never herself actually saying anything disloyal—only quoting the things others had said) she encouraged a kind of gossip that amounted to round-robin back stabbing. She was, in short, disloyal.

Loyalty is just the opposite. Being loyal to another person does not mean we have to agree with him. Quite the contrary. Loyalty usually requires us to express our disagreement. But loyalty also requires that we express our disagreement to his face—not behind his back—and often privately.

In all real friendships disagreements—painful arguments, strong differences of opinion—do arise. Friendship is defined not by whether you disagree with someone. Friendship is defined by how you handle the disagreements that inevitably arise.

St. Paul admonishes us to "speak the truth in love." Real friendship survives the inevitable disagreements that occur because real friendship is supported by loyalty—a long-term commitment that persists and endures through and beyond momentary flashes of anger and argument. And each time the truth is spoken in love, each time momentary hurt is overcome, each time reconciliation is reached, our friendship becomes stronger.

Most of us have experienced in some tough situation the remarkable, even costly, loyalty of a friend. In the sixties, in the fall after the Hough race riots, I saw a popular black football player at a predominantly black high school in Cleveland stand up for a white friend of his in school. It was a courageous thing to do in so volatile a situation. Late that afternoon as he returned home after football practice he was jumped by a gang of schoolmates and beaten up. "That'll teach you to stick up for whitey," they told him. Loyalty can be costly.

When the chips are down, when things are "for worse" rather than "for better," when things are "for poorer" rather than "for richer," we discover who our friends really are. "Fair weather" friends (so-called) are not friends at all. Real friends are loyal even when it's costly to be loyal.

There are, then, three qualities we can bring to friendship: hopeful commitment, openness, and loyalty. St. Paul wrote: "There are three abiding virtues: faith, hope, love, and the greatest of these is love." These three virtues are not unlike the three qualities I have spoken of—commitment, openness, and loyalty. Let me add, in harmony with St. Paul, "the greatest of these is loyalty." And let me conclude with a true story about loyalty that comes out of two men's experience of modern warfare:

A soldier named Tom lay gravely wounded in the no-man's land between the Allied position and the German position. Another soldier, George, a friend of Tom's, requested permission from the commanding officer to crawl out to Tom and pull him back to safety. The officer wisely refused permission: the chances of a safe rescue were negligible and he didn't want to lose two men rather than one. George, however, chose to disobey his officer and when the officer moved to a different part of the trench, George went over the top, crawled to his friend Tom, and dragged him back behind him. By the time he got back to the trench, his buddy Tom had died of his wounds and George himself had also been gravely wounded. The officer was naturally angry: "I told you not to do that," he said. "Your friend is dead and you are shot up. Now I've lost you both. You shouldn't have gone out there. It wasn't worth it." The young soldier, however, replied, "Sir, it was worth it. He was still alive when I got to him out there. He was still conscious and he said to me, 'George, I knew you'd come.'"

As we begin this new year together, my prayer for you is that you will find the courage to risk making friends, and that—through commitment, openness, and loyalty, above all, loyalty—you will experience the joy that comes from making and keeping friends.

36

Leadership—1

WANT TO TALK about leadership, because I think there's a lot of confusion about what it is. As nearly as I can tell, most people imagine that leadership is something you aspire to because it will bring you power, prestige, and happiness. People want to be leaders because they think, "Ah, finally I'll get to decide things. I'll get to make decisions. I'll get to do things my way." They also think, "When I finally attain such-and-such a position, everybody will look up to me. I'll have standing, the kind of respect I deserve, prestige. Then I'll finally be happy."

The bad news, however, is this. Whatever power a leader has is overshadowed by the cares and responsibilities that go with leadership. Whatever prestige a leader has is overshadowed by the second-guessing and criticism he receives for the decisions he makes. Leadership does not confer happiness.

Realism about Leadership

I hope all of you will be future leaders, but—before you decide to aspire to leadership—it's important that you have a realistic understanding of what it means to be a leader. Those who aspire to leadership because they fantasize that it will bring them unalloyed power, prestige, and happiness need to understand that the reality does not conform to their fantasy.

It would be wonderful if leadership simply entailed having a vision of how things should be and then putting that vision in operation. That would truly be "getting your own way." But, if a leader has a vision, he cannot simply impose it. He must try to persuade people to share his vision and, in the course of persuading them, he must respectfully listen to their visions. A leader must constantly, endlessly consult, listen, strive for consensus. Far from getting his own way, he must constantly seek the compromises that will bring people together. Far from getting his own way, a leader is constantly trying to understand the viewpoints of others and to persuade them to consider his own viewpoint.

Some years ago we had a boy who came to see me early in the fall to say that he had devised a new form of student government for the School. I said—quite genuinely— "Great!" He said he would unveil it in the school newspaper. And so he did: it was, I thought, an excellent scheme, elaborately thought out, and I told him so. But I added, "The hardest part lies ahead. You must persuade your fellow students that this is the way to go." He looked at me in amazement and said, "But I've explained it all in the article. I've already answered all the questions. I don't think I'll need to persuade them." A day or so later he went to the various homerooms. I tried gently to warn him that I thought he might be greeted with less than rapturous enthusiasm. And indeed, I heard from others that the prevailing response of the homerooms was, "Why do we need all this elaborate structure, when we can just cut through it all and say what we think and ask for what we want?" Furthermore, the few students who *were* interested in a student government challenged certain aspects of his plan—which infuriated him. His response to all challenges was "I've explained it all in my article." A couple of weeks later, he came to me and said, "The hell with it. If they're too stupid to want this, why should I bother? I spent all this time on it and they couldn't care less."

I have to tell you I had a deep sympathy for this boy, because I've felt that way in every leadership position I've ever held. Every person who's ever had a vision that others spurned has had that feeling of loneliness and rejection, that feeling of "why bother," that feeling of "the hell with it."

Leadership is not power to have your own way. It's not working hard on some glorious plan and then unveiling it to the applause of others. You have to have the patience, the fortitude, the guts to sell your idea, to persuade others to accept it. That is almost always an exhausting and discouraging task.

Whatever prestige a leadership position is alleged to convey is far outweighed by the underlying irrational feelings directed against anyone who is a leader. Leaders have always been subjected to people projecting things onto them. In my early days here to give you a trivial example, one boy remarked bitterly to me: "I'm sure you hate me because I have long hair." "How do you know that?" I asked him (I had never said anything to him about his hair.) He replied, "I can see it in your eyes." In actual fact, I had never, for a second, thought about his hair or disliked him because of it. When he focused my attention on his hair, in fact, it seemed to me he looked rather well in long hair. He had projected all sorts of views and attitudes onto me that I didn't hold. These views originated within him and were entirely emotional, irrational, and disconnected from reality.

I experienced a classic case of this kind of projection this summer in Budapest. My first morning there, during rush hour, I decided to take the Budapest subway. Now, as you may know, Hungarian is unrelated to any language in Europe except Finnish (and the Finns and Hungarians can't understand each other). I can read the papers in Spain and Portugal and France and Italy and Austria—and I even read the papers in the Czech Republic when I was in Prague earlier in the summer. But Hungarian is absolutely unfathomable and the only non-Hungarian directions in the subway were in Russian. So I was feeling quite proud of going to the window, plunking down my sixty florints, and getting a paper subway ticket. On the way in, I noticed others sticking their tickets in a machine for punching, and so I stuck mine in and it was duly punched. Within seconds, a man—a civilian—started shouting at me in Hungarian. I must have looked American because the only word of his rantings I could make out was the word American. It was rush hour and a small crowd gathered around us.

You'd have loved seeing the Almighty Headmaster getting dressed down in the Budapest subway. But I was not enjoying it at all and I had no idea what I'd done to get him so mad. I started several times to say to him—in English, of course—"I don't speak Hungarian," but I couldn't get a word in edgewise, and when finally there was an opening, I was so flustered—this is Jarvis the great leader at his best—that by the time I could utter the phrase, I said to him (if you can believe it!), "I don't speak English."

The second I uttered this immortal statement, "I don't speak English," my accuser erupted like Mount Vesuvius in broken English, shouting, "You thief. You liar. You steal from subway. You lie. You speak English." (All this punctuated with repeated assertions of "Americans lie. Americans steal," which soon elevated to "Americans rape Hungary. Americans rape the world.") Then suddenly a hefty woman—not one of Botticelli's Three Graces—grabbed my ticket out of my hands, marched five steps back to the machine and stuck the other end of the ticket in the machine for punching, returned it me, and then—with her very large handbag—whacked my accuser. The two of them then went at it toe to toe in exuberant Hungarian. I—being the courageous Good Samaritan that I am—beat a hasty retreat into the subway.

I tell you this story because it is about projection. This angry Hungarian obviously hated America and Americans. When he found an American who had innocently inserted his ticket the wrong way, he dumped a lifetime of accumulated rage on him.

If you aspire to be a leader today, you can count on all sorts of things getting projected onto you. At my previous school, a man on the faculty turned forty. Now back in the early seventies, the slogan was "Don't talk to anyone over thirty," so turning forty was serious business. A few days before his birthday, the teacher went to see the headmaster and told him what a terrible headmaster he was and then blamed him for just about everything that was wrong in his life. And when he finished, he said, "I quit." We all rather liked this guy, but most of us recognized that he was a very unhappy man looking for someone to dump all his unhappiness on. People nowadays refer to this tactic as the blame game. When you're unhappy, don't analyze what the causes within you might be (for your unhappiness). Look for some external victim on whom to blame everything.

The "No Win" of Leadership

Throughout history, people have gotten a perverse pleasure out of bringing leaders down, projecting evil motives onto them, focusing on their faults, finding their Achilles' heels, impugning their motives. Since Watergate, the media have made a national sport searching for leaders' weaknesses in order to bring them down. Leaders are caught in a Catch 22. If a leader is strong, undeterred by projection, blame, and calumny, he is then labeled as arrogant, as authoritarian, as dictatorial. If he sets aside his initiatives, goes with the way the wind is blowing, if he backs down at all, he is immediately labeled "weak" and "a waffler."

Before you decide to aspire to be a leader, you need to realize that leadership today does not bring prestige or adulation. Father Hesburgh, the great president of Notre Dame and dean of American college presidents, who was attacked relentlessly throughout his tenure as president, once remarked, "If you want to be loved, buy a dog."

In talking with former students now in business, I am struck by how naive they are about leadership. They expect that getting the promotion—being put in charge of something they've long wanted to "run"—will bring them happiness. Instead, it brings them anxiety, abuse, and exhaustion. And they comment poignantly, "It's not what I expected." So it is with all leadership positions. One very successful businessman remarked to me, "Leadership is taking all the blows and none of the credit." Shakespeare put it best when he said, "Uneasy lies the head that wears the crown." As then, so now. Leadership brings anxiety, pain, exhaustion, and loneliness.

Three Truths about Leadership

If leadership isn't simply power, prestige, and happiness, what is it? Let me conclude with three brief thoughts about leadership.

First, leadership is not an end in itself. You should not—particularly in the climate of our time—aspire to be a leader because you think the office itself—the position itself—will somehow bring you prestige and happiness.

Occasionally, you see boys, elected to some position or office here, who regard it as a sinecure or reward—who view it as simply a recognition of their popularity. When I confronted a captain several years ago for his lack of leadership, he said to me, "Being captain doesn't mean I have to do anything or say anything. They elected me because they liked me. I don't feel like being a leader." I have known class presidents over the years who were unwilling to lead—devoid of vision, desperately eager never to do anything that would make them unpopular.

Leadership, however, is about vision and courage. A real leader has a vision of what he wants to accomplish, an ability to articulate that vision, a willingness to hear criticisms of that vision and to modify it, and a willingness to spend hours persuading people to share that vision. A real leader has vision, tenacity, and courage.

Second, if you're a leader, be prepared to receive much more criticism and blame than prestige. If a class president decides that his primary goal is to be popular, he'll never make a good class president. Leadership sometimes requires taking a lonely stand. Abraham Lincoln once made a decision opposed unanimously by every member of his cabinet. Leadership sometimes requires showing enthusiasm when you feel exhausted. Leadership requires saying no when most others are willing to do something wrong, foolish, or dangerous. Leadership sometimes requires going against the tide. Leadership sometimes entails unpopularity. If you have a vision, the effort to persuade others will often be arduous. You will experience loneliness and anxiety. A true leader has the inner strength to lose in a good cause rather than to win in a bad one. A true leader has courage. In the midst of the Red Sea, with Pharaoh's troops fast closing in, the Israelites complained that Moses was going to get them all killed. They wanted to turn back. But Moses—alone—rallied them: "Stand fast, and see the salvation of our God!" Once they'd safely arrived in Sinai, the people once again turned against Moses. "We had it made in fleshpots of Egypt, and you (Moses) brought us out here to die." Moses was alone, rejected by his own people, but he rallied them again by saying, "God has not brought us out here to die," and they found manna and quail to eat in the wilderness.

By citing Moses, I don't want to give you the impression that leadership is all great and glorious moments of heroic courage—with all the world watching—as with Moses. For most of us, leadership is small acts. I visited the president of a mid-size company this summer. I'm sure he makes several hundred thousand dollars a year. I found him walking along the street picking up papers, adjusting hoses on the trees around his office. I nearly said, "Is that what they pay you your large salary to do?" But I didn't say that, because I know that leadership consists of just such tiny, quiet, and unspectacular acts.

Sometimes, of course, such tiny acts of leadership have spectacular consequences. Rosa Parks, the Negro lady in Montgomery, Alabama, who refused to move to the back of the bus, arguably ignited the incipient Civil Rights movement. She simply stayed put, but her tiny act of defiance inspired a nation.

Finally, leadership is costly. History tends to make things look easy and obvious. Historians all now regard Winston Churchill as one of the greatest leaders of all time, but we forget that he was bitterly opposed before he attained power, that he nearly lost a vote of confidence in Parliament in the middle of the war, and that he was voted out of office the minute the war was over. The whole time I was involved in the anti-Vietnam War movement, I was troubled by doubts. So many people told me that what I was doing was wrong—that I was a bad influence on young people. I could understand why they felt that way and at times I felt very hurt and very alone.

In the summer of '96 I was at the D-Day invasion beaches in Normandy. And while I was there I saw—maybe thirty yards away—a man who was nearly doubled over crying. When I walked over to him, his wife said to me, "He says he was in this very trench when the Germans lobbed a hand grenade into it and one of his best buddies leapt face down on it so that the others in the trench would not be killed, and it blew him to smithereens. My husband owes him his life."

Before you decide whether you want to be a leader, you have to decide if you want to pay the price of leadership. And leadership is always costly. Above all, it requires character: the ability to cling to a vision, the patience and endurance to persuade others, a thick hide for criticism and unpopularity, a tolerance for anxiety, and a willingness to lose in a good cause, even—as on the Normandy beaches—a willingness to die for your fellow man in a righteous cause.

I've seen some amazing examples of student leaders here—particularly in sports—who by their personal courage on the field, by their willingness to give the last true measure of devotion, have turned chaos into order, despair into confidence, defeat into victory.

At the heart of all leadership—at any age—is character: the courage to cling tenaciously to a vision, the grit to exhaust yourself in helping others to share that vision, and the toughness to endure the blame for every difficulty along the way.

That's the reason we care most of all not how smart you are, not what a good athlete or musician or whatever you are, but what kind of person you are. We dare to hope—dare to believe—that you will have the vision and courage to be a leader, that you will aspire do something great with your life.

Leadership—2

AST WEEK'S *NEWSWEEK* contained the following commentary on the Iran/Contra scandal: "Nor will the press leave go of it. When Ben Bradlee [editor of the *Washington Post*] exulted, 'We haven't had so much fun since Watergate,' he was speaking for a city where chopping down big men is a cottage industry."

None of us would wish to see the rights of the press curbed. A free press is fundamental to a free society. The commentary in *Newsweek* was not lamenting investigative reporting; it was, rather, lamenting an attitude that takes delight in debunking, that finds it fun to find fault, that enjoys discovering smut. If Washington can be described as a city that delights in chopping down big men, we as a people would have to be described as a nation that delights in tearing down. And Ben Bradlee perfectly expresses that exultant delight: "We haven't had so much fun since Watergate."

I could use this quotation as a launching pad to a general lamentation about the negative and destructive tenor of American society. Variations on that theme might include a discussion of radio talk show hosts who insult and pillory public officials. Variations on that theme might include a discussion of the destructive tone set by American TV with its menu of abuse, exploitive sex, violence, fighting, and murder. Variations on that theme might include a discussion of Monday morning quarterbacks—columnists with 20/20 hindsight who tell you what stupid mistakes the players made the day before. Variations on that theme might include a discussion of the rancor and disrespect with which we conduct public affairs and political discourse. And we would arrive at the hardly startling or original insight that ours is a sick society: that we value the critic more highly than we value the playwright or actor, that we are fascinated by scandal, titillated by the discovery of error and wrongdoing, and, worst of all, that we delight in finding fault and tearing down.

There's Nothing New Under the Sun

But this sort of negativism is not uniquely characteristic of America in our time. We didn't invent this attitude and we can't patent it. Such an attitude has pervaded all societies to one degree or another since the dawn of humanity. Tearing down is an old, old story.

The Golden Age of Athens produced Socrates. And Socrates has been held up ever since as the archetypal seeker after the truth. By relentless questioning, he sought to discover what was good and true and beautiful. Analytical questioning was always (for Socrates) the method by which he sought the truth: a means to an end. He asked questions in passionate pursuit of truth.

A group of young men in Athens, fortunate (like you) in their birth, were privileged to receive a superior education. They learned Socrates' method of questioning well, but they used it not as a means to an end (truth), but as an end in itself. These young men, the Sophists, used Socrates' questioning method to tear down and ridicule others, to embarrass others, to mock and deride others, to demonstrate how smart and superior they were. They used his method not in the constructive discovery of truth; they used his method to put down and to destroy.

Socrates—whom we think of first when we think of the Golden Age of Athens—was not typical of his age. The Sophists were typical of the age. Athenian society is a paradigm of all future societies: for every one Socrates (who uses his mental skills to do good and to seek the truth), there are ten Sophists.

On Friday I was having a quiet solitary lunch at a restaurant in Cambridge. I couldn't have avoided hearing the conversation at the next table even if I'd tried (which I didn't—I can eavesdrop with the best of them). A Harvard senior who had applied to medical school was talking with a friend of his. The Harvard senior was saying, "I like Brand X Medical School." The location of the school's hospital in a good neighborhood of Brand Y city meant that "You don't have to waste your time dealing with welfare types and people off the streets [his exact words]. You see people (you know) like us when you make your rounds every day. It's a real good neighborhood—no crime, no street people, no slime. You don't have to put up with all the garbage about providing medical care for people who can't pay for it. There are plenty of other hospitals where they can go." His friend, also a Harvard senior, nodded his head in agreement and replied, "That's great. "

Such cynicism did not originate in our country or in our time. That kind of cynicism has flourished—even among the best educated and the most privileged—in every age. The spirit of every age is cynical. It is never fashionable to be idealistic. People will always tell you you are a fool if you set out to help others, if you set out to do something constructive about the world around you. Cynical tearing down and selfishness have been the norm in every generation.

Leaders Are the Few, the Brave

You have the same opportunities as the privileged young men of Athens. From among you will come constructive idealists (such as Socrates was) who will be leaders for good; from among you will also come smart-ass moral cynics (such as Alcibiades and the Sophists were) who will stand on the sidelines and criticize and cut down.

It is far easier to be a cynic. It requires no risk whatsoever to identify on Sunday evening all the mistakes the coach made in the game on Sunday afternoon. Coaching is a high-risk endeavor. Right in the midst of the fray you have to puzzle out what is best. You know that every decision you make will be second-guessed. You are extremely exposed and extremely vulnerable.

So it is with all leadership. If you attempt anything constructive, there will be a chorus ready to denounce whatever you try to do. If you make a mistake (and inevitably you will) you can count on the vultures to swoop down eagerly.

One aspect of Socrates' story that is frequently overlooked is how alone he was. In the end he couldn't even make his friends understand what he was doing and why he was doing it.

This winter as I watched *Eyes on the Prize*, the TV series on the Civil Rights movement in the sixties, I was struck by how obvious it all seems now—with the hindsight of twenty years. But it was not obvious at the time. Far from it. At the time those who involved themselves in the movement often felt isolated, rejected, misunderstood: their motives questioned, their involvement attacked. There was tremendous self-doubt and tremendous loneliness. When you look at the TV series now it looks as if millions and millions of people involved themselves in what we now so obviously perceive to have been a righteous and noble cause. How quickly we forget that it was less than one percent of the citizens of our nation—less than one percent in that vaunted enlightened decade of the 1960s—who actually *did* anything about civil rights or about the Vietnam War. Less than one percent.

The great American poet James Russell Lowell was writing about that tiny band of people (that less than one percent) who in each generation decide to commit their lives to some greater cause than self-interest when he wrote these words:

> *Once to ev'ry man and nation*
> *Comes the moment to decide,*
> *In the strife of truth with falsehood,*
> *For the good or evil side;*
> *Some great cause, God's new Messiah,*
> *Off'ring each the bloom or blight,*
> *And the choice goes by forever*
> *'Twixt that darkness and that light.*
>
> *Then to side with truth is noble,*
> *When we share her humble crust,*
> *Ere her cause bring fame or profit*
> *And tis prosp'rous to be just;*
> *Then it is the brave man chooses,*

While the coward stands aside
Till the multitude make virtue
Of the faith they had denied.

It is indeed a "brave man" who chooses to lead constructively. And he will indeed experience the venom of the "coward" who stands on the sidelines and criticizes. "Chopping down big men is a cottage industry" in every age. Those who dare to be idealists, those who dare to lead constructively, who dare to share truth's "humble crust," face a life that will include discomfort and loneliness.

The Leader Has His Own Standards

Why, then, choose such a life? Why not take the easy way? Why stick our necks out? Life is tough enough without worrying about "society" and "others." Who needs to risk isolation, who needs to court unpopularity? Better just to look out for ourselves, mind our own business. I don't need idealism. Give me realism.

Over the holiday I chanced upon a recent book by Tracy Kidder called *House*. It's the story of four carpenters who live out in the western part of the state. They are content with their relatively simple lives as carpenters; they make ends meet. But it occurs to them that there would be nothing wrong with making a few extra bucks to augment their incomes. They therefore agree to build a large house for a wealthy man. The man is a lawyer and toward the end of their discussion with him he negotiates $660 off the price. As the four carpenters think about this relatively modest amount, they seethe with anger and resentment. The lawyer can well afford it. He has taken advantage of them. They will barely break even. And they say to one another, "OK, we'll get this so and so. We'll slap this house up for him, but we're not gonna do the perfect job we'd otherwise do." But as they proceed with their work, they find that they simply cannot compromise. All the fine details they had studied in books and learned from master carpenters they simply cannot bring themselves to leave undone. They have to do a meticulous job. And in the end the new house reflects their exquisite workmanship, the best work they can do. They are paid the negotiated price and they have made almost nothing for all the labor they have lavished on the house. But they have built a magnificent house and they have built it to their own high standards. Despite their resolve to build the house to a lower standard, they simply could not do it. They had to build the house to their own high standards.

So it will be for those of you who choose to do something constructive with your own lives, with those of you who seek to build something worthwhile with your lives. You may be angry with those who cheat you, who treat what you do with contempt; you may threaten to lay your high ideals aside, but something will compel you to build to your own high standard no matter what.

Lowell concludes his poem with these words:

> *Though the cause of evil prosper,*
> *Yet 'tis truth alone is strong;*
> *Though [truth's] portion be the scaffold,*
> *And upon the throne be wrong,*
> *Yet that scaffold sways the future*
> *And, behind the dim unknown,*
> *Standeth God within the shadow*
> *Keeping watch above his own.*

Those electronic evangelists who preach that Christianity brings prosperity and success are criminal liars. Judaism and Christianity are costly ways of life. The prophets of Israel were ridiculed and despised and stoned to death for what they said and did. Jesus of Nazareth was crucified. By the standards of this world they were not prosperous and successful; they were failures. But twenty-five hundred years later the prophets of Israel still influence us, and that Jewish peasant still attracts to himself a billion followers. Their lonely constructive lives, their ideals and values, could not be destroyed. "Though [truth's] portion be the scaffold," and though the powers of destruction seem everywhere enthroned, "yet that scaffold [the scaffold on which men have tried to extinguish the truth], yet that scaffold sways the future!" And we discover that, though we were apparently alone, "behind the dim unknown standeth God within the shadow, keeping watch above his own."

Soon the time will come when you must choose what sort of life you will live—what its basic purpose and tenor will be: "Once to ev'ry man and nation comes the moment to decide." I know many people my age who had the opportunity to do something with their lives, to devote themselves to "some great cause," to something worthwhile. But for them the "choice [has gone] by forever." It's too late. Do not find yourself in middle age saying, "It's too late."

"Remember now thy Creator in the days of thy youth." Think now what it is you want to accomplish in your lives. Think now what you want people to say about you after you have walked off the stage of life.

> *Near the snow, near the sun, in the highest fields*
> *See how these names are feted by the waving grass*
> *And by the streamers of white cloud*
> *And whispers of wind in the listening sky.*
> *The names of those who fought for life,*
> *Who wore at their hearts the fire's centre,*
> *Born of the sun, they travelled a short while toward the sun*
> *And left the vivid air signed with their honour.*

Stephen Spender wrote those words in his poem, "The Truly Great." He was writing about that handful of people in each generation who commit their lives to something truly great. My prayer for you, my dear children, is that your names will be found among those who

> *. . . fought for life*
> *Who wore at their hearts the fire's centre. . .*
> *[who] left the vivid air signed with their honour.*

38

"We Live in a Rapidly Changing World"

 I WANT TO BEGIN by paraphrasing statements we've heard here from two adults in recent months. These statements go, roughly, as follows:

The world of the twenty-first century will be qualitatively different from the world of my boyhood. Your lives will be very different from mine because of the changes in society.

We live in a rapidly changing world. No generation has witnessed such rapid change. The old values are, for better or worse, no longer valid in the world as we now know it. For a new age, there will be new values.

Now there's no question that we live in a changing world: we must either master modern technology or it will master us. It is also obvious that contemporary technology has brought us closer to people of different cultures, and we must acquire a knowledge of (and a respect for) our new neighbors in the global village.

Our Conceit About Our Own Age

Of course the world is changing, of course the world is different. But change has been happening for a long time—as in forever. Is the change occurring now qualitatively different? Do we really need basically new values to live successfully? I think not.

I had the great good fortune to have close and deep relationships with two great-grandparents and three grandparents. I often heard them talk of their childhoods in the nineteenth century and the changes that had occurred during their lives: the invention of the automobile and the airplane and two tumultuous world wars. An alumnus recently recounted how he built—here at school in 1924—a crystal set radio. I myself remember the Second World War, which raged for the first six years of my childhood, and which brought death to my own uncle (and millions of others) and apocalyptic destruction to every corner of the world. I also very directly experienced the social cataclysm of the sixties with the pill, drugs, the Civil Rights movement, and the Vietnam War. I remember my great grandmother telling me as a child that the First World War had changed everything. I recall the frequent assertions by pundits in the sixties that we now lived in a qualitatively different world and that the values that had served us in the past were no longer valid.

Each era, each generation, seems to have the same conceit, the same need to view itself as uniquely challenged by change. And each engages in hyperbole to describe its unique exposure to change. Each generation seems to decide that it is the first in which the old values are no longer valid.

A few years ago I saw the film *Wall Street* (or, perhaps, it was another film of that ilk) with its protagonist asserting—before he went to jail—that the new guiding principle of successful people was greed—simple, all-out greed. Shortly after I saw the film I was chatting with some parents and they said to me, "This is such a difficult time to bring up children, with movies like this telling them that the traditional values are no longer valid and that self-interest, ruthlessness, and greed should be their guiding motives."

I said in response—perhaps a bit too cynically and glibly—"There's nothing new under the sun. Greed has been advocated as life's guiding principle in every generation since Adam and Eve greedily grabbed the fruit in the Garden of Eden." I'd just been teaching *King Lear* and so I quoted Edmund (that great proclaimer of a whole new world in which old values are no longer valid), Edmund who greedily tricks his brother out of his inheritance, and then lies to and later betrays his own father (to death) in order to get the family fortune. Edmund laughs with utter contempt at

> *A credulous father, and a brother noble,*
> *Whose nature is so far from doing harms*
> *That he suspects none; on whose foolish honesty*
> *My practices ride easy. . . .*
> *All with me's meet that I can fashion fit. . . .*
> *This seems a fair deserving, and must draw me*
> *That which my father loses—no less than all.*
> *The younger rises where the old doth fall.*

There's nothing new about greed. Greed has an enduring, perennial appeal because it seduces us into following our basest instincts. Wall Street has nothing on Adam and Eve, Cain and Abel, and Edmund—to name only a few exemplars of that philosophy though the years. Maybe I'm cynical and worn down, but I couldn't share these parents' shock.

Far more insidious than a straightforward advocate of greed, in my view, is the modern adult who, while he may not advocate greed as a determining moral principle, has very few if any fixed values and who, if pushed, can't bear standing for something that might make him unpopular. I say "modern adult," but, of course, such adults are also an old, old story. Such adults inhabit every generation. And they are, I submit, more insidiously dangerous than those adults who straightforwardly advocate greed.

I've just been rereading the diaries of Sir Henry Channon who recounts how the great appeaser of the Nazis—British Prime Minister Neville Chamberlain—was wildly cheered in the 1930s each and every time he caved in to Hitler, while Winston Churchill, who warned against appeasing Hitler, was widely despised, a pariah and an outcast even in his own party, for wanting to defy Hitler.

The *Herald* did a story recently about a former representative, long a staunch opponent of abortion, who is now thinking about running for governor. He announced that he was changing his opposition to abortion because polls show that sixty percent of the Massachusetts electorate opposes restriction on abortion. I don't want to get into the pros and cons of abortion rights, but making your decision on the matter by looking at polls is certainly not what Churchill would have done. This candidate's guiding principle seems to be: lick your finger, stick it in the air, and go the way the wind is blowing. That is exactly what Churchill did not do. Principle, not popularity, motivated Churchill to stand up to Hitler.

I'm on the mailing list of several school newspapers. They make interesting reading. One school had a speaker—an expert from Children's Hospital—who talked about the toxic effects of alcohol on the adolescent body and who said, "It is about making choices. In my point of view there is no choice. You don't do it." According to that school's newspaper, the dean of students commented that the speaker didn't do what he asked him to do. Instead, "He gave the message to 'just say no.' I don't think that was the way to approach the issue. Too much moralizing." This dean of students was using a well-known spin technique: when you agree with someone, then you call him a bold and courageous spokesman for the truth. If you disagree with him, then you accuse him of "moralizing." I myself used this tactic with my parents. I frequently advised them to stop "preaching" at me and to "skip the moralizing." It's a cheap way to degrade someone who's speaking with conviction—and I was somewhat surprised to hear it from a dean of students.

Some adults who work with young people have a desperate need to be popular—to tell kids what they want to hear: "I'm on your side." Or perhaps, more accurately, some adults who work with young people can't bear to say or do anything that would make them unpopular. There's nothing new about that. It's been going on a long time. I remember, in particular, a mother in my hometown in Ohio who had a desperate need to be with adolescents all the time. She even dressed and talked like a teenager. She pandered to her son's friends, telling them what they wanted to hear about sex, for example, and alcohol. Pretty much every kid, I think, recognized her neurotic needs, though, of course, we repeatedly told her what a swinger she was in contrast to our "square" parents.

A boy told me recently about the mother of a friend of his who was passing out condoms. As she passed them out, she said, "Now don't tell your parents I gave you this. But I understand how you feel and I'm not saying I condone sex, but I know just how you feel." When the boy's date said, "No thanks, we don't need a condom because we're not having sex," the mother winked and said, "You never know what the future might hold."

Charles Glenn, one of the bright lights in American education, a professor at Boston University, calls this attitude in adults: preemptive capitulation. Such adults need to be thought of as swingers. "Here's a condom, before you ask, even if you don't want it. I'm ready as an adult to toss out the old values the minute you challenge them—or even before you challenge them. If it would make you unhappy or guilty for me to say sexual intercourse in adolescence is actually Not a Good Thing, or that drugs and drinking might be harmful, I'll just be quiet because I don't want to be accused of 'moralizing' and, above all, I don't want to upset you or run the risk of your not liking me anymore."

As I was hearing confessions this Christmas season, I was struck, as I always am, about how boringly similar sins are. I heard the same things—sex, cruelty, anger, selfishness—thirty-two years ago as a young priest. There's no difference at all. No qualitative change. And I think a priest fifty, one hundred, or five hundred years ago would have heard just about the same things confessed.

My father used to tell me how he taught his own father to drive in the late 1920s. And last summer Jake Russell—at a mere thirteen years of age—taught me (the illustrious headmaster) the computer. Cars make it easier for us to get from one place to another more rapidly and conveniently than a horse and buggy, and computers make it possible to communicate more rapidly and conveniently. And you can't live in the modern world without a car or a computer. But have they changed things qualitatively? I submit that they have not. Not anything like as much as the industrial revolution or the world wars changed society. I think you could make an excellent case that the pace of change in our era is actually less than that in many other eras. Has the world changed qualitatively when you get information off the screen on the Internet rather than from a book? I think not.

I was your age in the 1950s. We all thought we lived in a time of enormous change: the threat of nuclear holocaust, the breakup of old world structures (the end of empire), the beginnings of integration, etc. But historians now routinely regard the fifties as a time of quiet—even of somnolence. I think there's a good chance the present decade will be seen the same way. I've been working with teenagers for thirty-four years and you seem more like the kids I knew in the fifties than any kids I've known during the intervening years.

Every age wants to see itself as unique and every age is conceited enough to believe that it lives in revolutionary times in which the world is qualitatively changing and the old values are—after thousands of years—finally, at last, irrelevant if not defunct.

In the Cairo museum there is a tablet of stone—a six thousand-year-old tablet of stone—on which an Egyptian described his society. It reads: "Our society is degenerate. People no longer hold to the old values." That Egyptian, caught up in the same conceit we're caught up in, believed he lived in a rapidly changing world—one that was qualitatively changing—and that most people had stopped adhering to the traditional values.

Standing Against Our Time and Culture

The truth is that every age is an age of change in which people challenge the traditional values.

The survival of civilization in every generation depends on a few institutions and individuals—depends on a small minority of people dedicated to working for the public good.

My friend David Hicks, in a brilliant article in *The American Scholar*, points out that until very recently, the great American independent schools prided themselves on standing against contemporary culture. They didn't run after it or imitate it or cave in to it. They said, in effect: "These are the values we hold—honesty, simplicity, respect and concern for others, the acknowledgment of the Eternal in the midst of the transitory. Such values are never, in any generation, popular, but these are our values." In other words, the great schools stood unabashedly against the times and against the culture.

I was one of less than a handful of boys in my class at St. Mark's who was not the son of a millionaire. But I was never disadvantaged or made to feel a second-class citizen. We all slept in very Spartan quarters and were given very plain food (a euphemism, if ever there was one!). The school had no janitors because we boys cleaned the school every day from top to bottom. We went to chapel every single day and three times on Sunday. Our parents were told not to send us money, and each Saturday we were each given fifty cents to spend for the week. The school believed that there should be no distinctions between rich and poor, and it made sure that community life reflected that value. The lifestyle of the school, reflecting its strongly held values, went, believe me, very much against the spirit and values of the 1950s.

Unfortunately, in recent years, some (and I emphasize some) schools—on the principle of preemptive capitulation—have conducted market surveys to find out what people want so that they can provide it and attract more students. The last thing these schools want to do is to stand against the spirit and values of the times. The values of these schools are not fixed: they are changeable and variable, they depend on what people want.

I had a fascinating encounter with the mother and father of an applicant a couple of years ago. They had a very bright son and were trying to decide between Roxbury Latin and another school. They came to see me, and said that Roxbury Latin struck them as "rather rigid" in its values and in its rules. I asked them what gave them that impression. ("Rigid," of course, like "moralizing," is a classic debater's term to put a negative spin on something. When you like an institution's values, then you call the institution "courageous" and "inspiring" and "strong" for upholding its values. If you don't like the institution's values, then you call the institution "rigid" or "uncompromising" or "passé.") These parents said, speaking of the other school their son was considering: "It's more flexible, more understanding about families leaving early for weekends or vacations, for example." I said, "You're right. We are rigid about that." They then said they'd heard Roxbury Latin had required a student with high grades to leave because he didn't live by the school's values. I acknowledged that that happened every so often and told them we meant it when we said, "We care most of all what kind of person a boy is." They said they thought that was pretty "judgmental" (another great spin word). I said, "You're right, we are judgmental with boys who don't live up to the high standards we think they're capable of reaching." The conversation continued in that vein for some time and I finally said—I hope charitably—"From all you say, it would seem best for your son not to come to here. You don't seem to share our values, and I think you'd be much happier at Brand X School (which they kept telling me was much more accommodating and less judgmental)." To my surprise, I discovered a few days later that their son was coming here. When I asked them the following September why they'd decided on us, they said, "We may not agree with you about some things, but, when all was said and done, we were impressed that Roxbury Latin stands for something, that it says what it is and is what it says. It dares to say: 'This is who we are; you can take it or leave it.'"

The Importance of the Few

What's true for institutions (such as Roxbury Latin) is even truer for individuals. I submit that the quality of life in each generation is determined by a very small number of people who dare to stand against the times, against the culture. This School was founded to create—dare we say it—just such a leadership elite: an elite of responsibility and obligation, not an elite of privilege.

You are, already, quite different from most young men in your generation. You actually spend hours each day studying. You actually read books for pleasure. You actually treat your bodies well—lifting weights, eating right, exercising. You actually aspire not merely to exist but to do something great with your lives. Most of you are courageous enough, tough enough, strong enough, to face life squarely: not to run away from life by anesthetizing yourselves with drink and drugs, but courageous enough to engage life actively with courage and hope.

At the holiday concert I had a conversation with the parents of a Roxbury Latin boy. They said, "Did you really tell our son that he'd know if he was studying hard enough for his exams if it hurt, if he was miserable." "Yes," I said, "I wished him a week of great pain. I think he's strong enough to push himself till it hurts." I'm pretty sure they didn't agree, but the boy was delighted when I told him his grades. "Now that it's over," he said, "I'm really glad I did it." (I hope he told his parents.) Few boys your age in the world can postpone gratification to the degree most of you can. Few are tough enough to consider pushing themselves to the limit.

You are already different. You already live by values that relatively few young men your age share. As adults, you will, I hope, live by values that relatively few adults in your generation will stand up for.

In every generation the world is saved by a few people who stand for something: Socrates, who said it was more important to live well (to live lives of value) than merely to live (to exist); Moses, who had alone to confront the Israelites for worshiping a Golden Calf the minute his back was turned; Jesus, who said to his followers, "You are the salt of the earth" (the few tiny grains that can transform the taste of a whole society); Winston Churchill, who appeared to throw his career away standing, unpopularly, against Hitler in the thirties; Little Rosa Parks, who went against the law of the land when she refused to go to the back of the bus; and Mother Teresa, who, when asked why she chose to live and die among the destitute and hopeless, replied, utterly against the spirit of our time, "I wanted a very hard life!"

In every generation, not just your generation, it is a tiny number of such people who preserve and transform society. In every generation, it is a tiny number of people who stand for something, no matter how unpopular, dangerous, or costly such a stand may be.

In every generation, most people choose the easier, more comfortable way, living lives of what we called in the sixties "self-fulfillment," lives without vision, lives without any great purpose, lives without costly commitments. T. S. Eliot memorialized this large majority in these biting words:

> *A Cry from the North, from the West and from the South*
> *Whence thousands travel daily to the timekept City;*
> *Where My Word is unspoken,*
> *In the land of lobelias and tennis flannels*
> *The rabbit shall burrow and the thorn revisit,*
> *The nettle shall flourish on the gravel court,*
> *And the wind shall say: "Here were decent godless people:*
> *Their only monument the asphalt road*
> *And a thousand lost golf balls."*

That is the epitaph of the many, of those who travel the conventional, easy road. That is the epitaph of the self-indulged, the epitaph of the dull.

There is another way. It is the way of the few who want to do something great with their lives, who do not fear unpopularity, who dare to risk defeat and even death standing for what they believe in. This is the better way. This is the only path to the good life. This is the way of the few—the few who dare to care, who dare to try to make a difference. This way, I submit, is much more exciting, much more rewarding, and dare we say it, much more fun.

39

Anything Worth Doing Is Worth Doing Badly

CLERGYMAN ASKED ME if I would talk with a sixteen-year-old in his parish who had recently been charged with breaking and entering and theft. The boy was from an affluent suburb; he had no need to steal, so I asked him, "Why'd you do it?" "The guys I was with," he replied. "They said 'If you don't do this with us, you're chicken'." "What'd you say?" I asked. "Nothing," he said. "Nothing?" I asked. "I didn't want them to think I was chicken—that I didn't have the guts to do it—so I went along. I thought I had to."

I start with this conversation because it illustrates one of life's great ironies: wanting to demonstrate that he had guts, this kid demonstrated that he was gutless. He was too weak to resist his friends, too cowardly to risk unpopularity.

Another conversation, another boy—an eighteen-year-old, also from the western suburbs. He was speeding along a country road with his date, failed to negotiate a curve, and totaled his car into a tree. He walked away with barely a scratch; his date went face first through the windshield. Her face was destroyed; she will have to undergo years of plastic surgery that will only partially restore her looks. "What happened?" I asked. "I was speeding," he replied. "How come?" I asked. "I wanted to impress her. I was just showing off." And then in tears, "I was showing her what a man I am." The same irony: in trying to show how tough he was, he demonstrated how weak he was. Those who have to drive fast—or steal—to show what men they are, really, of course, demonstrate that they're not men at all.

Another conversation, this one not with a teenager, but with a sexually active man in his twenties who had had intercourse with a girl without wearing a condom. (She was protecting herself.) Unbeknownst to him—and she claimed unbeknownst to her—she had had intercourse with someone who had AIDS. Through intercourse she transmitted AIDS to him and he's now dying. "Why didn't you protect yourself?" I asked. "It was just a hassle. I just couldn't be bothered," he said. "Didn't you hear all the warnings about AIDS?" I asked him. "Yeah," he said, "but I never thought it would happen to me." "Wasn't she concerned about the dangers?" I asked. "Actually," he said, "she was pretty impressed that I wasn't afraid." And so, playing the role of macho stud, this guy sentenced himself to death. Anybody who has to do what this guy did—to prove to his girlfriend (and even more to himself) what a man he is—is of course no man at all. He wasn't courageous; he was stupid.

So often as a priest, you get called in to talk with people when it's too late. I couldn't be angry or judgmental with these three young men. How could you feel anything toward them other than an immense sadness? Nothing I can say will remove the court record or the destroyed reputation of the boy who went along with the break-in and robbery. Nothing I can say will restore the face of the girl who went through the windshield or take away the remorse that the boy who was driving will live with for the rest of his life. Nothing I can say will cure the young man dying of AIDS. It is too late for them and there is very little anyone can do to help.

It is not, however, too late for you and I want to address just one issue with you this morning—the relationship of risk to courage. I've given you examples of three young men who—in the name of courage—took foolish risks that required no real courage. There are, however, risks worth taking in life, risks that are not foolish, risks that require real courage.

You all know the cliche "Anything worth doing is worth doing well."

I want to challenge you this morning with what appears to be its opposite. What I want to say to you today is this: "Anything worth doing is
worth doing badly."

"Anything worth doing is worth doing badly." There is a tendency
on the part of all of us only to attempt things we think we can do well.
We're afraid of being humiliated by doing something poorly.

Let me give you an example. When I was assistant director of the
Upper School at University School in Cleveland, one of my advisees—
also a student in my Western Civ class—was a wonderful young man
who was a fine tennis player. He asked me one day if I played tennis.
Now, in the town I grew up in in Ohio, tennis was considered an effete
snob sport played by rich people who weren't tough enough to play a
real sport like football. There was not a tennis court in the town, so
there was no danger that any of us would be tempted to indulge in this
deviant activity. But some of my classmates at St. Mark's had taught me
the rudiments of the game and I had also hacked around at tennis every
now and then in the years that followed. Anyway, this fourteen-year-
old kid asked me if I'd like to play and I said, "Sure." To make a long
story short, he was a superb tennis player and the few times my racquet
touched the tennis ball that afternoon I drove it directly into either the
net or the back fence. I've never played since. Playing tennis had never,
admittedly, been something high on my life agenda, but certainly one
factor in my never playing again was the embarrassment I felt at being
badly beaten by a mere fourteen-year-old. I don't think I am untypical:
we are all apprehensive about doing things unless we can already do
them well. As a result we do the things we're good at over and over, and
pretend (or convince ourselves) that we don't care about the things we
don't do so well.

Some years ago in Paris, I met a former student of mine from Cleveland. I've never taken French, but he'd studied it for four years in high
school. Would he utter a word in French? Not on your life! He was even
embarrassed when I bumbled along with my fractured French. (I've
always longed to have someone compare me to Winston Churchill but
I'm afraid the only way I'll ever be compared to Churchill is that, like

him, I speak atrocious French.) This boy—beautifully trained in French—was so fearful he'd say something incorrectly, so terrified of being embarrassed, so afraid of humiliation, that he couldn't bring himself to utter a word.

And let's be honest. Such fears of embarrassment and humiliation are real. If you attempt something you're not already good at, there are risks. If you risk trying out for a team, you could be cut from it. If you risk asking a girl for a date, she could refuse you. Such fears paralyze some people so that they crawl away into a shell and don't risk anything. If you don't risk anything, you can't be embarrassed. If you don't try out for a team, you don't have to fear being cut. If you don't ask a girl out, you don't have to fear being turned down. If you don't set high goals in the classroom, you don't have to worry about not doing well.

When I say "Anything worth doing is worth doing badly," what I mean is that there are risks in life that are worth taking—that require real courage. Despite the risk of failure and embarrassment, it is worth attempting things even if you will, in all likelihood, never do them particularly well.

I want to give you just one example of what I mean: a young man I met twenty-five years ago when I was at divinity school in Cambridge, Massachusetts. I was twenty-four years old; I had finished two years of graduate study in England and all I needed in order to be ordained was one year of seminary. It was my seventh year of higher education and I was very low on money.

Through a friend of a friend of a friend, I heard there was an opening for a pianist at a cocktail bar about ten minutes from the seminary—stints of a week or two every few months with odd nights in between, covering for the real pianist. The job was ideal, time-consuming but not demanding—an evening's work in a haze of smoke playing popular jazz, blues, the general bar mishmash including the inevitable requests of the latest sentimental love songs. ("Moon River" was big that fall. Yuk.)

The first week I was playing in came the younger sister of a college friend of mine and her boyfriend. When I'd finished the set she came over and invited me to join them at their table. Her date—a hulking young man of twenty-one—was a member of the Harvard football team: a clean-cut wholesome youth (of course from the Midwest!) who was a starter on the varsity.

We chatted a while, I went back to the piano, and they left before I finished the next set. To my surprise, they reappeared the next night. He never broke training, just sipped a coke while she sipped a glass of wine. On the third night, they appeared again, and I went over to their table to say hello. I assumed that she must like music and be dragging him each night, but it was he who said, "Man, I'd like to play the piano like you."

I laughed, enjoying the compliment even though I knew that if Bruce liked the way I played he was not much of a judge of musicianship.

"Man, I'd like to play the piano like you!" He was not complimenting me; he was uttering a longing in his heart to make music. Later in the season my then-girlfriend and I took her little brother to a game to watch Bruce play and then to meet him after the game. The little kid was thrilled: "I want to be a football player just like him," he said. Meanwhile, back in the cocktail lounge, this football player was expressing the same sort of longing as my girlfriend's little brother, "Man, I'd like to play the piano just like you!"

As it turned out, he came from a completely nonmusical family. There was no piano in his home, no interest in making music. He was struck by the beauty of it and longed to be able to play it himself. A few nights later he said, "Man, how about showing me how to play?" I said, "Bruce, are you sure you want to learn? It takes a long time and you have huge time commitments." "Yeh, I really do," he replied, and so I started to give him lessons at the seminary. He offered to pay me and I said no, though he gave me fabulous tickets for the Harvard home games—the best seats I've ever sat in in Harvard Stadium.

I taught him with the same book that is used all across the country for children. He had as little natural talent at the piano as it's possible to have. It's astounding how brilliant people can be at one thing while being entirely hopeless at another. Every step forward was labored.

Only for one brief moment, however, did he show the slightest sign of discouragement. (He said one day, in a spasm of despair that was over as quickly as it came: "Oh man, I can never play well.") Otherwise he was always buoyantly optimistic. After about six lessons, he could play the first song in the book and he invited me to Dunster House for dinner: "I'm having Dory [his girlfriend] and some guys from the team over. I'm going to play my piece for them," he said. So there we were—six of us—in the Dunster House Junior Common Room after football practice—with this 6'4", 225-pound hulk, sitting at the piano playing the first song in the children's piano book—"Twinkle, Twinkle Little Star," if I remember correctly. At supper one of the football players started to kid him a bit and he said: "OK, dumb-dumb, you try it! I'll tell you something. Football's easy. This is the toughest thing I've ever done."

That's what I remember about this kid—what John Cheever would call his "blue-sky courage." He wasn't afraid to go all out, to try really hard at something for which he had no natural talent, at something he would never be good at. He didn't care. He wanted to learn how to play the piano. Even though he would never be able to do it well, it was worth doing. He exemplifies what I mean when I say that "Anything worth doing is worth doing badly." He didn't have to be good at it for it to be a worthwhile experience. There he was, this hulking jock, beating his brains out at age twenty-one to play something with his huge hands that many little children of eight or nine could play better than he could. "OK, dumb-dumb, you try it! Football's easy. This is the toughest thing I've ever done." That is the perfect definition of courage: to risk trying something that's worth trying that you're not already good at.

It is easy to ignore schoolmates whose interests and friends, whose personalities and backgrounds, are different from yours. It's easy to avoid getting to know them. It requires no guts at all: gutless wonders do it every day. It requires guts to make an overture to someone who is different from you—whose background, personality, and interests seem far removed from your own. It requires guts because it's a risk. You may get a cold response, you may get snubbed; he may make you feel little or stupid. Don't minimize the risk. And yet it's a risk worth taking because—maybe, possibly, perhaps—your overture will be successful, will enrich you by enabling you to get to know someone who adds new dimensions to your life.

If you're with a group, it's easy to go along with the group. It was easy for the sixteen-year-old boy to go along with the break-in and robbery—gutless wonders give in to peer pressure like that every day. It's a risk to say no to something that's wrong. Your peers may scorn you, reject you, make you feel alone and out of it. On the other hand, some may admire (perhaps only silently admire) the inner strength that enables you to stand alone. Some may even join you. It's a risk—one that requires courage.

It's a risk to present yourself to others as you really are. It takes courage. Most people hide behind masks. They're afraid that if people see them the way they really are, they won't like them. Therefore they always wear a mask. But in my experience people admire the courage of those—like Bruce the football player—who don't hide, who make themselves vulnerable, who dare to risk openly revealing themselves, expressing their hopes and their desires.

Every day you have an opportunity for courage. A situation will arise in which you will choose either to take a worthwhile risk—or to run away from it. Each day a situation arises in which you can risk reaching out to someone, or in which you risk apparent unpopularity with your peers. Pray every day. Pray that God will give you the necessary strength to be courageous in such situations.

My prayer for you is that you will have the guts to avoid stupid risks, and that you will have the guts to take worthwhile risks. For, while it is certainly true that anything worth doing is worth doing well, it is also true that anything worth doing is worth doing—even worth doing badly.

40

Tough and Tender

 MAN MY AGE shared with me this summer the story of his boyhood. His mother was psychotic, his father alcoholic. From the time he was twelve he received from them no understanding, no support, no love. He was often abused, falsely accused, devastated. No one in his school seemed to notice or care. No one reached out to him. He was utterly alone. His life was a living hell.

Later in the summer I visited a friend in the hospital who is in the last stages of brain cancer. Once a joyfully exuberant bon vivant, he stared at me without a flicker of recognition, his once sparkling eyes eerily vacant.

Life is tough.

It is tough even for the lucky. People are always talking to me about "the lucky few" who are selected to attend Roxbury Latin. Occasionally I respond flippantly by saying, "Yeah, you're right, they're lucky. They get to work three times as hard as most of their contemporaries. They get to take the toughest courses taught in an American high school. They are pressured to immerse themselves in the burdensome demands of athletic teams and activities." I'm sure people have told you how lucky you are. If your luck continues you will find yourself at a pressure-cooker college, and next scrambling madly up the greasy pole of success in a demanding job, wondering how you'll pay for your house and how you'll feed and educate your children. All this if you're lucky. Life is tough, even for the lucky.

When I first went as a parish priest to St. Paul's Church in Cleveland, I looked around this very large parish and saw literally hundreds of families who seemed to have it all. They had luxurious homes, expensive cars, high-paying jobs, beautiful children, all the advantages and opportunities one could wish for. I served in that parish for ten years and when I moved away there wasn't a single family left in that category. Every single one—in the intervening years—had been forced to deal with some significant difficulty or suffering or loss or tragedy.

We are inclined to think that life for most people imitates television. We are inclined to think that when conflicts arise in most families, they are resolved, as they are on TV, in twenty-two minutes, and that every family member is then hugging, kissing, reconciled, and happy. How often boys have said to me something like: "My dad is not a typical dad; he never takes me to baseball games and stuff like that." Or, "I used to be able to talk to my mother, but she's so tired when she comes home at night that I don't want to upset her. It's not like what happens in other families: she's not waiting there with chocolate chip cookies and milk to ask me how school went that day. It's almost like I should be asking her how her day went."

But life does not imitate television. There are no such families. Real fathers and mothers have their own problems. Adults who remember their own childhoods very selectively keep telling people your age that these are the happiest years of your life. While you who are living them know them often to be hard, uncertain, and painful. I had as happy an adolescence as anyone could have, but I have found life beyond adolescence far happier. In real life, conflicts and anger and hurt are not resolved in families or anywhere else in twenty-two speedy and amusing minutes. Life does not imitate television. Life is far more complex and far more difficult.

Some people just can't face up to life's toughness. They can't hack it. They run away from it, try to blot it out by alcohol or drugs. When things get tough, the weak deaden themselves to reality, flee from life's toughness. It is cruel to call such people cowards, because they are pathetic. Victims of life.

One way some men respond to life's toughness is by putting on thick coats of armor. I'm a tough guy with a thick skin and nothing affects me! One of history's classic macho men was Marc Antony, parading bare-chested through the streets of Rome. In the end, of course, Marc Antony turned out to be a wimp who ran away from the battle. Like most men who have to make a show of flexing—whether the flexing is literal or figurative—he had a deep sense of inadequacy that he was trying desperately to hide, and a deep need to prove (to himself and others) how tough he was. Any man who has to throw his weight around and put on the tough-guy macho act might as well wear a sign around his neck saying "I'm inadequate, I'm insecure." Men who have to show you how tough they are are not tough at all.

A variation on this macho pose for men is what we might call the "no-emo" pose. You show what a tough guy you are by your blasé attitude. I'm "cool, man," detached, self-contained. I could really care less, nothing fazes me. This carefully constructed image of invulnerability is a mask. Those who hide behind the mask aren't cool or self-contained. They're afraid, fearful of opening themselves up to others, fearful of expressing or sharing their feelings, fearful of the risks of getting involved in real relationships with others.

Alcohol, drugs, the macho pose, the no-emo mask—these are all pathetic attempts to run away from the reality that life is tough.

Real men don't run. They stay and fight.

Preparing for the Tough Life

One of this school's principal aims is to challenge you now so you will develop the confidence and toughness to face life's future challenges.

You couldn't put yourself in a more challenging school. Not only are the demands great, but the demands sometimes seem to come all at the same time. The important test, the long paper, the big game, the critical rehearsal all seem to fall on the same day. Much of what you accomplish here is done under the intense pressure of conflicting priorities and merciless deadlines. No boy graduates from here who doesn't ask himself at times, "Can I hack all this?"

Every boy here experiences heartrending disappointments and frightening failures: whether in the classroom or in sports or in friendships. You work really hard and get a mediocre grade while the guy next to you does nothing and gets an A. You go all-out in practice every day and you never start, and somebody half as committed as you is a star. You try to make friends with someone who doesn't care whether or not you exist.

It is precisely at that point when you are under the pressure of conflicting simultaneous demands, or when you are knocked down, face in the dirt, that you discover who you are. In that moment of truth you have to decide whether you are going to cut and run or stay and fight.

If you have the courage to stay and fight you will have to dig deep within you to find the strength to pick yourself up, dust yourself off, and go on.

I have found myself face down in the dirt a number of times. And I have often wondered whether I could get up and go on. It's impossible to overstate how terrible and gut-wrenching such moments are. One of the many joys of middle age is that you have gotten up often enough to have confidence that you can do it again, tough as it is. Each time that you are able to get up and overcome defeat you add new muscle for the battle of life. Viktor Frankl, the great Viennese psychiatrist, reflected while imprisoned in a Nazi concentration camp, "That which does not kill me makes me stronger." Those who are really strong, who are really tough, don't deny the hurt, they don't pretend there's no pain. They face the hurt and pain and they struggle to get up and to go on. The macho act and the no-emo pose are gutless denials of pain; alcohol and drugs are gutless escapes from pain. Right now in your life in this place you have the opportunity to discover and develop the inner strength (the spiritual muscle) to face the pressures, the pain and the defeats, the disappointments that are an ongoing part of everyone's life.

The former head of a tough independent school wrote recently: "Newspapers love to refer to private school students as preppies, the consummate country club set, the coddled rich, when the truth is, if everyone on the Detroit assembly line had been putting in the hours of honest-to-God labor that [the private school] student does, there would be more Chevies and fewer Toyotas on American highways."

You wouldn't be here if we didn't think you had the "right stuff," the inner strength to cope with and surmount the most rigorous of challenges. When talk-show host Chris Lydon, Class of '58, was interviewed in the *Globe* a few years ago, he said, "After Roxbury Latin the rest of life has seemed easy." Perhaps that's an overstatement, but it is certainly a long-standing goal of this School to prepare a small group of young men who learn today courageously to face up to life's inevitable demands, setbacks, and injustices and who therefore will have developed the inner strength to be the world's leaders tomorrow.

The Courage to Risk Vulnerability

What makes a man strong? What distinguishes a strong man from a weak one?

The most painful experiences in life are those in which we are vulnerable to hurt: When, for example, we go all out to achieve a good grade or a starting position and fail to achieve our goal. Or, when, for example, we reach out to someone and are rebuffed. Or when we invite someone to do something and receive a disinterested or cold response. Or when we help someone and go unthanked (taken for granted). Or when we express affection and are mocked or ignored. In these terrible moments, we feel humiliated, belittled, exposed.

And we are exposed. All of us, even the greatest. At the Harvard 350th Convocation, the Prince of Wales had to wait through an hour and forty minutes of speeches in front of a throng of eighteen thousand, before his turn came to give the final and major address of the day. When he was at last introduced he began by saying, "I cannot tell you how the suspense of this mammoth occasion has been killing me. You've devised an exquisite torture. . . ." By sharing with them how vulnerable he felt, he captivated the throng seated before him. He, the featured guest, he the man of the world who has lived his entire life in the public eye, he who has spoken with notable success in almost every country on the face of the earth, was man enough to admit he was scared.

How much effort and energy we expend hiding—even from ourselves—our loneliness, our need, our weakness, our fear of embarrassment. It takes enormous courage to face squarely our own vulnerability, and even more courage to expose ourselves to rejection or ridicule by reaching out to others.

When I was at University School in Cleveland we had a formal served lunch and each master and boy were assigned to a table. I had at my table perhaps the shyest boy I've ever known. Try as I—and others—did to pull him into conversation, he was obviously too timid to say a word. Finally, one day after several weeks, to our astonishment he began haltingly to tell a joke. It was a joke I'd already heard—and probably most of the others had—but we held our breath as he finally risked opening his mouth. Just as he got towards the end, a boy at the end of the table loudly interrupted with the punch line and then said in the most contemptuous tone, "Everybody's heard that story." Such cruelty takes about the same courage it takes to trip up a crippled man. I tell this story not to illustrate the fact that there are emotionally retarded bullies who need to beat up the weak in order to feel strong. I tell the story because I think most of us are sensitive and honest enough with ourselves to understand and enter into that shy boy's fear. We can see in him our own vulnerability writ large. Nothing takes as much courage in life—nothing—as risking opening ourselves up to others.

Only those who are strong will risk such vulnerability. Only the truly tough will dare to be tender.

If this School's most precious asset is the diversity of its student body, the greatest challenge to a student here is to find the courage to open himself up to others who by background and interest are very different from him. I think of two boys in the same class here, now graduates (and to protect them I shall alter the details of their story): One boy lived in a housing project in Dorchester. The other lived in a large home with a swimming pool in Dover. One was black and the other white. But they became close friends at school. The Dorchester boy invited the Dover boy to spend the night. "I'll use my Beaver Brook sleeping bag," said the Dorchester boy. "You sleep in my bed." A few weeks later, the Dover boy came into my study and said, "I stayed with John in Dorchester and I'd really like to invite him to spend the night at my house. But if he sees where I live and all the things my family has, he won't like me any more."

Somehow he overcame his fear of rejection. And now, years later, these boys (now men) are still very close; they have been ushers in each other's weddings. Both had to take risks. There is no friendship or relationship worth having that doesn't involve risk. There were times when their relationship hit a snag (all relationships hit snags), and both had to take still greater risks. Both dug deeper and found the courage to do so, and both now share the reward of friendship.

It is just when relationships hit a snag, it is just when we encounter problems or frustrations or failure in our lives, just when we feel humiliated, that we find out who we are. We either run or we dig deep. It was only when the prodigal son reached the nadir of life—wishing he could eat the slop that he (as a hired hand) was feeding the pigs—only then did the prodigal son, as Jesus tells us, "come to himself." It is, says the psalmist, in the valley of despair that we find the meaning of life: "In going through the vale of tears we find it to be a spring." (Psalm 84)

Growing Through Our Setbacks

Paradoxically, then, we learn the most about life not through our triumphs and successes, but through our failures and our sufferings. We develop the inner strength to cope with life by facing up to life's difficulties, by hunkering down to overcome life's problems.

Life is tough and we are vulnerable. The real man doesn't run away from life; he's not afraid to admit his vulnerability.

One great benefit of admitting our own weaknesses and vulnerability is that in doing so we become aware of the weakness and vulnerability of others. Some years ago Mother Theresa spoke at the Harvard commencement. She looked out on the great sea of satisfied graduates on their way to success and glory, and she dared to offer them as her graduation present the poor and suffering of the world. She told of visiting a family in Portugal. The youngest child in this large family was grotesquely deformed and hopelessly retarded. "What is his name? What do you call him?" she asked the mother. And the mother replied,

"We call him our Professor of Love, because he has taught us how to love. "

This helpless child—whom many families would regard as a curse and a burden—was seen by this family to be a blessing: In his helplessness he evoked the attention, the sympathy, and the affection of every member of the family. "We call him our Professor of Love, because he has taught us how to love."

Every failure, every defeat, every bit of suffering that we experience (as we risk vulnerability in opening ourselves to others) makes us stronger. Stronger—among other reasons—because we become more aware of the sufferings of others. Our sufferings, our failures, our defeats can become for us professors of love: they make us sensitive to the burdens and sorrows that others must bear.

My beloved children, now and in the years ahead you will suffer and fail and know despair. My prayer for you is that when you experience such suffering you will dig deep and from your suffering build the spiritual muscle you will need to cope with life's many difficulties, and that in your own suffering you will grow to understand with compassion the suffering of others.